ILLEGIBLE WILL

ILLEGIBLE WILL

Coercive Spectacles of Labor
in South Africa and the Diaspora

Hershini Bhana Young

Duke University Press   Durham and London   2017

Typeset in Garamond Premier Pro by Westchester Book group

Library of Congress Cataloging-in-Publication Data
Names: Young, Hershini Bhana, author.
Title: Illegible will : coercive spectacles of labor in
South Africa and the diaspora / Hershini Bhana Young.
Description: Durham : Duke University Press, 2017. | Includes bibliographical
references and index. | Description based on print version record and
CIP data provided by publisher; resource not viewed.
Identifie rs: LCCN 2016038931 (print) | LCCN 2016037623 (ebook)
ISBN 9780822373339 (e-book)
ISBN 9780822363095 (hardcover : alk. paper)
ISBN 9780822363200 (pbk. : alk. paper)
Subjects: LCSH: Performing arts—Social aspects—South Africa. |
Blacks in the performing arts. | Southern African literature—
Themes, motives. | African diaspora. | Slave labor—History. |
Forced labor—History. | Will.
Classifi cation: LCC PN1590.B53 (print) | LCC PN1590.B53 Y68 2017 (ebook) |
DDC 792.089/96068—dc23
LC record availablea t https://lccn.loc.gov/2016038931

Cover art: Levern Botha in *Cargo*. Photo by Garth Stead.

FOR MY FATHER

CONTENTS

ACKNOWLEDGMENTS

Between my last book and *Illegible Will*, my life has undergone a series of sea changes. The term is particularly apt, as in its original context, Shakespeare's *The Tempest*, a sea change suggests a metamorphosis that follows drowning. These pages represent the drowning and the metamorphosis, the watery grave and the sunlight.

The people who have helped me tread water and learn how to swim are many. The community of scholars that has developed out of the Black Performance Theory Group has shaped this book in more ways than I can count. Thanks especially to Jennifer Brody, Fadeke Castor, Sarah Cervenak, Tommy DeFrantz, E. Patrick Johnson, Omi Osun Jones, Uri McMillan, Matt Richardson, and my brother from another mother, Jeffrey McCune. Thank you Stephanie Batiste for always getting me to the ocean. You have all anchored me with your grace, fabulousness, and spiritual depth.

Numerous people helped me put the book together. Yvette Christianse was extremely helpful and gave me the courage to believe in what I was doing. Saidiya Hartman was her lovely self. VéVé Clark helped from the other side. H. F. Heese was kind in providing me with a copy of Tryntjie's sentencing. I am grateful for the assistance of Arvin Bhana, Chiman and Nirmala Govind, Nigel Penn, and Goolam Vahed, who found archival material for me when I was far away from home. My various anonymous readers helped sharpen the book's focus. Miriam Angress is an amazing editor—I am so happy we found each other. Patrick Walter was the developmental editor for the book. He did a fantastic job, despite my bouts of sullenness when he insisted that poetic language was not a stand-in for focused analysis. My colleagues at the State

University of New York, Buffalo, have been supportive, in particular Jang Wook Huh, Damien Keane, and Mike Rembis, who brightened many a gray day. The department's administrative staff made my life so much smoother and happier. Thank you for candy and constantly resent e-mails, even though I often ignored the latter: Wendy Belz, Sophia Canavos, Jennifer Elinge, Nicole Lazaro, Karen Serrianne, and Joyce Troy.

My students have been phenomenal, as well as phenomenally patient with me. Thank you especially to Ana Grujic, John Hyland, and Nick Lindsey. Aleksandra Szaniawska has been a lifeline, helping me take care of Drees. Numerous people have co-parented my son, feeding him, driving him to soccer, and loving him. In particular I thank Gwen Howard, Laurie Ousley, Laura Sommer, and their families. Thank you to LaKisha Simmons and Jason Young and to little Layla, who brings so much joy in her wake.

My chosen family in Buffalo has been there for me in more ways than I can count. Susan Cahn and Tandy Hamilton have opened their home and their hearts to me. Susan has modeled what it means to be a generous intellectual and lifelong friend, while Tandy changed my bandages, carried me to the bathroom, and hugged my son at school. They are the perfect balance. I thank Dana, John, and Fiona Rigney. Dana was always there to run away with me on rainy days, to make art, and to remind me of myself. Patrick Walter is the eye to my hurricane. I cherish his kindness and his ability to see me.

Chamara Kwakye drove incredible distances, dove to great depths, bought her godson shoes when I could not afford them, and held my head above water. Palvih Bhana is beautiful and always makes me smile. Hemant, Angie, Kiri, and Aiden Bhana make summers worthwhile. My father, Surendra Bhana, has encouraged, prodded, and listened. For showing me what it means to live gracefully with illness, to be a good academic and an even better person, I dedicate this book to him. Idris Young is the river and its banks, the reason I remember to breathe. Through everything there has always been my mother to remind me that change is neither good nor bad. It just is. And I should just get on with it.

INTRODUCTION

Imagine a beginning—always arbitrary. A woman stands on stage in London, clad in a black dress that hugs every curve. Across the Atlantic in New Orleans, a group of women wearing high-necked blue dresses, with well-oiled hair and scrubbed fingernails, answer questions from buyers eager to procure a deal. These women, separated by an ocean, know nothing of one another. They cannot even dream one another up. These women have everything to do with one another. And with us.

This volume attempts an excavation of the historical and present-day limits of liberal, capitalist notions of individual agency. It does so by exposing the continuities between the forms of labor literally embodied in slavery, indenture, and the commodified raced and gendered spectacle. *Illegible Will* is structured around a series of disparate and far-flung (geographically and temporally) case studies/performances, which include the tragic life of Tryntjie (a Madagascan slave at the Cape of Good Hope), a novel by Andre Brink, Indian indenture in Natal, the Miss Landmine Angola beauty pageant, Saartjie (Sarah) Baartman's time in London, Joice Heth (one of P. T. Barnum's first freak shows), and Yvette Christianse's brilliant novel *Unconfessed*. By juxtaposing "case studies" such as these, my historiographic approach situates southern African performances within African diasporic circuits of meaning. I do not mean to suggest that these historical case studies are teleological explanations. Instead, as C. Riley Snorton writes, these "prior moments and events ... foreshadow [black will's] emergence to suggest that our contemporary moment finds precedents in other times and places" marked by a crisis of meaning in black will.[1]

This book is deeply indebted to the works of performance and disability scholars such as Saidiya Hartman, Joseph Roach, and Rosemarie Garland Thompson. Intervening in histories that privilege the written, I argue that everyday performance practices such as selling beer and sighing or limping reveal a diasporic repertoire of shifting creative and embodied responses to imperialism that exceed the textual and verbal. This study, then, attempts what Dwight Conquergood has described as "a riskier hermeneutics of experience, relocation, copresence, humility and vulnerability: listening to and being touched by the protest performances of [subjugated] . . . people."[2] Chapters on Miss Landmine Angola or Sarah Baartman for example, are obvious exemplars of this approach as I analyze pageant participants' poses, the spectacle of their disability or Baartman's "rude" and reluctant demonstrations of her musicality. However, one of Performance Studies' most radical contributions lies in its refusal to simply replace the romance of textual authority with the seductive immediacy of performance. In "Performance: Blunders of Orpheus," Joseph Roach suggests that over-privileging the living repertoire can result in the widening of the gap between performance studies and textual studies. Should they neglect the textual "resources that stand behind the critique and representation of social differences," performances could find themselves "adrift in the present, unmoored from prior [imagined or known] iterations of them."[3] Performance scholars, then, must be attentive to the complex interaction between textuality and embodied memory. We must know when to remember and when to reinvent and when to search out fugitive traces and echoes of prior moments in the gloom.

Illegible Will struggles with how best to think through and write about embodied practices/repertoires of behavior as inextricable from literary and historical claims. As numerous scholars such as Saidiya Hartman and Diana Taylor insist, reading the textual for the performative and making the archival performative lead us toward an understanding of history and performance as overlapping modalities that distill meaning from the past. Robin Bernstein argues that the historical and the performative work together, "with neither form of knowledge . . . pre-existing the other. Within each scriptive thing, archive and repertoire are one."[4]

It is for these reasons that I use performance studies as a methodology in chapters that seem less obviously about performance, such as those dealing with the contemporary novel *Unconfessed* or the narrative history *Rogues, Rebels and Runaways*. Whether textually based or embodied, the various scenes in each chapter then are about making meaning through performative histories of transatlantic and trans–Indian Ocean circuits and exchanges. The construction of racialized bodies via the spectacle, as well as the creation of various viewers and consumers, becomes the engine and the function of the historical circulation and exchange that this book traces.

When faced with the undocumented "event," performative histories have a unique ability to alter how we make history and conjure memory. Moving away from understanding the past as only chronological and behind us, Diana Taylor asks us to imagine it "as also vertical, as a different form of storage of what's already here. Its iterative, recurrent quality functions through repeats, yet breaks out of them." The "repetition with difference" of performance offers an alternate modality for thinking about an always reiterative history. Taylor goes on to say that the "bearers of performance, those who engage in it, are also the bearers of history who link the layers past-present-future through practice."[5]

How does one engage performatively with the archive as a vertical and chronological space?[6] How does one remember histories that depart from traditional notions of the archive and archival process? Anjali Arondekar suggests that "even as the concept of fixed and finite archive has come under siege, it has simultaneously led to an explosion of multiple/alternate archives that seek to remedy the erasures of the past."[7] In her attempt to "queer the archive," what I have described as reading the archive performatively, Arondekar proposes "a different kind of archival romance, one that supplements the narrative of retrieval with a radically different script of historical continuation."[8] Rather than presuming one can find what has been missing, Arondekar theorizes a reading practice that departs from the assumption that recovering lost or new evidence can somehow excavate illegible subjectivities. Instead of the search for an object that leads to a subject, the scholar's search should be for a subject effect: a ghostly afterlife or a space of absence that is not empty but filled. In other words, rather than insisting on excavating factual evidence that may or may not be there, but that can never adequately fill the holes in the archive, my work performs politically urgent narrations or informed critical conjurings, a method at which some historians might balk. Given the dearth of traditional archival material written by and about black people, what is required is an engagement "with the material imprint of archival evidence as a 'recalcitrant event.'" To do this requires moving beyond arguments about missing or present documented evidence into what Arondekar calls "the realm of narration."[9] Such an engagement requires navigation across disciplines: a remapping of the disjunctures, chasms, and nodes of connection between different historically located fields of knowledge that can help us more fully flesh out the afterlife of black diasporic subjects.[10]

My manuscript relies heavily on the primary research done by historians such as Clifton Crais and Pamela Scully and Nigel Penn to provide new insights into the political dynamics of certain black historical actors and to problematize standard assumptions about their subjectivity. That I rely on the primary research of others might be construed as a weakness of this manuscript, and to some extent it is. But the focus of *Illegible Will* is on exploring the *process* of reading the archive across existing literatures and connecting fields. How do historians and other thinkers, given their particular investments and theorizations of the archive itself, encounter black presence and absence? What kinds of associative thinking are possible if we look at how historians attribute historical will rather than simply being reassured that they have located evidence of its existence?

Illegible Will thus attempts a queer imaginative conjuring through critical theories of redress. The filled empty spaces call out for critical imaginings or alternate visions that suggest moments in which agency could reside. These critical imaginative moments lie side by side with hegemonic discourses, providing not only an avenue to think through the power of historical fiction but also a way to reconceptualize the relationship between historical process and narrative structure. While not necessarily empirically true, these performative moments offer us equally valid outlines of history's afterlife. Black performance studies thus provides me with a messy theoretical body, as well as with a methodology that can animate, suture together, and disrupt disciplinary investments in writing black histories.

Alexander Weheliye reminds us that black (performance) studies has to account for how the field contributes to the creation of primary, particular objects of knowledge such as black culture.[11] Using the work of Hortense Spillers and Sylvia Wynter, he suggests that instead of a descriptive field, black studies must operate as mode of knowledge production. For Weheliye, this mode allows us to theorize the "ideological and physiological mechanics of the violently tiered categorization of the human species in western modernity, which stand counter to the universalizing but resolutely Europe-centered visions embodied by bare life and biopolitics . . . without demoting race and gender to the rank of the ethnographically particular, instead exposing how these categories carve from the swamps of slavery and colonialism the very flesh and bones of modern Man."[12] I am careful not to use the term "black" uncritically in this project to suggest a uniform and shared identity that is unmoored in time and space. *Illegible Will* resides in the uneasy and fraught spaces among specific African peoples, African Americans, and various other peoples whom modernity has excluded from a "humanity" that is coterminous with white, liberal Man. Along with Weheliye, scholars such as Oyeronke Oyewumi and Chandra Mohanty warn against falsely universalizing methodologies and constructs that can either retroactively map contemporary meanings onto historically located bodies or, under the guise of universality, use naturalized Western concepts such as "gender" while subjugating indigenous worldviews and systems of meaning.[13]

In keeping with black performance studies as a mode of knowledge production, I set transatlantic sites in conversation with one another not so much to apply the same universal identitarian categories to different historical situations as to map their uneven development and application. I place seemingly disparate performative sites in conversation with one another precisely because racialized bodies across the diaspora were displayed and defined against one another while also being compared to the bodies of their viewers, all in order to develop modern transatlantic systems of race and gender that enable capitalism and its attendant modes of political power. The differing sites become coherent *as sites* only in their relationship to one another.[14] The coherence of these sites is precarious because systems of power constantly change, necessitating time-specific performances of blackness. Race, as Ann Stoler writes, "is a discourse of vacillations. It operates at different levels and moves not only between different political projects but seizes upon different elements of earlier discourses reworked for new political ends."[15]

It is important to remember that racial formations, as Stoler tells us, are "shaped by specific relations of power and therefore have different histories and etymologies."[16] In her comparative study of race, class and gender, Zine Magubane pays close attention to these histories and etymologies. As a result, she is loath to propound "a general theory of the articulation of race, class, and gender that is capable of explaining the very different social relations of, for example, England in the nineteenth century and Brazil in the twenty-first . . . [Rather the] utility of historical case studies [or performances] lies less in their ability to generate a totalizing theory than in their ability to suggest ways of looking at the world or at social situations that may be taken up and deployed, with modification, in other contexts."[17] Magubane wishes to foreground what might be called a diasporic methodology that highlights the connections between economic processes and racialized gender. In other words, as Stoler insists, discourses of sexuality, race, and labor must be placed "within a common frame as productive sites in a broader process of [the] nor-malization [of the white bourgeois body]."[18] I would amend Magubane's dia-sporic methodology to foreground performance. I argue that the connections between economic processes and racialized gender are embodied, tactile, and repeated with difference by various actors in a wide array of locations. These actors re-imbue blackness with meaning through their performances so that it is historically located but also always new.

The population at the Cape during the seventeenth century was pheno-typically, religiously, linguistically, and culturally very diverse, with slaves originating from areas such as Malaysia, Mozambique, the Indian subconti-nent, and Madagascar. Also included were Khoikhoi and Baastard Hottentots (the children of slave or settler men and Khoisan women) who, while legally exempt from slavery, joined the ranks of coerced labor. Although blackness in the Cape during this period was not the inflexible naturalized racial category that it imagined itself to be later, it would still be a mistake to think that color prejudice did not affect slaves such as Tryntjie of Madagascar, whom I discuss in chapter 2. As the renowned historian John Edwin Mason argues, while the Cape "had yet to elaborate a well-developed racial ideology, 'respectable' whites subscribed to a pervasive color prejudice that cut across divisions of class, ethnicity, and religion."[19] This color prejudice, though unstable and not yet forged into the rigid concepts of race that some argue were "firmly established" by 1820,[20] articulated a link between the inherent deviancy of the "nonwhite"/less human and systems of coercive labor. The attempts to define slavery revolved around a racialization of coerced labor that gradually cemented the mutable links between race and slavery itself. The scientific codification of older racial prejudice became crucial to the justification and structural development of the slave trade and imperial policy. As whiteness became essential to the category of the human, slavery and other forms of coerced labor began to be inextricable from notions of blackness.

An example of racialization that uses the phenotypic to fuse slavery with blackness can be seen in the struggles around the racial classification of the Khoikhoi, or "Hottentots," as they were derogatorily known. By describing "Hottentots" as "fair"-skinned, seventeenth-century and some eighteenth-century travel writing threatened to disrupt the growing codification of race into a "visual science" of skin color that underpinned slavery. This literature on the Khoikhoi insists that they are not black or brown but yellow, tawny, fair-skinned, with their babies being born white-skinned. For example, Linda Merians describes how, in a report to the members of the Royal Society, John

Maxwell "describes 'Hottentot' skin color as 'naturally as White as ours,'... 'a race onto themselves' [and therefore] *'unfit' for slavery*."[21] Subsequent historical changes to this racial discourse result in the "Hottentot" being the exemplar of the primitive. Sarah Baartman's putative elongated labia and steatopygia are re-read, not only as signs of lesser humanity, but also as evidence of fitness for enslavement. Blackness, as Magubane reminds us, is a variable, historically located tool, etched onto the body and intimately linked to capitalist systems of labor.[22]

Recalcitrant Bodies

The performance scholarship I will be engaging with insists not only on the materiality of the body, but also on what Taylor calls performance's manipulation and experimentation of historically located notions of embodiment.[23] My work builds on performance scholars in its focus on southern Africa and site-specific spectacles of laboring bodies. How well does black performance theory travel, given that there is no universal, transparent notion of the (black) body? What does the performing body look like from the vantage point of the Cape of Storms, for example, where the Indian and Atlantic oceans break against each other?

The famed African scholars Jean Comaroff and John Comaroff remind us that "the body... cannot escape being a vehicle of history, a metaphor and metonym of being-in-time."[24] Similarly, Magubane asks us to consider how "embodiment articulates the evolution of capitalism and colonialism."[25] As Timothy Burke cautions, one cannot simply translate a local African or African American vocabulary for the body into a more general scholarly language because understandings of the body as a unit of analysis are not consistent across time and space. Burke suggests, "Regarding the body as an invariably significant or coherent subject in any culture must be regarded as a suspect notion; the body as a subject is specifically a product of the peculiar and convoluted history of Western and Christian insistence on mind/body duality.... In particular, bio-power... makes sense only in reference to historically specific and modern figurations of the body in Western history, and thus has dubious relevance to the pre-colonial and perhaps even contemporary cultural experiences of many Africans."[26] Burke's argument sets the groundwork for Weheliye's warning that biopolitics as a mode of analysis often figures racial difference as a primitive vestige located prior to contemporary thought as such. Weheliye suggests instead that the "conceptual tools of racialized minority discourse augment and reframe bare life and biopolitics discourse" by inhabiting "the nexus of differentiation, hierarchy, and the human" and imagining different modes of being human that do not center on the liberal bourgeois Man.[27]

The case studies in all of the chapters work through the temporal and geographic specificities of the body. Consider, for example, the Miss Landmine Angola pageant, as discussed in chapter 3. As Neville Hoad points out, largely unemployed, amputee contestants have "very little in common with a standard-bearer pageant like Miss World beyond adherence to the basic generic form of a pageant [and its typical contestant]."[28] The material body, what it stands for, how it is represented, and how gender or beauty or any number of discourses are embodied and inscribed has everything to do with what Hoad describes as the "enormously complicated set of transnational exchanges, precisely connected at the level of the economic to the global histories and their libidinal economies" that led to the military conditions that caused these women's injuries in the first place."[29] The history of the West's encounter with the Other has pivoted around the creation of the injured spectacle of Otherness. The ways in which women's bodies were viewed and represented underwrote the (sexual) exploitation of those bodies that is essential for the capitalist appropriation of empire.

Illegible Will claims that in order to open up the question of agency, coercion, and consent, one needs to prevent the collapsing of the material and discursive body. I wish to engage not with the body functioning as a symbolic surrogate for personhood but with the messy realities of bodies that bleed, heal, dance, and die. In a chapter titled "Rotten Worlds," Elizabeth Povinelli tracks the discursive production of a large sore on her shoulder. Studying the way in which her sore is framed by doctors, healers, and colleagues as they offer various explanations, treatments, and affective responses, Povinelli distinguishes between two social aspects of embodiment that she terms corporeality and carnality. For Povinelli, corporeality functions as discursive strategy, while carnality emphasizes a material, fleshy body located in an environment. She distinguishes between these bodily registers "in terms of the difference between flesh as a juridical and political maneuver and flesh as a physical mattering forth of these maneuvers."[30] The fact of flesh is not opposed to discourse, instead "the uneven distribution of the flesh—the creation of lifeworlds, death-worlds, and rotting worlds—is a key way in which ... [individual agency and social constraint] are felt, known, and expressed."[31] In many ways, this formulation is indebted to Hortense Spillers's argument about the distinctions between "body" and "flesh" revolving around captive and non-captive subject positions.[32] Spillers posits that "before the 'body' there is the 'flesh,' that zero degree of social conceptualization that does not escape concealment under the brush of discourse, or the reflexes of iconography. . . . If we think of the 'flesh' as a primary narrative, then we mean its seared, divided, ripped-apartness, riveted to the ship's hole, fallen, or 'escaped' overboard."[33] Like Povinelli's carnality, Spillers's flesh is not a natural substrate that exists prior to racialization. Rather, it is crucially produced through acts of violence. The unprotected, ungendered slave body becomes what Spillers calls a text *and* a methodology for reading life and death, subjugation and survival.

Understood, then, as both flesh and body, Povinelli's body is subject to numerous, often incommensurate discourses. Contemporary science might understand her sore as a symptom of staphylococcus or anthrax spores, whereas culturally prejudicial discourses might read the lesions as evidence of the "filthiness" of Aboriginal communities where she works. Conversely, Aboriginal communities themselves might diagnose her sore as the result of contact with a living, breathing ancestral site. While all these discourses exist simultaneously, they are differentially empowered. For instance, as Povinelli and Kim DiFruscia discuss, the diagnosis of staphylococcus is more likely to be taken as scientifically true than one about ancestral contact.[34] But no matter how the sore is understood (a matter of vital importance in terms of treatment), it causes the material body to sicken. And, as Povinelli points out,

Depending how one's body has been cared for, or is being cared for, it sickens it in different ways and different degrees. . . . And this slow corrosion of the life is part of the reason why, if you are [a person of color], your life runs out much sooner than [that of white people]. And if the state provides you rights based on longevity . . . but you are dying on average ten to twenty years sooner than non-Indigenous people, then the carnal condition of your body is out of sync with the apparatus of recognition. . . . Carnality therefore becomes vital to understanding the dynamics of power.[35]

The body and the flesh, corporeality and carnality, therefore become crucial to understanding the dynamics of power that crosshatch the African diasporic body as each chapter works through notions of labor, illness, and performance.

This idea of material embodiment is distinct from the social and structural death discussed by Achille Mbembe and Orlando Patterson. Theorizing dance and gesture, death and dying, I wish to add a fleshy carnality to the discourse of necropolitics to more adequately open up questions of will and personhood. Povinelli's discussion of the material deterioration of bodies and the state's interest in certain people's (and not others') longevity provides an opening to discuss what Mbembe terms "necropolitics," or technologies of control that subjugate life to the power of death.[36] Rather than revolving around various notions of state and individual autonomy, sovereignty becomes an exercise in defining life and controlling mortality. Mbembe writes that, under the conditions of necropolitics, "power is infinitely more brutal than it was during the authoritarian period. . . . If it still maintains its tight grid of bodies (or their agglomeration within camps or so-called security zones), this is not so much to inscribe them in disciplinary apparatuses as to better inscribe them, when the time comes, within the order of that maximal economy that has become the 'massacre.'"[37] Within site-specific, late modern colonial contexts, Mbembe describes the endless states of racialized terror such as continual warfare or (I would argue) the withholding and distribution of health care that lead to totalizing forms of domination over human lives and the control of death. This becomes particularly relevant in my chapter on indentured labor where the work accomplished by the death of the laborers ultimately proved more valuable than their labor when alive. Orlando Patterson's groundbreaking *Slavery and Social Death*, on the power relations that undergird plantation slavery, also recognizes the centrality of death in colonial regimes. Patterson's argument uses "bare life" and the politics of exception to think through master-slave Hegelian relationships. He argues that these relationships ultimately *produce* the slave through the slave's "social death."[38] His concerns are with the making of the slave through her negation, through her social unmaking.

Mbembe's and Patterson's social unmaking must be placed alongside the fleshy body's illness, decay, and death, or what could be called a material death. Looking at the body in a historically contextualized manner that incorporates material death and social death allows us to interrogate the politics around life-stealing labor that have become so normalized as to be rendered transparent. Thus, in the instance of the slave who works herself to death on the plantation, her rotting body as well as the social death she experienced as a slave reveal the embodied ways in which domination works. The interplay between her corporeality and her carnality gestures toward the plural notions of identity and agency that diasporic Africans were and are able to practice even within conditions of extreme violence.

To further explore embodied practices of agency, this volume also pays close attention to meaning-making forms of movement. My analyses of a pageant contestant's pose as she awkwardly reclines next to a pool and of Sarah Baartman's slow recalcitrance as she appears on stage are attempts to write a history contextualized within the body itself. Gesture is not merely a product of socialization. Rather, as Carrie Noland reminds us, "The lived experience of executing a gesture is as important as the [culturally and historically specific] symbolic dimension of the gesture."[39] The body achieves a kinesthetic awareness of itself as nerves tingle, synapses fire, and the body creates and discovers itself. The symbolic dimension of gesture cannot simply be translated into verbal language. On the contrary, as Juana Rodriguez points out, "Sometimes the point of gesture is that it can register what cannot or should not be expressed in words. And sometimes it signals what one wishes to keep out of sound's reach."[40] In their emphasis on the kinetic, those things that one cannot say or does not want to say except with a hand caressing a cheek, rubbing, pushing, and falling, gestures refuse determined meanings as they constantly search for social connection. While gestures reveal what Rodriguez calls the "inscription of social and cultural laws [that] transform our individual movements into an archive of received social behaviors and norms," kinetic energy shapes and reshapes the body.[41] This embodied kinesis reroutes normative processes of meaning making, troubling social norms even while indexing them. Let us imagine the simple act of holding one's hands up, for example, as if a policeman is pointing a gun at one's chest. This gesture has accumulated a constellation of social meanings. It tells the police officer to pause and not shoot just yet. Through the careful raising of my arms and opening of my torso, I recognize the potential violence to my person embodied in the policeman's stance. The body of both police officer and suspect enact a culturally determined script of power and surrender, without which gesture would just be uninflected, meaningless motion. The plea "I can't breathe" or "Don't shoot" expressed through vulnerable torso and arms held to the sky accrues meaning as it resonates throughout the African diaspora. Yet each performance, even as it reiterates a culturally specific gestural vocabulary, houses the possibility of multiple other meanings. Thus, approaching a police officer (who may or may not have his gun drawn) with arms up is not so much a gesture of supplication as a threat, a parody of subservience. Instead of enacting my normative gestural role of freezing or supplicating, my gestures turn vulnerability into aggression. They refuse social scripts, demanding another type of relationality. Another example would be the Cake-Walk performed by slaves that mimicked the rigid, stiff movements of their owners. Slave owners perceived slaves' gestural vocabularies of straight limbs as flattering imitation.

What they overlooked was the West African belief that straight limbs characterized death. By taking on the characteristics of white dancers, Susan Phillips argues, slaves performed white ownership and exhibited control over the dead, thus countering the social death of slavery.[42] Or as Rodriguez writes, dance "reflect[s] how social forces exert corporeal power, and how as pulsating kinetic subjects, we find out own ways to groove to the tracks."[43] The example with the police officer and the Cake-Walk both reveal, according to Noland, how gesture becomes the connecting link between "discourses privileging the biological body, subjectivity, and somatic experience on the one hand and, on the other, discourses indebted to a deconstructive critique of embodiment as a staging of the body through structures of signification that are not necessarily the body's own."[44] Throughout *Illegible Will*, I hope to think through the historical and spatial contingencies by which gestures migrate, repeat, and acquire (new) meanings. The body as gestural archive and inventor, as monument and stylus, is paramount to any understanding of diasporic performance.

Time and Space

Despite covering large swaths of time, *Illegible Will* is a postapartheid study in that it tells stories that the grand drama of apartheid obscured for so long. Throughout the book, I render visible South Africa's long history of international contact that becomes apparent only following the end of apartheid and its myth of global isolation and autonomy. Thus, this book focuses on certain historical texts, cultural production, and moments while de-emphasizing other, equally important ones. One of the most important forms of southern African labor that this manuscript does not discuss is migrant labor—whether we go as far back as the Mfecane (the dispersal and militarized upheaval that attended the consolidation of the Zulu kingdom in the nineteenth century) or focus narrowly on recent labor disputes in the South African mining industry. Since the beginning of the twentieth century, the South African mining industry has set up a transnational infrastructure of labor migrancy that transported workers from undeveloped "homelands" and rural townships to the mines, where these workers were crowded into a system of compounds. As Jonathan Crush and Clarence Tshitereke tell us, the mining industry has wielded significant authority over the management of migratory labor diasporas.[45] The story of the proletarianization of rural agricultural economies continues to be told. For example, Phaswane Mpe's

Welcome to Our Hillbrow (2001) highlights the centrality of migrant labor in the southern African landscape.[46] Showing how other African immigrants to South Africa are scapegoated as the primary carriers of HIV and AIDS, Mpe uses the trope of contagion to think through a contemporary Hillbrow, which is inundated with migrant workers desperate for paying jobs. While my study recognizes the importance of those laboring Southern Africans who remained relatively stationary and did not cross large bodies of water, I focus primarily on the wake of the Black Atlantic and the sea tack toward the Indian Ocean.[47]

The book thus crisscrosses oceans to include African Americans, black British, East Africans, Madagascans, Goans, and South Asians. It insists on recognizing the flow of labor both away from and toward the African continent. As a result, *Illegible Will*'s chapter on Indian indentured labor, in particular, makes visible the other ocean central to coercive labor regimes and largely occluded in the current, Paul Gilroy–derived academic discourse: the Indian Ocean. While there are several continuities between the Atlantic and Indian oceans in the historical performances of slavery and coercion, we need to trace the differences between these oceanic sites to keep from collapsing them into each other or ignoring one in favor of the other. "Narratives of migration, diaspora, settlement, and naming on and around the Cape of Storms" as Loren Kruger states, "introduce currents that blur new and old maps of cultural traffic."[48] A thoughtful perspective on Cape slavery necessitates the inclusion of the African continent and the Indian Ocean and Red Sea in the African diaspora. The dispersal of Africans across the Atlantic has had a near-monopoly in studies of the African diaspora, marked particularly by the popularity of terms such as "Black Atlantic." In particular, as Pier Larson reminds us, "the use of new social identities in the African continental portion of the diaspora during the age of enslavement was in many cases linked to a social amnesia of enslavement, differing from the formation of African American identities in the western Atlantic and their link to memorialization of trauma and victimization by enslavement."[49] While the transatlantic slave trade was the largest forced migration of Africans (approximately twelve million), many African slaves were captured and moved to destinations within the continent itself. One needs to also remember the numbers recounted by Larson, the trans-Saharan trade (nearly eight million), and the Indian Ocean and Red Sea trades (more than four million).[50] The African diaspora thus consists of intimately linked brutal dispersions that were transatlantic, trans-Saharan, trans–Indian Ocean, and internal to the African continent itself.

Thus, the slaves stolen from Mozambique who made the Cape their home are just as essential to the African diaspora as those who were shipped to the Caribbean and the United States.

Madagascar in particular has been overlooked and proves key to this project, particularly in the chapter on Tryntjie, a Madagascan slave at the Cape. The island is often considered a world apart, excluded from African studies and only sometimes included in South Asian history. However, as Larson posits, the island nonetheless represented a "cultural and economic crossroads and its peoples experienced a variety of slave trades between the fifteenth and nineteenth centuries as both captives and captors."[51] Africans of the Indian Ocean diaspora were therefore subjected to a host of experiences that, while distinct, bear remarkable similarities to those of Africans who were crisscrossing the Atlantic Ocean. One needs to contest the marginalization of East Africa and Madagascar from historical considerations of slavery. Instead, this history needs to be located within what Tony Ballantyne and Antoinette Burton call "imperial webs" that function as "systems of exchange, mobility, appropriation and extraction, fashioned to enable the empire-building power to exploit the natural resources, manufactured goods, or valued skills of the subordinated group. . . . These webs include systems of contact and exchange, and displays of power and domination, that shape the imperial landscape."[52] The stories of the various historical people in this manuscript enable us to situate Cape slavery, under the control of the Vereenigde Oost-Indische Compagnie (Dutch East India Company; VOC) from 1652 to 1795 within larger discourses of slavery.

While not as involved in the slave trade as its partner, the Dutch West India Company,[53] the VOC did need to supply the Cape Colony with slaves. Confronted with international competition for slaves and having been excluded from regions such as Dahomey and Guinea by the Dutch West India Company, the VOC looked at alternative potential slave markets such as Delagoa Bay and Ceylon. Thus, Cape slaves were not from West Africa and Central Africa but instead hailed mainly from Asia and the southwest Indian Ocean.[54] In the seventeenth century, most slaves were from Madagascar. The eighteenth century showed demographic shifts: early in the century, almost half the slaves were from India and Sri Lanka. Twenty percent were brought to the Cape via Batavia (modern-day Jakarta). Toward the end of the VOC's reign, the number of slaves from Asia had declined considerably as they were replaced by men and women from Mozambique. The total number of slaves between 1652 and 1808 can be estimated at 63,000, comparable to the total number of slaves brought to the Americas in a single year.[55]

One-third of all slaves in the middle of the eighteenth century were owned by the VOC and housed in the company slave lodge in Cape Town that Worden describes, crucially for our later discussion, as "the best known brothel of the colony."[56] These slaves performed public works and any other services that the VOC required, such as carpentry and building. The rest of the slaves were privately owned and mainly performed domestic service on isolated farms and in independent households. Thus, Cape slavery was characterized by the small scale of slaveholding units as the average slaveholder had only ten slaves. This number must be qualified due to the presence of indigenous Khoikhoi laborers who worked alongside slaves but who, as Worden points out, "entered into a social structure already conditioned by the slave system, and although nominally free, became subject to similar means of coercion and control which were later to be applied in a modified form to Bantu-speaking laborers."[57] The small number of slaves and their intimate proximity to white masters, mistresses, and indigenous workers has sometimes been mistaken to suggest the mildness of Cape slavery. In actuality, slavery everywhere it existed operated by a brutal exercise of power over fungible slave bodies. In the Cape, the relative isolation of many farms where male slaves often outnumbered male colonists led to extreme forms of coercion and control. For evidence of such brutality, one need only glance at the Court of Justice's proceedings to find documentation of torturous punishments such as spanning a slave's body into *poolsche bok*.[58] Throughout the seventeenth century and eighteenth century, Cape law allowed the master to lay up to thirty-nine lashes onto a slave with a whip, *sjambok*, leather thong, rattan, cat-o'-nine-tails, or other such instrument as retribution for "domestic offenses" such as running away, neglect of duties, and impudence. Court records document how Justinus Rens beat his slave Camies with a sjambok for refusing to "bark like a Dog and Crow like a Cock."[59]

As was the case in most colonial transatlantic slave societies, male slaves greatly outnumbered female slaves. Only in the final years of the VOC's rule did female slaves exceed 25 percent of the slave population.[60] Female slaves in the records are characterized both by their absence and simultaneous overwhelming presence. These women's voices are missing, but their bodies are all over the records as subjects of racialized discipline. When going through the transcripts of trials from the Council of Justice between 1705 and 1794, for instance, one is struck by the extent to which female slaves appear as victims of their owners and fellow slaves. Case after case tells us of female slaves such as Regina van Ternaten, who, after being whipped for absenteeism, was found dead in the veld, or Diana, who was whipped to death after her master ordered another slave named January to beat her.[61] The slave woman, Suzette Spencer argues, left "no written body of records, yet her body functions as both the invisible enigma and the open or naked surface upon which historians inscribe multiple narratives."[62] What all these cases highlight is an extensive cataloguing of women's bodies as sexual objects but a comparative absence of women's voices as subjects. The construction of black femininity is indexed by a historical invisibility that is not challenged but, rather, supported by the injured bodies of brutalized women that populate the archive's pages. As Nell Painter suggests, the "truth" about black female subjects lies in which critical methodologies we use to interpret their consenting and coerced bodies located within slavery's politics of violent intimacy.[63]

Consider the statement of an indignant Reverend William Wright of Trinity College, Dublin, who writes

> [Cape] slaves are in the habit of living in unrestrained concubinage ...
> with Europeans. . . . Shall I enlarge on the effects of such a system? Is it
> necessary to tell the inhabitants of a Christian country, that when the law
> and usage sanctioned adultery, thus converting every private house into
> what should not be named in these pages, the tendency and effects of such
> a system must have been demoralizing in the extreme. . . . How unpleasant
> [to be exposed to a system] so general and so public, that it never shuns the
> light, and seldom excites a blush.[64]

Wright sees this sanctioned adultery as evidence that the "incurable evil of slavery" corrupts the European slave owner but not the slave, who is already morally lax and sexually wanton. Wright, as well as other diarists and travelers to the Cape, had difficulty grasping the meaning of the sexually exploitative behavior they witnessed. As Mason observes, these colonialists "refused to acknowledge the vulnerability and powerlessness and the overt and covert forms of coercion that forced the women into these liaisons [with white men]."[65] Rather than slave owners' being victims of their slaves, they were victims to their own sexualized and racialized performances of power. In the early 1770s, Anders Sparrman, a Swedish naturalist and abolitionist, shared a meal with a white overseer over which they discussed concubinage with slaves in terms that actualized Reverend Wright's deepest fears (or fantasies). Based on his own sexual experiences, the overseer provided Sparrman with a sexual ranking of (slave) women according to their ethnicity, beginning with Madagascan women, who were the "blackest and the best," then Malabars, followed by Bugunese or Malays. The bottom of the list was reserved for Hottentots and then, "worst of all," white Dutch women.[66] Such a candid list reveals not only that the sexual enjoyment of slaves was common, but also that all of that erotic life was located in what Sharon Holland terms the "messy terrain of racist practice."[67] White male settlers sexually abused female slaves housed in the company Slave Lodge so routinely that travelers to the Cape complained that the women were the source of the high occurrences of venereal disease among white men.[68] O. F. Mentzel describes "female slaves . . . as always ready to offer their bodies for a trifle; and towards evening, one can see a string of soldiers and sailors entering the lodge where they misspend their time until the clock strikes 9 . . . Three or four generations of this admixture (for daughters follow their mother's footsteps) have produced a half-caste population—as mestizo class—but a slight shade darker than some Europeans."[69] As Wright observes, so blatant was the sexual abuse of slaves by white men that a *plakkaat* (an ad hoc ordinance used as common law in the Cape) was issued in 1678 prohibiting whites from openly going about the streets with slave women from the lodge. Such public behavior supposedly undermined the authority of European men. In 1685, High Commissioner Hendrik van Rheede of the East India Company noted during his visit to the Cape that many of the slave children in the Company's Lodge had Dutch fathers. To wit, he reiterated another plakkaat that he felt was being ignored, which prohibited sexual intercourse between female slaves and white men, as well as systems of concubinage. He also ordered that these "half-castes" be taught useful trades and emancipated upon adulthood.[70] Other plakkaats attempted to ensure that a slave woman who had children with her master could not be sold during his lifetime and that both she and her children would be entitled to their liberty when the master died.[71] These laws speak more to white anxieties than to the actual political dynamics of sexual violence. White men did not undermine their authority by identifying their slave mistresses or openly walking the streets with them, as Commissioner van Reede feared. Instead, such performances of sexual access reasserted the vulnerability of black femininity, thereby consolidating the power of white masculinity to sexually plunder at will. Black femininity became defined precisely through white sexual enjoyment and exploitation.

No matter how commonplace these repertoires might have been, it is important to note that (middle-class and upper-class) slave-owning society did not legally, religiously, or socially condone sexual intercourse between master and slave. Both masters and mistresses took significant measures to hide what was occurring in their households and at the Slave Lodge. Perhaps the anxieties of white slave owners that they would be exposed revolved not so much around sexual reputation as around the dissolution of white paternity on which claims of slavery and freedom ultimately rest.

Recalcitrant Events and the Crisis in Liberal Notions of Agency and Consent

Using the concept of the laboring body, *Illegible Will* critically explores the liberal, binary notions of individual freedom and social constraint. The discursive ideals and fantasies of self-sovereignty and the value of individual freedom arise from the Enlightenment's basis in contractual democracy and speculative capital. According to Magubane, the shift to "capitalist social relations is always depicted . . . in terms of freedom and choice" as individuals are strongly "encouraged" to sell their labor.[72] Classic formal Marxism posits that workers are "free" under capitalism in that they are separated from the means of production and therefore have to work for an employer. Thus, the worker is "free" to sell his or her labor. The liberal state recognizes (with varying degrees of enthusiasm) workers' rights. As Donald Donham explains, this "ideological framework" implies that "everyone is seen as having something to sell (and buy), which concentrates efforts of encouraging exchange, the underlying assumption being that everyone benefits from smoother and ever more extensive exchange."[73] The failure of existing forms of capitalism to live up to these ideals is painfully obvious. Sara Ahmed shows us that even for Marx, property relations depend on "objects 'being willing' in such a way that they would be forced if they were not."[74] Bound or unfree labor, as I argue particularly in chapters 1 and 4, is not only created by and intimately connected to global capital flows.[75] The liberal discourse of an individual's freedom to sell his or her labor supports the ideological constraints of various inheritances such as race. The interplay of freedom and the tethers of race is essential to the creation of the liberal subject, as these concepts refract each other, bouncing the individual between liberty and constraint. The workings of ideology, constraint, and coercion are blatant in slavery and similar forms of unfree labor. However, commonplace distinctions between free and coerced labor become murky when we begin to look at specific historical cases. As Donham astutely formulates the matter, not only does free labor not exist in any uncontaminated form, but it also "reflect[s] a certain naturalization of wage labor itself—in fact, an inability to see the complex mix of truth and falsehood, or ideology and reality, in all forms of labor control."[76]

Consent and coercion rests on an Enlightenment notion of the self in possession of a rational, self-contained individuality. The self becomes the core of subjectivity, what Rosemary Wiss formulates as the "center from which the person looked out and acted upon the world, and at the same time an object which could become self-conscious and subject to self-restraint."[77] The European, bourgeois man was the epitome of this conceptualization, with women, children, and Others (both male and female) needing various degrees of education and guidance to fully realize their selfhood. The political theorist Carole Pateman argues that consent, as a political theory in the seventeenth century and eighteenth century, rests on Lockean assumptions of participating human individuals naturally "free and equal" to one another who voluntarily or tacitly commit to enter into social relationships to preserve this freedom and equality. " 'Free and equal individuals,' to use Lockean terminology, own the property in their persons and their attributes, including their capacity and competency to give consent. Thus children were not competent and as such were unable to give consent. The individual is the 'guardian of *his* own consent.' "[78] Locke, according to Pateman, posited that fathers became patriarchs through the tacit consent of their sons. As a result of the marriage contract, wives were "naturally" subjugated to their husbands, accepting their will in all things concerning them both. Through marriage, women appeared to consent to the authority of their husbands in what was regarded as merely a formal acknowledgment of patriarchal power relations. Paradoxically, this naturalized subordination excluded women from the very definition of consenting individuality, for in the contractual arrogation of her will to her husband, a woman was no longer a "free and equal" individual within civil society. Thus, her consent, like her dissent, was rendered illegible.[79]

There have been many criticisms of Pateman's now famous critique of the (marriage) contract and women's ability to consent. For example, in "Demeaning of Contract," Carl Stychin insists, quite correctly, on the need for a more "nuanced analysis focusing on the conditions in which many women enter contracts [and an understanding that] the meanings of masculinity and femininity are subject to cultural contestation."[80] He goes on to critique Pateman for overlooking the possibility that "some women resisted the sexual contract throughout history and did manage to engage in forms of exchange in civil society."[81] I would further suggest the impossibility of adequately reconciling the marriage contract's resulting arrogation of women's will with slavery and colonialism. A contract between person and property is largely meaningless in these contexts in which bodies and countries are occupied and relegated to terrains of otherness. The failure even to see a need to couch the violence of colonialism and slavery in contractual terms, for the most part, excludes the subjectivity of slaves and the colonized from liberalism's language of individual autonomy, choice, and coercion. As Spillers reminds us, our "plight [as African and diasporic peoples] marked a theft of the body—a willful and violent . . . severing of the captive body from its motive will, its active desire."[82]

Despite these limitations, however, Pateman's critique of the individual as a volitional subject proves useful when thinking about the institution of slavery. Consider the preoccupation in early abolitionist writings with the atrocious abuses of individual slaves by corrupted masters. Elizabeth Clark describes the cataloguing of various horror stories in early texts, such as Theodore Dwight Weld's *American Slavery as It Is: Testimony of a Thousand Witnesses* (1839). Documents such as these are replete with examples of individual atrocity—for example, the case of Thomas Jefferson's nephew who responded to a sulky slave by chopping off small bits of her body and feeding them to the fire until no part remained of the slave in the morning, or the case of a slave woman beaten to death with a fire shovel for the infraction of burning the dinner.[83] Terence Ball has posited that such meticulous documentation of devastating cruelty reinforces an individualist "ontology which holds that the world is composed of discrete, distinct, and wholly separate entities ('individuals'); therefore, causal—and coercive—relations are seen as contingent relations between individual elements."[84] Antislavery rhetoric in the early 1800s relied on the suffering black body. This figure, an individualized spectacle, was brutalized not by the system of slavery, but by his or her master. Abolitionists could critique slavery only via the white reader's identification with the authenticated spectacle of the suffering body of the slave which, as Saidiya Hartman develops, ran the "risk of fixing and naturalizing this condition of pained embodiment [and] exploit[ing] the spectacle of the body in pain."[85]

Using the same logic as the early abolitionists, slaveholders insisted that these documented instances of barbarity were anomalous; a result of a few "bad" masters or the overzealous application of discipline by otherwise well-intentioned owners. In this way, slave owners, too, circumvented critiquing the system of slavery, assuming and insisting that it was a generally benign and kind institution. Whether articulated from an abolitionist or pro-slavery perspective, this argument is premised on the existence of atomized, self-determining individuals. What both early abolitionists and slave masters missed is that slavery is a process of commodification. Understood as a commodity rather than an individual, the fungible black body occupies interchangeable positions within systems of exchange. These positions are never new but, rather, inherited, passed on, and reinvented by those performers who occupied the roles previously. As Roach elaborates, "In the life of a community, the process of surrogation does not begin or end but continues as actual or perceived vacancies occur in the network of relations that constitutes the social fabric. Into the cavities created by loss through death or other forms of departure . . . survivors attempt to fit satisfactory alternates."[86] Individual people, whether Sarah Baartman or Thomas Jefferson's ax-wielding nephew, can be seen as such alternates. As Ball suggests, these historical figures "do not so much 'play' their roles as they are 'bearers' . . . of them."[87] In other words, one cannot read the embodied performance of a single individual slave or master without reference to other bodies and performances, whether similar or dissimilar. The staging of the slave's and master's bodies exists within specific semiotic flows of meaning where no one body can be understood without the apparitional appearance of other relational bodies within the circulation of commodities. Instead of an individualist ideology of liberalism, *Illegible Will* posits a relational ontology in which the meaning of objects and people is forged out of the relations between them. Therefore, to rehearse Ball's theorization, "causal—and coercive—relations hold between elements in a socially structured ensemble of relations."[88] The intentions and motivations of individuals thus are constituted and constrained by their systemic relations. The "good" master and "bad" master and the "caring" capitalist and "ruthless" capitalist have to be seen as one and the same because coercion is ultimately "a feature of structures" and integral to the workings of capitalism itself.[89]

By arguing for a relational ontology rather than an ideology of individualism, I am not suggesting that we abandon the individual labor contract. Rather, we need to reread the labor contract with a different set of eyes to return to the promise embedded in its actual form. Instead of an appropriation of the contract for individual gain in which one party sees the other as a means to a set of unshared ends, we need to think about how the relations enabled by a contract give rise to a limited set of shifting communal obligations. As Daniel Markovits develops, "Rather than deny that the contractual versions of community are thin and formal, or that it arises against a backdrop of self-interest, I argue that even the most self-interested, discrete, and purely transactional contracts . . . invoke the moral relations of respect and community that . . . present the foundations of promissory and contractual obligation."[90] This "collaborative form of community," Markovits goes on to say, is not about ensuring and sharing the other party's ends. Rather than having all involved parties feel that "we want the same end thing," collaborative contractual community or a relational ontology shares a concern for the other person's point of view and demonstrates a mutual responsiveness to the joint engagement. So if two people contractually share the intention to go for a walk together, they may not want to walk to the same place, or one may have a sprained ankle and perhaps no longer wants to walk. Mutual responsiveness might entail walking on another day, slowing down, picking another path or an abbreviated route, or even bicycling to accommodate the shared intention, as well as the sprained ankle.[91] This may seem naïve when thinking about mine workers, for example, but the form of the contract presupposes a temporally delineated collaboration that can be the basis of a community built not around sameness but around a shared intentionality.

Using the issue of same-sex marriage legislation, Stychin similarly refuses to abandon the language of contract (no matter how patriarchal and racist) because it provides him with a useful tool with which to engage the limitations of liberalism and sentimentalism's gendered narratives of individualized romance.[92] Stychin moves beyond the traditional opposition between privatized ethical relationships that revolve around a non-self-serving desire and commercial relations that privilege the acquisition of property above all else. Rather than oppose self-interested commercial relations of exchange to patriarchal and racist familial relations of love or intimacy, Stychin asks us to yoke a reformulated notion of contract to relationships normally deemed private. He insists on what he terms a "relational contracting" that consists of collaborative intentional performances. Adjusted to historical and contextual specificities, this performative contracting revises the principle of self-gain characteristic of the classic contract. I illustrate this kind of collaborative, shared performance at the end of chapter 2, in which I discuss the contractual relations between a servant (the descendant of slaves) and her white master, a renter and her landlord.

By foregrounding a process of surrogation that moves away from individualist ontologies, I pay close attention to performative moments as they occur within a variety of sources: the archive, court cases, contemporary histories, novels, visual art, and websites. The shape and contours of these performances that bear the traces of forgotten surrogations allow me to speculate on absence and silences. They allow me to engage with the "recalcitrant event" by critically imagining places where agency could reside. This project, then, is *not* a search for the "will" of black performers hidden within problematic representational and historical structures. Given that our access to the past relies on legal, criminal, and narrative records often written by deeply implicated and hostile adversaries, locating the agency of black laboring bodies is largely impossible. This is not to say that these bodies had no will. On the contrary: I have *no* doubt that within the constraints of domination, black historical figures made meaning that exceeded the confines set on them. They did it well and often and with significant results. However, as Arondekar suggests, moving away from the romance of retrieval means moving away from "giving voice" to those who have long been silenced. Instead of finding lost voices, my project asks about the possibilities of critical narration that engage with the absence instead of merely attempting to fill the void. By superimposing disparate aporias in the historical record, each chapter allows for "will" to be imagined and set into conversation with traditional historical evidentiary processes.

In some ways, my project overlaps with Ahmed's *Willful Subjects*. Rather than writing a history of "will," Ahmed turns to the "entangled emergence of will and desire" in various philosophic and literary works.[93] She assembles brief and episodic eruptions of the willful figure, creating a "willfulness archive" even as her own intentionality pushes at the boundaries of linear teleological histories. Her lovely reading, for example, of the Brothers Grimm's "The Willful Child" gives us a stubbornly determined female child who refuses to be buried, to submit, and to stop desiring. *Illegible Will* is less about assembling an archive of such "feminist killjoys" as about insisting that the illegibility of (black) will within the historical archive requires performative critical engagements with absence. The intimate loop of freedom and slavery and coercion and consent does not require a retrieval of willfulness or will-lessness. Taking up Spillers's charge that new grammars be invented for certain categories under crisis, the will of black diasporic bodies must be imaginatively and critically performed rather than simply unearthed.

An example of such a critical performance is *Cargo*, the seventh of a series of collaborations between two South African movement theaters, Jazzart Theatre and Magnet Theatre. According to the Jazzart Theatre's website, *Cargo* "uses performance to re-imagine the archive of slavery in the Cape, bringing it to the attention of a wider audience while linking the past to our present reality." At the heart of the performance is a stunning solo performed by Levern Botha as the historical figure on whom chapter 5 of this volume focuses: Sila van der Kaap. The stage is covered in sand, with a shallow trough of water surrounding what appears to be a wall of a cargo hold. On each side of the wall, two women dressed in white salvage pieces of paper from the trough of water, alternating between reading aloud from them and placing the wet pages over the edge of the trough to dry. Botha moves across the stage, between land and water, reeling between the set of archival papers on the right and that on the left. When the women read aloud at different moments, Botha stops her movement across the stage to stand before them. A particularly poignant moment comes when the woman on the right reads out loud from archival criminal proceedings that outline van der Kaap's attempts to murder her children and then kill herself. The wet pages give us a reductive record of her actions while telling us almost nothing about her feelings and motivations. Botha's body, as she stands in front of the woman reading, breathing heavily with her arms held loosely at her sides, insists on the adequacy of the archive's words. Botha as Sila van der Kaap embodies archival absence and presence, the trace and the deep silence. When the woman stops reading and starts looking for more pieces of paper, Botha begins to repeat her heartbreaking choreography of vulnerability. She flings herself across the stage, falling and desperately pushing herself up, across land and water, between this archive and that, until it appears that she can no longer keep moving. She collapses, her body partly in the water, her head on the ground. Botha's performance of van der Kaap lies at the heart of my book. Flinging myself between this reading of the archive and that one, I gesture toward the seething absences of will. Listening to historians as they give us bare outlines, this book is a choreography of vulnerability and exhaustion as I struggle and fail to grasp the meaning of various historical characters. Instead, breathing heavily, I am left with the precious gift of their unintelligibility as I lie across the borders of history, fiction, and performance.

Chapter 1 begins with the repatriation of the body of Sarah Baartman. Instead of continuing the historiographic overemphasis on her body, I focus on issues surrounding her labor by turning to a court case in 1810 in which the African Association for Promoting the Discovery of the Interior of Africa brought suit against Baartman's exhibitors, Henrik Cesars and Alexander Dunlop. The association's claims that Baartman was enslaved converted her performance into a platform for debates about the "free" will of contractual labor. I argue that it is impossible to determine how willingly or unwillingly Baartman entered into a "contract" with Cesars and Dunlop. Her "will" becomes accessible only if we creatively read her performances in London against other ethnographic performances of "will." Specifically, I imagine Baartman's "rude" performance of her "Hottentotness" alongside the performances of slaves in New Orleans as they stood on-stage for auction. The omnipresence of this transatlantic genealogy reinforces the hegemony of racialized spectacles of subjugated labor and the ongoing crisis around person and property. Also embedded within the performances of Baartman and auctioned slaves lie alternative theaters of memory that claim the resistance to and the injury of bondage as birthright.

Chapter 2 examines the strange case of Tryntjie. Kidnapped from the coast of Madagascar and brought to the Cape in 1696, Tryntjie surfaces in the records of the Council of Justice, where she was sentenced to public execution in 1713 for having had sex with her mistress's husband, Mennsink; the attempted poisoning of her mistress; and the murder of her "bastard" child. In *Rogues, Rebels and Runaways*, Nigel Penn attempts to recover Tryntjie's lost story.[94] Reading Penn's historical narrative using a literary eye, I continue my argument about the illegibility of "will" in the archive. "Rape," "desire," "love," "coercion," "fatal passion," "seduction," and "romance" all appear repeatedly to describe the relationship between Tryntjie and Mennsink. But none of these words come close to understanding what would drive a slave to "comply" year after year with her master's sexual and other dictates. The yoking together of captive person and property places our notions of consent and "will" in crisis. To critically reimagine her will, we can only examine the contemporary notions of submission and coercion that anchor our present-day understanding of habitual sexual violence. I thus end with an analysis of the recently deceased Andre Brink's historical fiction *The Rights of Desire*, in which the ghost of Tryntjie lies buried, literally and figuratively, under the house of the aging Afrikaner Ruben Oliver.[95] Brink's writing allows us to conclude that love between Mennsink and Tryntjie would require not just that they cared for each other but also the emancipation of Tryntjie and all other enslaved peoples in the Cape.

Chapter 3 uses the genealogical performances of disability by women such as Joice Heth, who was exhibited by P. T. Barnum, to understand the spectacle of Miss Landmine Angola, a beauty pageant organized by Morten Traavik for the survivors of landmine detonations in which the winners receive a prosthetic limb. Focusing on the staging of disability by Joice Heth, whom Barnum claimed was George Washington's mammy and 161 years old, I construct a genealogy of performance that links the freak show to the beauty pageant and the Miss Landmine Angola pageant. Bringing together disability studies with performance studies, I show how disability is produced via the spectacle of Heth's contorted hands and unemployed Angolan women with amputated limbs lying next to sparkling pools. There can be no simple understanding of the "will" of Heth and her decision to be exhibited or of the unemployed Angolan women and their "choice" to participate in the pageant—not because their "will" and choices are absent but because their "will" remains largely illegible within structures of representation and history making such as P. T. Barnum's diary and the Miss Landmine Angola website, with its multiple links.

Chapter 4 complicates postapartheid portrayals of the origins of Indians in South Africa by comparing Natal indenture to the enslavement of Indians in the Cape and the indenture of the indigenous Khoikhoi. Using the work of Achille Mbembe and Jin-Kyung Lee, I argue that indentured plantation work constitutes a form of necropolitical labor that necessarily incurs physical and mental injury on a continuum with death. I thus turn toward various histories and historical fiction that describes the exceptionally high rates of suicide among indentured servants on South African plantations. Rather than describing suicide as exceptional examples of crisis premised on individual notions of free "will," suicide allows us to see the plantation in its various surrogations as a space that routinizes violence, overestimates the differences between enslavement and free labor, and underestimates the violence of "free labor." I conclude by turning to the critical reimagining of "will" in the short story "High Heels," from Agnes Sam's collection *Jesus Is Indian and Other Stories*.[96] Reflecting Sam's heritage as the descendant of kidnapped Indians forcibly brought to South Africa, these short stories think through notions of "will" around religious conversion and desire. In "High Heels," the negotiation over a pair of red shoes and a door behind a curtain articulates multiple queer religious and sexual allegiances. The story introduces a concept the final chapter develops in more detail: Gloria Wekker's notion of "mati work."[97] Mati work moves "will" beyond the liberal realm of the individual to a relational ontology and acknowledges self and community through the foregrounding of remembered and re-performed erotic acts of creation.

In chapter 5, Yvette Christianse's stunning historical novel *Unconfessed* takes up the challenge of theorizing "will" as queer relational performances of vulnerability.[98] The narrative of the novel spins out from a kernel of archival evidence about Sila van der Kaap, who was sentenced in 1823 to life imprisonment on Robben Island for the murder of her son Baro. We can never understand what motivated the historical van der Kaap to kill Baro, Christianse writes. Knee deep in the Cape Archives, she asks, "How, then, does one approach a story whose referent is constantly circling back and around itself in the archive or, rather, constantly circling the moment in which a slave woman becomes the subject of legal action and punishment, namely that moment in which she killed her son?"[99] I argue that *Unconfessed* is less about murder than about relationships such as mothering in crisis both during and after official emancipation. The novel explores relationships predicated on shared vulnerability, debility, and "slow death": "All we have is each other and that too is our downfall."[100] Thus, *Unconfessed* figures "will" as the particular instantiation of three moments of relational ontology: van der Kaap learning to love the women and children on the island; her discovery of the power of laughter as a black noise that generates community; her ability to listen from a position of vulnerability. To be in relationship with another requires being undone and, in this way, to be remade relationally.

Illegible Will ends with an epilogue that discusses the photographer Zanele Muholi's "Queercide," a series of images that document violence against black African queers. The original "Queercide" photos were stolen from Muholi's hard drives and backup drives in 2012. I read these missing photographs by looking closely at another series of Muholi's photographs that include depictions of Katlego Mashiloane and Nosipho Lavuta. Through her exquisite portrayals of these two black lesbians, Muholi uses her camera to re-theorize "will" in ways that are queer, relational, and inextricable from homophobic and sexist violence in South Africa. The deliberate attempt to erase such women from the (visual) landscape constructs these women's "willful" desire in the spaces of vulnerability between them.

RETURNING TO HANKEY

Sarah Baartman and Endless Repatriations

I found myself grappling not with the safe residue or inert traces
of history removed from the present, but with a vital, visceral plumb-
line of historical ghostings questioning neatly marked categories of
difference. . . . Dreams become literal visitations . . . actual encounters
irrupting onto the scene like disavowed grandmothers.
—REBECCA SCHNEIDER, *THE EXPLICIT BODY IN PERFORMANCE*, 175

Given this book's emphasis on material bodies, recalcitrant historical events,
and performances of labor, there are few case studies more appropriate to
begin with than the ubiquitous story of Saartjie (Sarah) Baartman. Rather
than focus on her time in France and scientific racism, this chapter develops two particular historical moments. First, I trace Baartman's "afterlife" that,
through its relationship to time, reveals how absence and presence weave
through our histories. Next, I examine the various performance traditions that
situate her display in London, ending with the African Association for Promoting the Discovery of the Interior of Africa's suit against Baartman's exhibitors Hendrik Cesars and Alexander Dunlop in London in November
1810, in which they were accused of enslaving her "against her will." While it
may seem counterintuitive to move backward in time, such a strategy refuses
a narrative of performative origins. Instead, through this sequencing I enact
what Joseph Roach has called "vortices of behavior"—those transhistorical
processes and physical spaces that "canalize specified needs, desires and habits in order to reproduce them."[1] What happens when we read Baartman's

early years, particularly in London, through her repatriation and rumors of her missing body? Can thinking about her repatriation and burial refuse the closed circuit of scientific racism she and discourse on her has remained ensnared within? Instead of understanding contemporary society by making recourse to her past, how do our present concerns shape her history?

I begin this chapter, then, with a discussion of the present-day labor performed by the repatriation of Baartman's remains. Her return home, as Jin-Kyung Lee argues, shows how the "moral and material economies of death are mediated by individuals, households and communities who have a historical affinity towards movement."[2] Like the exhumations of numerous displaced Africans such as migrant workers from the late nineteenth century on, Baartman's reburial reimagines a cultural politics of national belonging. For the post-apartheid government, the return of her remains supposedly sutures together a new figure of national citizenship. My consideration of Baartman's complicated burial, however, focuses less on questions of nation than on questions of will within the black diaspora. This chapter asks whether we can use Baartman's remains to rethink subjectivity as characterized by diasporic resonances, fragments, and inauthenticity. What do a plaster cast, a skeleton, preserved organs, and wax molds of genital parts—none of which are verifiable as belonging to Baartman—say not just about the "body" that was buried in Hankey and the way it functions, but also about the post-apartheid diasporic subject?

The second part of the chapter uses the stunning archival work in which Clifton Crais and Pamela Scully identify several moments of transatlantic performance that informed Baartman's exhibition in London.[3] Using their research, I show how the convergence of ethnographic spectacle, the freak show, and the exotic display/sex inscribes meaning onto Baartman's body and the black female body in general. In addition, I focus on the African Association's lawsuit against Baartman's "captors" in London. While clearly not the intention of the litigants, the case foregrounds issues of consent that play out in the present. Descriptions of court proceedings reveal the African Association's reading of her embodied performance as one that resonated with the performances of transatlantic slaves for sale, especially in New Orleans. Using this comparison, I argue that Baartman's performances did indeed resemble the spectacular staging of slaves. However, the conclusions I reach from these resonances differ from those of the African Association, whose real concern was to establish clear-cut distinctions between contractual free labor and slavery (abolished on British soil only in 1807). I find the question of whether

Baartman had signed a contract of secondary importance and instead argue that systems of free and unfree labor are versions of each other whose relatedness becomes obfuscated by the illusion of choice. Rather than trying to read the archive for whether Baartman chose to be exhibited, I engage critically with the illegibility of her will. To do this, I read her afterlife for the various ways post-apartheid figures have stepped into the void of her will, claiming to speak for her. Through close readings of descriptions of her performances, I place Baartman's embodied gestures alongside those of slaves for sale to conjure the ghostly possibilities of her agency within the close confines of free and unfree labor.

Performances of Death and Displacement in Hankey

Testimony in front of the Truth and Reconciliation Commission (TRC) about the human rights abuses that took place in South Africa between 1960 and 1994 abound with the mention of bodily remains. From the "baboon hand" of Sicelo Mhlauli preserved in a bottle,[4] to the brains of Sony Boy Zantsi buried in the ground by the policeman who shot him, one is repeatedly struck by the materiality of bodies torn apart. Death did not mark the end point of bodily violence, as corpses were hacked to pieces, set alight, and otherwise mutilated. Not only the murder but also the savage treatment of the corpse was used to inflict terror on the living, whose dead often returned to them as fragments—as "scraps of hair attached to parts of his scalp" or limbless torsos. It was no accident, then, that TRC witnesses insisted on the recognition, recovery, and repossession of bodily remains. For example, Joyce Mthimkulu took pieces of her son's scalp to a TRC hearing as a form of testimony, not just about the injustices of the past, but also about the continuation of violence into the present.[5] For those without even those macabre fragments, such as Ncediwe Mfeti, pleas were made often for the return of some part, any part, of their loved ones. Ciraj Rassool, Leslie Witz, and Gary Minkley record Mfeti as saying, "Even if it is his remains, if he was burnt to death, even if we can get his ashes, the bones belonging to his body, because no person can disappear without trace. If I could bury him, I am sure I could be reconciled."[6] Possession of the fragment comes to stand in metonymically not for the recovery of the whole body but, instead, for the ability to memorialize the dead and demonstrate the continued suffering of the living. By respecting the dead, the state (represented by the law) thus does not suture the wounded body together but acknowledges the injury inherent in the fleshy scrap. As Rassool claims in "Human Remains," "Heads and burials, bodies and returns . . . provided an inventory of human rights violations and an archive of symbolic reparations."[7]

From the late 1900s onward, the repatriation of dead bodies increasingly became an issue, particularly in the cases dealing with the bodies of resistance leaders and fighters who waged much of their struggle from across South Africa's borders. The state was incredibly reluctant to take on such a herculean task, involving not just a logistical nightmare of identification, exhumation, and transportation but also an economic quagmire of financing. Most individual repatriations were privately funded and facilitated. Starting in 2005, the state began to respond to the demands of the TRC by locating burial sites, identifying the dead, and returning corpses and remains for state funerals. Ironically, given their powerful historical complicity with scientific racism, forensic analysis and physical anthropology became key to the identification of the remains of cadres who died as political prisoners or were otherwise killed by the apartheid government.

Along with such high-profile cases, however, the issue of repatriation affects many South Africans who were not resistance leaders, soldiers, or ethnographic spectacles. Since the second half of the twentieth century, the politics of death and displacement in South Africa has been profoundly altered by the growing mobility of Africans, and particularly of the Xhosa peoples. Given the state's misuse of the migrant labor system, the forced removals of "illegals," coerced relocations, and the near-impossibility of wage labor in rural areas, "ways of dying" have had to be reimagined across distance.[8] Rebekah Lee stresses the ways that community and kin have navigated the moral and material economies of death and mobility. "In what way," she asks, "has this more mobile orientation influenced the perception of rites and responsibilities surrounding death? And how have more mobile 'ways of dying' in turn created new subjectivities and new ways in which to imagine relations between the living and the dead?"[9]

In the late nineteenth century, for example, Sotho migrants developed idioms and *sefala* songs of comradeship to contest and endure the dangerous conditions in the mines, the omnipresence of death, and the longing for "home." Consider, for example, the following lyrics: "I am a cut sprout, ever resprouting. A poor man has no place in the country . . . Poor men, we are long-legged; You know we shall die far away" or "I am not dead; even now I still live. I am a wanderer of the mines; Sootho."[10] Awarded little respect in life, Sotho migrants had little chance to be buried with any kind of ceremony, let alone the appropriate cultural rites, and it was unlikely that the mining company would transport workers' bodies to their ancestral homes. In fact, the mines established their own cemeteries at the start of the twentieth century and began unceremoniously burying Africans in unmarked graves. Eddy Maloka documents how Basotho miners responded by establishing the first South African burial societies, through which families were informed about the death of their relative and efforts were made to return the body to Lesotho for proper burial.[11] He goes on to tell us that in case the body of the deceased failed to arrive home, some people "had a customary provision for a 'fictional' burial [involving] a ritual for the 'burial' of the belongings of the deceased," followed by customary mourning.[12]

The repatriation of ancestral remains in South Africa thus has a significant history that deals with, among other things, disrespect and violence against dead and living African bodies; varying "traditional" and "Christian" rites and rituals around death; and the exorable link between death as material and death as symbolic. Our historically contingent interactions with and interpretations of actual bodies are key to how we imagine ourselves individually and collectively. Our treatment of the dead forms what Diana Taylor calls scenarios or acts of transfer: "meaning-making paradigms that structure social environments, behaviors, and potential outcomes . . . , [the] portable framework [of these paradigms] bears the weight of accumulative repeats. The scenario makes visible, yet again, what is already there: the ghosts, the images, the stereotypes."[13] Thus, corpses that are buried, exhumed, and reburied work through what Roach calls "surrogation," where bodies are reinhabited across time, allowing for the construction and diasporic transmission of memory.[14] Surrogation works as embodied ritual, providing social actors with the means to reincorporate the corpse into various living communities and restore meaning to what is left. I would argue that this process is always incomplete. There are always pieces left over that make no sense, like a scrap of scalp.

Sarah Baartman was merely one of the traveling dead. How do we then account for the role her body performs in post-apartheid South Africa? How do we make sense of her fame, her spectacular homecoming, and her burial? Why is it that scholars, including me, continue to focus on her? Even if we consider the repatriation of ethnographic spectacles, she is not alone. Consider the case of "El Negro of Banyoles," the name given to a stuffed human body displayed from 1916 to 1997 at the Francesc Darder Museum of Natural History in Banyoles, Spain. According to Connie Rapoo, "El Negro" was supposedly buried around 1830 in Botswana or South Africa, then stolen from his grave and stuffed by French taxidermists named Edouard and Jules Verreaux.[15] He was displayed as "Le Bechuana," or a person of Tswana descent, and the museum's deeply racist ethnographic installation went unremarked until December 1991, when Alphonse Arcelin, a Haitian doctor living in Spain, began a series of protests that coincided with preparations for the Barcelona Olympics in 1992. Spain's anxiety about adverse international publicity most likely expedited the repatriation of the stolen corpse. The nameless man was repatriated and reburied in Gaborone, Botswana, on October 5, 2000.[16] Unlike Baartman, "El Negro of Banyoles" remains an obscure, anonymous tragedy.

Rapoo writes that the reason for this discrepancy may stem from El Negro's and the Hottentot Venus's different "dynamics of identification and social relations: two genders, two nations, complex meanings of diaspora and assimilative tropes of tradition, family and postcolonial national belonging."[17] Gender, in particular, as well as the global reintegration of South Africa as a beacon of racial reconciliation, played a huge role in this disparity. After the release of Nelson Mandela and the "fall" of apartheid, the eyes of the world were fixed on South Africa. Thus, the performance of repatriating and reburying Baartman became crucial to the country's articulation of itself as a post-apartheid nation with shifting identities, desires, and fears. Her corpse became a stage on which historical introspection, land claims, and an emerging concept of indigenous rights and rites were played out. In April 2002, the remains of the Khoikhoi Sarah Baartman were finally repatriated to South Africa after an eight-year campaign.[18] People of Khoikhoi descent, particularly the Griqua, were instrumental in claiming Baartman as kin and demanding her return. The Griqua had not heard of Baartman until the genealogist Mansell Upham brought her plight to their attention. Motivated by the growing international interest and burgeoning economies around indigeneity,[19] Upham returned to South Africa shortly after the elections of 1994 to become the legal adviser for the Griqua National Conference (GNC). In late 1995, the GNC's leader A. A. S. LeFleur II approached Nelson Mandela and the French Embassy, arguing for Baartman's repatriation.

Thus, three agendas—the Griquas', Upham's, and LeFleur's—converged to result in Baartman's return. Demonstrated knowledge of ancestral burial sites has been crucial to land claim disputes, as Lee argues, with reburials helping to "consolidate families' legal and material entitlement to land."[20] For the Griqua, Baartman provided a way to consolidate their long unrecognized and complicated identity, their land claims based on that identity, and their place within the new South Africa. Baartman performed their displacement and lent a name to their loss across time and space. Thus, for example, France was initially reluctant to open the door to what could become a flood of repatriations, given the country's possession of a large number of ethnographic bodies and objects from Africa. However, attempts to preserve national reputation, alongside increasingly contentious internal racial politics, led the French government grudgingly to hand over Baartman's remains.

France's actions in connection to Baartman partly stemmed from the nation's desire to obscure its treatment of an increasingly politicized and vocal second generation of African and Arab French citizens descended from sub-Saharan African immigrants who began arriving en masse in the 1980s. These immigrants and their children met with increasingly virulent racism and ethnocentrism, greatly aided by the growing popularity of the French right in the 1990s. France saw Baartman's return as a means of exonerating itself from increased accusations of racism as African migrants either struggled to eke out a living or continued to be deported. As Lydie Moudileno argues, for the nation-state, Baartman's return has putatively "delivered the ghost from its wandering 'revenant' condition," even while her contemporary counterparts still search the streets of Paris for the justice that is their birthright. This diasporic population remains "an embarrassing body and presence for French laws and Republican ideals, an awkward reminder that the historical circumstances of today's global immigration continue, in fact, to produce tomorrow's ghosts."[21]

For the African National Congress (ANC), Baartman presented a perfect opportunity to recruit the "Coloured" vote as the party failed to carry the Western Cape in the elections of 1994. "Coloureds" were struggling with post-apartheid politics, as many identified with white Afrikaners with whom they shared a language and a history in the Cape. At the same time, these white Afrikaners has subjected them to terribly racist abuse as nonwhite. In addition, the apartheid government's labor preference laws no longer protected "Coloureds" as black Africans moved into previously restricted areas, competing with them for housing and jobs. The ANC felt that its treatment of Baartman would send a clear message to a people in transition that the congress was an essential part of post-apartheid South Africa. Thus, it saw the reintegration of Baartman as crucial to incorporating "Coloureds" into the new nation.

The primary rationale for repatriation, however, had to do with the post-apartheid project of rebuilding a global capitalist nation, anchored by a "return" to traditional ethnicities and narratives of African recuperation. President Thabo Mbeki's brilliantly scripted performance at her gravesite presents Europe's treatment of Baartman as an example of the violent legacy of scientific racism inscribed onto Africans. By performing rituals of mourning, Mbeki's monolithically imagined Africa was supposedly throwing off the yoke of colonialism, emphasizing its powers of self-determination, and lending credence to indigenous African belief systems. This was the African diaspora in reverse—as "wandering" children returned to an independent Africa that was now firmly part of the twenty-first century. Ideally, then, for the state, as Rapoo observes, such "theatres of reburial and re-membering [on African soil] subvert her colonial imaging as an ethnological, racialised and sexualised specimen [and] express African agency and determination."[22] Reclaiming Baartman became a way to reclaim agency for a nation and for individual citizens. As Crais and Scully articulate, "South Africa would, in effect, speak for Sara Baartman, defend her human rights, and in doing so claim her as a citizen of the fledgling democracy."[23]

To think about what this repatriation and burial accomplished, it might be useful to think about the performances themselves around the repatriation and burial: script, costume, ritual, and rite. What kinds of embodied performances were used to convey so many different messages to a diverse viewership? When her remains arrived in Cape Town, the performative rituals began with a small "enrobement," or *aantrek*, ceremony sentimentally called "Flowers for Sarah Baartman" and involving a small welcoming party of dignitaries. Women featured prominently in the ceremony, which included an "authentic" San dance by Yvette Abrahams. While evocative and moving, Abrahams's dance fixed the "traditional" in an imagined past to which indigenous people are often relegated. Knowledge of what constituted tradition was fraught throughout the process by the failure to understand how such customs grow and change with time and by the gaps in the archival record about what certain rites and rituals looked like. Also, this notion of the traditional was complicated by the ANC's performative deployment of certain rituals and customs as shorthand for national legitimacy and authenticity. The construction of the traditional thus had everything to do with contemporary attempts to reconstruct a "pure" indigenous past that had somehow survived colonialism and apartheid untouched.

Unable to determine the contours of "tradition," the Reference Group in charge of Baartman's repatriation eventually hired an archaeologist to produce a description of "authentic" Khoikhoi burial practices. However, Christianity also had to be incorporated into the ceremony, as Baartman's conversion was deemed very important to her. As Crais and Scully observe, one of the two documents that Baartman clung to until the end of her life was a copy of her baptismal record.[24] Thus, the funeral in Hankey combined Khoikhoi "traditions" with Christian burial rites to create an indigenous Christian burial. Instead of being buried on her knees, as is the Khoikhoi custom, Baartman's skeleton and remains were buried flat in a coffin decorated with aloe wreaths. On the actual day there was all the fanfare necessary to consolidate national and regional pride, as well as to celebrate the passing on of the dead: parades, slogan chanting, spiritual songs, animal-horn blowing, Khoi music and dance, food stands, and considerable media coverage. Participants were costumed in "traditional" loincloths, clothes made in national colors, and ethnic garb such as brightly colored saris and animal skins. The national anthem was followed by state tributes and a presentation of Khoikhoi music. Khoigoed, a Khoikhoi herb, was burned to purify the air. President Mbeki made a dramatic entrance via helicopter, eventually transferring to a motor cavalcade that slowly wound its way toward the site. Anticipation built. Mbeki finally delivered a very long, if somewhat rambling, speech about "our grandmother, Sara Baartman" to the approximately seven thousand people who had gathered. Khoikhoi leaders then scattered arrows across the grave to recognize her as an ancestor. There were hymns, scripture readings, a sermon, and, finally, the laying of a pile of rocks atop of the grave, as was traditional among the Khoikhoi in the eighteenth century. Red soil surrounded the grave, and a *boegoe* bush was planted to help purify Baartman's spirit so she could become part of the earth.

Much like the Parade of Nations at the Olympic Games, here was a spectacular performance designed for both the national and the world stage. This set of rituals did not require proximate physical presence at the site of the performance; on the contrary, participation at times appeared even more intimate via distance as the media provided omniscient views with close-up shots and historical commentary. As both a localized performance and a media event, the spectacle of the burial emotionally conjured the idea of a nation without the racial and ethnic fractures, economic strife, and gendered violence that plagues South Africa today.[25] As Mbeki informed mourners, "The story of Sarah Baartman is the story of the African people. It is the story of the loss of our ancient freedom."[26] Mbeki implied that, by claiming Baartman, Africans were reclaiming their freedom to govern themselves. South Africa's entrance onto the world stage, not as the former last bastion of racism but as a representative of all that was liberally progressive, was complete.

The one exception to this liberal progressiveness was the role of science. Rather than embracing scientific positivism as a tool for technological and medical advancement, Mbeki argued that Western science and indigenous knowledges were antithetical to each other. By appropriating Baartman's body and subjectivity in the interests of denouncing hard science, Mbeki did what scientists like Georges Cuvier did all those years ago: he stepped into the void of Baartman's will. The illegibility of Baartman's will allowed scientists to mold her body into a problematic exemplar of scientific classifications of the human. This inability to read Baartman's will also allow her to be reappropriated as a vexed symbol of an anti-science indigenous rhetoric. This rhetoric of indigeneity is not only discrete from, but also hostile to, science, which is reduced to its role as a tool of imperialism. I am not denying that Western positivist science has played a fundamental role in imperialist regimes. However, like Katherine McKittrick, I refuse to consider science and indigeneity as fundamentally antagonistic. If we recall Elizabeth Povinelli's sore from the introduction, we remember that it received multiple diagnoses that reflected the particular worldviews from which they originated: staphylococcus or anthrax spores, aboriginal "filth" or contact with certain ancestral sites. Based on his rhetoric of indigeneity, we can infer that Mbeki would be deeply suspicious of the notion of staphylococcus spores, insisting as he did with the AIDS virus that notions of staphylococcus and anthrax were part of a racist conspiracy and needed to be jettisoned to preserve the dignity of black lives.[27]

Mbeki was not alone in his stance. Similar issues arose when it was proposed that Baartman's remains be genetically tested. According to Moudileno, the French museum directors, the South African government, and the Khoisan descendants could not verify that the body parts in the jars were actually Baartman's. Testing the remains for DNA evidence that they did indeed belong to a Khoikhoi woman was proposed and soundly rejected by the Reference Group—in particular, by Yvette Abrahams, who took a firm stance against "hard science." Invoking the notion of the rights of the individual (whether dead or alive), Abrahams wrote a six-page memorandum in which she claimed to speak for Baartman as her descendant. She insisted that Baartman would not have consented to additional testing. Stepping into Baartman's shoes, Abrahams laid claim to her by filling the archival void with the fantasy of a knowable presence. To test the remains would be to continue the biological exploitation of Baartman. Whether or not the remains were Baartman's was not a question to be settled by "hard science" but would, instead, remain a question of belief for her descendants. For Abrahams and Mbeki, winning

Baartman's remains meant the triumph of African self-governance and sim-plified African cosmologies. They could not imagine a world in which science and culture are not on opposite sides of the war for black bodies. It is only by burying Western science, according to Mbeki, that African agency can be reclaimed. And it is only Mbeki's and Abraham's imagining of Baartman's will that enables their dismissal of Western science.

I agree that the knowledge claims of Western science often been have ad-vanced through the brutalization of black people. Even today's kinder, gen-tler version of science has much to account for in terms of its treatment of populations deemed disposable and its treatment of animals. Western sci-ence, particularly in the case of Baartman, is deeply implicated in creating and perpetuating hierarchical regimes of race. Even though repatriations, for example, might have changed the practices of sciences such as physical an-thropology and archaeology, they have not "transformed the basic positivistic and universalist premises with which these sciences operate."[28] Repatriation is often seen as a loss for science and a gain for indigenous people receiving the ancestral remains. An example of this kind of thinking is encapsulated by Martin Legassick and Ciraj Rassool when they quote the eminent archaeolo-gist Tim Maggs likening "his" bones being taken away from him in 2002 to "the act of burning the archive."[29] In an attempt to rectify this violent disre-gard for other worldviews, postmodern models of scientific inquiry theorize a single material world and multiple cultural perspectives that lend various meanings to that materiality. But these multiple perspectives can't be given interpretative equivalency as the perspective that clings closest to the puta-tive material reality is the most transparent, the truest. And this happens to be modern Western reality.[30] Even in the recognition of other perspectives, Western science accords itself greater veracity.

However, I am unwilling to simply jettison "hard science" as a tool of rac-ism for a number of reasons that the focus of this chapter prohibits. Suffice it to say that the difficulty of separating categories of "Western science" or "hard science" from indigenous knowledge systems cannot be underestimated. In addition, neither category has singular agendas, trajectories, or approaches, and they both change over time and space. McKittrick's work on science and creativity provides an important intervention here. Using the work of Sylvia Wynter, McKittrick refuses the opposition of scientific and creative knowl-edges, arguing instead that combining the two perspectives allows for new understandings of the liberal human subject. She writes that this is what "the promise of science can do for us as intellectuals interested in race, racism, and the body: attention to the functioning of scientific racism as a closed system (a loop) provides an opportunity to reconsider the political work of science within our reading practices."[31] This is not an attempt to reach back in time and dispel the violence done to Baartman and other colonial subjects. It is, instead, a call to read this story of violence using a different paradigm that does not oppose science and imaginative ways of knowing but rethinks them as in dialogue with each other. The embodied creative cultural labor necessary for such dialogue exposes the limits of scientific knowledge while simultaneously remaining open to scientific practice and its outcomes. Thus, McKittrick goes on to say, critically imaginative readings of Baartman's gestures enable us to develop what Marlene Nourbese Philip calls a "collaborative language" that binds the creative/cultural to the biological.[32] The material body, in its enactment of this "collaborative language" or "corporeal orature,"[33] exceeds the biological and creatively reimagines the human through haunted gestures and seething absences.

I would argue that Baartman's remains require us to think through strategic political choices, borrowing from various conflicting worldviews with an eye toward redress. The explanation for Povinelli's sore lies in both spores and ancestral contact, which require different medical and spiritual interventions at different times. Instead of either a scientific oddity/exemplar of primitivism or "our African grandmother" whom we can feel in our bones, Baartman becomes a multiplicity of different objects and processes as she travels across space and time: she is the package shipped across the ocean; she is the body that traverses continents; she is the "traditional dances" performed by South Africans upon her "return"; she is the rocks that cover her grave over which we weep. Baartman travels not just across space but also across time. The multiple meanings she has accrued swing toward and away from the contemporary moment. The work she performs, before and after repatriation, actually enables her remains to shape-shift and time travel. As they move through contradictory cultural and political contexts, the remains acquire multiple meanings via the coalescence and dissolution of histories to become new objects. Whether to abandon Western science for its racism is not the point. Instead, we should be asking whether and how science can work creatively *with* culture to acquire new meanings that benefit those who are suffering and surviving in its aftermath.

Baartman's returned remains include a plaster cast, preserved organs, a skeleton, and waxed molds of genital parts. What has been buried and memorialized are a mix of body parts and copies of the original body made of plaster and wax. According to Crais and Scully, Griqua women have "long fashioned blankets recalling their history of dispossession and scattering, bits and pieces of cloth which they wear around themselves during the winter, fragments of the past stitched together reminding them of their history and that, one day, their land shall be returned and restored [and] one day they will make blankets of whole cloth."[34] Baartman as a series of objects and processes spanning time and space is not unlike this blanket assembled from fragments. Instead of longing for a time when this blanket can be made of whole cloth, Baartman's repatriation insists on the power of what Moudileno describes as the "systematically re-assembled and disassembled, abandoned and reclaimed."[35] Baartman perhaps can be understood as an incomplete performance that foregrounds the spatiotemporal gaps and silences of the recalcitrant archive. Haunted by colonial reason, her repatriation is not a resurrection but an insistence on the torn organic and inorganic substances that are her remains. Plaster and wax, bone and organ—this Baartman is incompletely forged, a consistently shifting object that refuses to allow us to close the door on this chapter of history. Rather, her still changing gravesite throws it further open as we gaze into the abyss of her afterlife. Immediately after Baartman's burial, visitors wrote her messages on nearby stones. As the months passed, some removed chips as keepsakes from the cement boundaries enclosing her grave. Soon, the stream of visitors dried to a trickle. People began complaining about the deterioration of the site as graffiti covered the information board, wind-blown garbage snagged on boulders, and the grave itself was vandalized. Rumors began to circulate that the grave was now empty and Baartman's stolen remains had once again been relocated.

After-After Lives

A Charou who makes caskets for a living was on his way to deliver one of his coffins to a Funeral Parlour when his car broke down. Trying not to be late, he put the coffin on his head and began heading toward his destination. Some policemen saw him and wanted to make money off him for a bribe, so they chooned him: "Hey you! What are you carrying, and where are you going?" You know Charous can think on their feet, so he said, "I didn't like where they buried me, so I am relocating!"[36]
—RACIST JOKE MADE BY THE SOUTH AFRICAN CARTOONIST RUAN KEMP ON FACEBOOK, FEBRUARY 6, 2014

In September 2003, two years before the theft of the bronze plaque that marked her grave, two men ostensibly deposited the body of four-year-old Makhumandile "Trompies" Bantom near Baartman's grave. The boy had been abducted from outside a day-care center, and his throat was cut. Trompies's identity and why he was murdered is an important story for another time. It is his carefully chosen placement next to Baartman's gravesite that I wish to think about. I argue that the dumping of his body near Baartman's grave makes sense only if we consider two specific aspects of indigenous beliefs around the power of death and bodily remains. The first aspect has to do with how death changes a particular landscape, while the second thinks through the role of the bodily remains as medicine or poison.

The (spiritual) investment in the site reveals the spatialization of power, a unique geopolitics of death in which the land itself—rocks, red soil, bushes—becomes imbued with the power of death. Thus, the terrain of the gravesite, formerly a piece of land of little interest, is forever charged, pulsating with the power that, while originally created by the interment of Baartman's remains, now encompasses this entire area, including the body of Trompies. As Adam Ashforth writes, "Despite the fact that the business of death and dying has been medicalized, sanitized, and commercialized, an intense, if vague, aura of danger ('infectivity')—quite distinct from the sadness and grief—still surrounds it."[37] This "infectivity" can work like a gas, according to some South Africans, where it pollutes the air around dead bodies. Still others claim that the site's power derives from being in the presence of spirits and souls that could sicken or harm the living. Those who have been exposed to the dead, from closest loved ones to mourners and gravediggers, must undergo purifying rituals, including washing their hands in cold water in which pieces of aloe have been soaking and burning herbs such as Khoigoed to purify the air. To have exposed Trompies intentionally to this poison, as appears to be the case, is to have set in motion a chain of malicious forces that continue the spread of this "death" to those close to the boy, such as his mother. Thus, exposure to the infection of death can be used as a weapon against one's enemies.

The possible disappearance of Baartman's remains also suggests the use, by indigenous healers, of her body parts and other items to make what is commonly called *muti*, which Crais and Scully translate into English as healing or toxic "medicine," "poison," or "herbs."[38] According to a study by the journalist Candice Bailey, one in five inhabitants of rural areas in South Africa have firsthand knowledge of ritual killings that result in the trafficking of human body parts for muti.[39] Both Bailey and Mary Braid document the rise in the number of ritual killings and the harvesting of body parts necessary for muti.[40] The creation of muti is specialized information to which only a few specialists have access. Further, its "ingredients" and rituals of assemblage necessarily change to respond to new misfortunes and sicknesses, such as HIV/AIDS. Muti is not just tool to be used by human agents. Rather, once assembled, it literally acquires a life of its own. The healer/witch interacts with the power of the muti "so as to effect specific desired ends in concert with these forces."[41] Thus, muti becomes an actor who performs alongside the healer or witch. One of the crucial functions of muti is to aid in the communication and transfer of power between human and spirits. Baartman's celebrity status affords her exceptional value in this economy of death. Thus, muti made from Baartman's remains is believed to be strong enough for a healer to cure AIDS or for a witch to kill a village, for example. In order not to objectify indigenous practices and relegate them to the past, one must contextualize such practices and fears in the present day.

Popular media, as Gareth Van Onselen and Mary Braid discuss, often labels muti and witchcraft as "medieval, a throwback to the dark ages," as primitive vestiges of a "superstitious" past.[42] Instead, muti is an absolutely modern, albeit often disturbing, response to the post-apartheid state. The end of apartheid saw the rise of what Ashforth calls "spiritual insecurity," a state characterized by "doubts and uncertainties aroused by both the inherent indeterminacy of 'invisible forces' and the existence of competing, and often contradictory, schemes and authorities for interpreting their nature and actions in a context of widespread ignorance about how best to act."[43] Instead of quieting certain fears, the end of apartheid made many people feel as if spiritual malice and violence formed an ever tightening noose. The failure of government policy to address increasing socioeconomic inequalities, the spread of AIDS, and the continued lack of resources led many to feel that witchcraft was shaping their lives. The spiritual insecurity of living in a world in which the promise of justice is endlessly deferred, in which the very state that was supposed to rectify past wrongs becomes the source of injustice and continued subjugation, belies the myth of a past buried, of remains returned and given a home. Whether or not Baartman's remains have been left alone, the rumors of her empty grave maintain her political vitality. She shape-shifts and time travels, gesturing toward the failure of the postcolonial state to address the growing tides of spiritual insecurity. Ashforth writes, "No matter how culturally sensitive a court system might want to be—and South African courts have long taken the belief in witchcraft into account as a mitigating factor in sentencing[—]there is simply no getting around the fact that the category of the person to which the term 'human' in modern doctrines of human rights refers is not a being capable of inflicting harm in the manner widely presumed by people who speak of witchcraft."[44] It is in this space between incommensurable worldviews that Baartman's body thickly resides and pulsates, forming anything but a bridge.

The rest of this chapter turns back to when Baartman was still alive. I situate her time in London within particular historical performance traditions, such as the ethnographic spectacle and the freak show. I do so not to rehearse a history that has already been elegantly written by scholars such as Rachel Adams, Robert Brogdan, and Clifton Crais and Pamela Scully but, rather, to identify gaps in the archive from which the afterlives of women like Baartman can emerge—for example, how Baartman appears to deviate from performative expectations or how she over-saturates them can lead us toward the embodied production of alternate meanings. I also discuss the stagings of Baartman and others on the auction block and in the courtroom to demonstrate how racialized spectacles permeated every level of society, greasing the wheels not just of slavery and imperialism, but also of abolitionism and commodity capitalism. Too often the story of freedom is narrated as a finished event, with slavery and freedom clearly demarcated from each other temporarily, geographically, and culturally. However, my comparison of Baartman's performances to slave auctions demonstrates that bondage and freedom were less distinct than traditionally claimed. In addition, by focusing on black audiences and not just black actors, I complicate the notion of the spectacular, fungible black body. Black bodies are not just the object of the gaze; they also look back or refuse to look back, as the case may be. While we may never ascertain the will of Baartman or any of these other black historical actors, perhaps emphasizing the breaks, sutures, and seams in their flattened performances will allow for an interrogation of possessive individualism and provide insights into the structural workings of coercion and consent. Any determinations of agency that I arrive at in this chapter are examples of my unwieldy engagement with the absence of black will in the archive. Given this illegibility, when instances of will do erupt in this chapter, they exemplify my own informed ghostly critical imaginings.

Crais and Scully's work on the Hottentot Venus has rewritten much of what we thought we knew about Baartman. They devote a significant amount of their study to her life before she set sail for London, deducing that she was born some ten years earlier than was commonly thought, in the 1770s, about fifty miles north of the Gamtoos Valley. They sketch out the various journeys that Baartman makes away from rural areas to eventually arrive in Cape Town, where she labored for more than ten years before embarking for London in the mid-1790s, and not in 1807, as previously thought.[45] This new timeline allows us to better contextualize Baartman's life in London, which saw the British government's gradual colonization of the Cape. Claiming that the Netherlands had proved unworthy of the task by failing to civilize the native population, Lord Caledon, governor of the Cape, ushered in Britain's new role as protector of the mistreated natives via the proclamation of the Caledon Code of 1809, or the "Hottentot Code," as it was also known. Among other consequences, the Caledon Code prevented colonists from removing Khoikhoi from the Cape. Thus, Baartman's arrival in London with Alexander Dunlop and Hendrik Cesars as her "keepers" could not go unnoticed. Indeed, as Yvette Abrahams describes, Baartman's body became the battleground for larger questions about the competence of Lord Caledon, imperial native policy, and Cape colonization.[46]

On October 11, 1810, Zachary Macaulay traveled to 225 Piccadilly, paid his two shillings, and saw Baartman as she stood clothed in a tight brown dress meant to simulate nudity and emphasize her behind. Macauley was well known for his evangelical fervor and his campaigns for social reform, including the abolition of the slave trade. He had made his journey to see Baartman supposedly not to gawk at her. Instead, he stated in a later affidavit, as a representative of the African Association he was "desirous if possible of learning under what circumstances she came to England and whether she was made a public spectacle with her own free will and consent or whether she was compelled to exhibit herself and was desirous of returning to her own country."[47]

Macauley directed his questions to Cesars about whether the exhibition of Baartman was in fact an instance of slavery and a violation of the Caledon Code. Cesars's reluctance to answer his questions or provide any written contracts, along with his abrupt demeanor toward Baartman, convinced Macauley that Baartman was indeed enslaved. After a public furor that included a return visit by Macauley to see Baartman, this time with the famed abolition-ist Thomas Babington and Peter Wageninge (who spoke Dutch fluently), the King's Bench agreed to consider a single question: had Baartman been forced to come to London and exhibit herself, or had she come of her own free will? As the attorney-general notes, the African Association had "every reason to believe, that the unfortunate female in question was brought away from her own country without her consent, was kept here for exhibition without her consent, and that the appearance of compliance which she evinced was the result of menaces of ill-treatment."[48] Cesars supposedly answered such accu-sations in a letter published by the *Morning Chronicle* on October 13, 1810, by insisting that Baartman "was my servant at the Cape, and not my slave.... [S]he is brought here with her own free will and consent, to be exhibited for the joint benefit of both our families."[49]

The African Association saw a direct connection between the spectacular nature of enslavement and the spectacle of Baartman ordered about by Ce-sars. During his first visit, Macauley was "disturbed" by the way Cesars issued directives to Baartman—ordering her to turn around so audience members could prod her buttocks. The "poor wretch," Macauley wrote in a letter to the *Morning Chronicle* dated October 12, 1810, "is made to walk, to dance, to shew herself, not for her own advantage but for the profit of her master, who, when she appeared tired, holds up a stick to her."[50] One's understanding of Cesars's actions, as Crais and Scully remind us, needs to take into account important questions about audiences, as Cesars was racially interpolated dif-ferently in the British and South African contexts. In the Cape, Cesars was a Free Black with slave ancestry, a racial category that came with its own set of social stigmas and disenfranchisement. Most Londoners, however, under-stood him as white (a mistake that has survived numerous historical retell-ings). Thus, British audiences perceived the interactions between Cesars and Baartman not as free exchanges between two people of color but, rather, as reenactments of Boer-slave relations. Many considered the Boers European savages who had deteriorated into primitivism due to the length of time spent living among native peoples and slaves. The putative barbarism of the Boers manifested particularly in their vicious treatment of their slaves and thus motivated the British to take over the Cape and thereby "rescue" the na-tives. According to Crais and Scully, the jarring tone that Cesars used toward Baartman was particularly offensive to the British, whose "romantic human-ism and [sentimental] identification with suffering" allowed them to imagine themselves as more enlightened than the Boers.[51]

Rather than dwell on its fascinating intricacies, I am interested specifically in how Baartman's case stages a legal debate and consolidates definitions of free and unfree labor. Edlie Wong writes about how the "earliest legal contests over slavery in Britain were fought over the status of those slaves whom slaveholders had brought into the realm. *Somerset* [*v. Stewart* (1772)] was the culmination of a score of earlier freedom suits that abolitionists had initiated on behalf of these slave attendants, and it established a powerful antislavery precedent favoring freedom for slaves once on free soil."[52] The African Association's legal proceedings against Baartman's exhibitors in many ways were part of this attempt to challenge slavery through the figure of the traveling slave who geographically traversed slavery to freedom. What distinguished Baartman's case, however, was its focus on whether or not Baartman was a slave in the first place, not whether the condition of her slavery followed her into Britain. Such emphasis allows us to intervene critically in the very terms of the debate, focusing not so much on whether Baartman was a slave as on the extent to which freedom was dependent on and productive of slavery. As the legal question of Baartman's status illustrates, the exaggerated differences between contractual black labor and slavery become less important than the ways that so-called free labor operated simultaneously and symbiotically with slavery, specifically with regard to the theorization of "free" will and its legibility.

The African Association's direct comparison of Baartman's displayed body to the performance of slaves was by no means natural, given the unique history of Khoikhoi people in South Africa, who were assigned various racial designations at different times.[53] The African Association's lawsuit suggested a type of reading of Baartman's body that overlooked her ethnic distinction to incorporate her into the visual economy of black subjection and thus into the wider debates of racialized slavery. As Sadiah Qureshi points out, "Baartman's exhibition occurred at precisely the moment when the abolitionist issue was gathering strength and pro-slavery campaigners were actively creating an image of *the* black that erased ethnic differences between culturally diverse black peoples so as to lend force to their political agenda."[54] The association's reading of Baartman's performance provides an opportune example not only of the transnational consolidation of blackness via the spectacle of the racialized body, but also of a growing British investment in the "common sense" and economic soundness of the free market. Baartman's exhibition provided the association with a perfect opportunity to flex its political muscle and bring its cause to the British public. Rather than seeing the kinds of exploitation that can occur under the guise of "free" labor, the African Association attacked the institution of slavery by attacking Baartman's shows, thereby actively defending a capitalist colonial order, which as Zine Magubane reminds us, is based "on the 'voluntary' commodification of the self and a 'willing' capitulation to the dominant logic of capital."[55] Magubane and Rosemary Wiss demonstrate that the African Association was motivated not so much by a humanitarian and abolitionist ethos as by the doctrine of economic liberalization. Magubane writes that the association desired the "proletarianization of the indigenous labor force" in the Cape, and in Africa in general, to satisfy the need for new markets for British goods that would ensure the association's members' interests as landed and mercantile elite.[56] Africans, according to Wiss, were thus "strongly" encouraged to enter into British society "by rational and individual self-improvement, the very embodiment of the spirit of capitalism" and to market their labor which they presumably owned.[57]

To add to the tensions between free and unfree labor, Macauley (a former Jamaican overseer) had a personal investment in decrying slave labor. During his time in Sierra Leone as governor of the Sierra Leone Company, Macauley had "contracted" black apprentices. He took these "boys" to England in 1799 after his term as governor was over, but their period of indenture had yet to expire. Thus, his "apprentices," it was charged, were his de facto slaves. Crais and Scully write that these accusations of "practicing slavery under the cloak of a linguistic sleight of hand" damaged the reputations of Macauley and other reformers, such as William Wilberforce and Thomas Babington, who thought of themselves as heroically ending Britain's participation in the slave trade.[58] Perhaps in an attempt to distance himself from the scandal, Macauley completely ignored the two young slaves (one of them named Matthias) who accompanied Baartman to England. For Macauley, the slaves who accompanied Baartman might have conjured up the debates about his own apprentices' ambivalent status as permanently indentured/enslaved. Baartman mentions them in official testimony, so Macauley could hardly have been unaware of their plight. This elision of Matthias and his companion foregrounds the vulnerable female slave as spectacle, thereby exploiting the erotic desires of captors, rescuers, judges, and the public. More important for my argument, it also allows Macauley to neatly sidestep the inherent contradictions that arise when one attempts to distinguish free and unfree labor. Rather than see the continuities, Macauley exaggerated the differences in an attempt to advocate for free-market economies.

It is worth noting that in November 1810 the King's Bench pointed out to the attorney-general that it might be easier to bring a case of public indecency against Cesars than a case about the violation of antislavery laws. The African Association refused: decency came second to its cause of liberty. Macaulay, Babington, and Wageninge testified as to Baartman's unhappy state of mind and absolute (although sometimes reluctant) obedience to her master's commands. A writ of habeas corpus was issued, and several men interviewed Baartman without the presence of her keeper, Cesars. It is unclear whether Dunlop was present. The statement we have on record, a translation from Dutch into English, paraphrases the interview. Heavily influenced by contractual language, it suggests that Baartman was aware of the grounds on which the African Association had brought suit against Cesars and Dunlop. Yes, she was there of her own consent. No, she had no desire to change her current situation or to return home. Yes, she was well cared for by Dunlop and the two young men formerly from the Slave Lodge who waited on her and helped dress her. Yes, it was a little cold, but despite that, she wanted to stay in England. Baartman's putative testimonial emphasis on contract, consent, and her desire to earn money defines and consolidates the differences between free and slave labor. Rather than being an example of the continuities between them, the framing of her testimony posits free and unfree labor as antithetical.

Pivotal to defining Baartman's status as free or enslaved was the issue of whether she had signed a contract. Crais and Scully, unlike many previous historians, managed to locate the document written by Dunlop, which had remained in the possession of the Musée de l'Homme after Baartman's death. Retroactively dated to October 29, 1810, the contract stipulated a term of service of five years. It stated that Baartman was to perform domestic chores, as well as to exhibit herself in England and Ireland.[59] She would be paid twelve guineas, and her passage to and expenses in Ireland would be paid for, as would her passage back to the Cape, should she desire to return. Baartman appeared to be largely unaware of the terms of the contract, not least because it was written in English before she acquired fluency in that language. Apparently, one of the court officers who interviewed her translated the document into Dutch for her. The contract became a fetish object for all those involved. The court regarded it as evidence of her free status; it enabled Dunlop to construct a fiction of nineteenth-century employer-employee relations; and it temporarily thwarted the political and economic agendas of Macauley and the African Association. What Baartman thought of the document remains illegible. However, Crais and Scully tell us that she "carried this document all the way to Paris.... The contract was perhaps a sad talisman of that moment when the law knocked at her door in London."[60] Their description of the contract as "sad talisman" converts the document into something that should have been but that never was. For Crais and Scully, the contract itself is not the problem. Instead, they take issue with the inadequate and dishonest use of the contract—that is, the fact that it was retroactively written, and all participants did not sign it freely, with equal knowledge and intent. However, I would argue that Crais and Scully, like the King's Bench itself, fail to interrogate the more fundamental distinction between contractual free labor and unfree labor that the contract both presupposes and inscribes. The decision eventually reached by the King's Bench, on November 28, 1810, was that Baartman was not "deprived of her liberty."[61] The case for habeas corpus could not be made because of Baartman's contractual "consent," although, ironically, the case established a legal precedent with regard to habeas corpus that still is cited today.

Concluding that the derogatory display of Baartman's body was voluntary constitutes what I feel is an overestimation of her agency. The court's chilling conclusion that her labor was "free" and that her performance was "voluntary" raises crucial questions about whether the concepts of coercion and consent prove too reductive to capture the dynamics of performances that require the simulation of consent within a context of subjugation. Baartman was not enslaved per se, but she also was not free. What happens if we think of her as performing not only while on display but also as she testifies in front of a group of men who are determined to cast her in various ways? Can she be seen as paradoxically being coerced into performing her consent in the courtroom, just as in the instance of her exhibitions? Can we imaginatively trace, in the shadows of all these moments, the actor speaking for herself even as she speaks for the master?

The African Association underemphasized capitalism's reliance on relations of coercion even while relegating coercion and force primarily to the realm of slavery. By conceiving of Baartman as an isolated individual, the association figured her coercion as the result of the unscrupulous action of Dunlop and Cesars. In the same manner, the association imagined that the injury of individual slaves resulted from the personal excesses of particular masters. In other words, Baartman's situation was folded into the abolitionist discursive tradition that documented the particular and spectacular abuses of slaves rather than the quotidian, mind-numbing routine violence of the system of slavery that slaves endured for entire lifetimes.[62] Thus, as Wiss argues, her subjectivity and "will" were deemed "not the product of a political system of meanings, but rather [the result of] the experience of individual consciousness [that] prescribes the basis of social reality."[63] The lack of a structural critique meant that Baartman was no longer a suffering martyr but instead something almost impossible to understand within the discourse of liberal humanism: an agent who willingly chose domination, a person who chose to become an object sans will.

Ironically, it is within *pro-slavery* arguments just twenty years after Baartman's case that one can find descriptions of the coercive labor endemic to capitalism. In the 1830s, southern apologists such as George McDuffie and Chancellor William Harper responded to abolitionists' attack on slavery with reports on the horrific conditions of "free" labor, particularly in northern factories. Wilfred Carsel notes that by 1860, structural critiques of capitalism had become essential to proslavery arguments, with writers such as the infamous George Fitzhugh insisting: "(1) that the condition of the so-called free worker of the North was already fearful and was becoming increasingly more horrible; (2) that the free-labor system enslaved the worker just as much as the chattel-slavery system; and (3) that wage slavery was infinitely worse for the worker than chattel slavery."[64] Indeed, using stories from northern newspapers, legal investigations into labor conditions, administrative reports, and the heart-wrenching testimony of workers of all colors, pro-slavery proponents advanced the critique of capitalism missing from the African Association's lawsuit, showing the coerciveness of exploitative wage systems. Pro-slavery advocates recognized these wage systems as transnational. For example, Carsel notes that the fate of free laborers in America was foreshadowed by the condition of the worker in England, where, according to Fitzhugh, the system of free labor had had more time to develop and therefore reveal its terrible consequences.[65] The "free" laborer of England and America was seen as equivalent to the chattel slave of the South. However, instead of concluding that the free market needed to be substantively reformed so as not to resemble slavery, pro-slavery advocates argued for the superiority of slavery as a benevolent coercive system. Ironically, then, it was not abolitionist writings but, rather, pro-slavery arguments that better articulated the inherent coerciveness of free labor. In a remarkable paradox, however, such proponents would insist not that Baartman be released from her demeaning contract, should she so desire, but that she be enslaved and more thoroughly subjugated in order to be freer.

The struggle to determine what it is that Baartman thought and felt becomes increasingly obvious as we make our way through the archival material.

Macaulay noted that Baartman "gave evident signs of mortification and misery at her degraded situation in being made a spectacle for the derision of bystanders without the power of resistance." He goes on to state, "From the dejected appearance of the said female and from the obedience which she pays to the commands of her exhibitor [I am led to believe] she is completely [*sic*] under restraint and controul [*sic*] and is deprived of her liberty. . . . [She] appeared very morose and sullen."[66] Macaulay's affidavit was riddled with contradictions produced by his simplistic binary of individual agency and victimization. He made much of Baartman's complete inability to resist and her total obedience even as he pointed to those parts of the performance in which her resistance was evident in some shape or form. He thereby read her "will" to argue that this performance was against her will and talked about her total obedience to her master even though he shortly thereafter recounted an instance in which Baartman refused to display herself. Her refusal necessitated that the "exhibitor . . . let down a curtain. . . . After the curtain was let down [he] looked behind it and held up and shook his hand at her but without speaking and he soon afterward drew up the Curtain and again called her out to public view and she came forward again upon the stage."[67] The tension that appears between willfulness and domination in this incident speaks volumes, not only about coercion involved in the spectacle of the contractually obligated Baartman, but also about the vectors of "will" and submission that crosshatched the performative sale of the slave. Rather than locating "will" only within the realm of "free" labor and coercion only within the quintessential realm of unfree labor/slavery, an examination of these troubled stagings of blackness allows us to see the coercion and severely constrained workings of agency in both types of performances. Saidiya Hartman warns us about the dangers of framing certain performances as illustrative of the slave's consent to hegemony. Rather than "arrogating to the enslaved [and obligated] the illusory privileges of the bourgeois subject or self-possessed individual . . . , [what needs to be] considered . . . are precisely the ways in which performance and other modes of practice are determined by, exploit and exceed the constraints of domination."[68] While Hartman largely focuses on pleasure in its various modalities as possibilities for agency and redress, I wish to focus on the labor of performing one's fungibility and resistance to that fungibility as possible sites where "will" can be conjured. Such a tracing acknowledges that resistance, in both form and content, is shaped by domination as people negotiate the daily violence of coercive systems and performances.

Macauley proved to be more interested in framing Baartman as a synecdoche for the suffering female slave than in actively engaging with her as a subject. Language difficulties aside, he thus neglected to engage with her during his first visit to 225 Piccadilly, instead asking Cesars for information about Baartman's state of mind. During a second visit, Macauley, Babington, and Van Wageninge carefully observed her behavior, paying particular attention to instances when she sighed. Crais and Scully tell us that when Van Wageninge asked her in Dutch whether she was treated well and whether she desired to return home, Baartman refused to answer.[69] Instead of respecting this refusal, the men constructed a narrative of her subjugation on her behalf. Later, after being interviewed by the court for three hours, Baartman gives a careful statement in Dutch regarding her putative freedom that does not stray too far from the language of contract and free labor. However, this statement was not only paraphrased but also translated from Dutch into English, and this process of translation could also account for the statement's emphasis on the issues of contract and freedom. The sound and the fury of critical and historical interpretations of her life, the attempts to discover what really happened and how she really felt, constitutes an example of Anjali Arondekar's narratives of retrieval. Rather than assigning meaning to Baartman's carefully constructed refusals, either as the silence of consent or as the anger of resistance that led her to bite her tongue, what happens if we accept her silence for what it is. As discussed in the introduction, instead of assuming that by uncovering new evidence we can recover Baartman's subjectivity, I suggest searching for her ghostly afterlife, the space of her absence. By searching for this space, I hope to respect her "rights to obscurity," her access to a meaningful silence that withstands the numerous ascriptions of meaning on her body and her history.[70] I thus began this chapter with a discussion of her literal "afterlife"—her posthumous repatriation and reburial. But what about the absent present moments contained within the historical records of her exhibition? What can Baartman's imperfect occupations of various roles in ethnographic spectacles and freak shows tell us about the legibility and illegibility of black women's will?

The Speaking Savage and the Weaving Shadow

The prologue of Andrea Levy's novel *Small Island* (2004) opens with Queenie, a young British girl named after the queen, recounting a visit to the British Empire Exhibition in 1948, which she mistakes for a visit to Africa.[71] To foreshadow the fraught relationships between white British citizens and black Caribbean postwar immigrants, Levy focuses on Queenie's encounter with the ethnographic spectacle of a homogenized and timeless Africanity. Queenie and the two adults accompanying her, Emily and Graham, get lost in "Africa" while Graham is looking for the toilet. The three of them find themselves in a supposed jungle, complete with mud huts, dirt floors, and a black woman weaving. "In a hut sitting on a dirt floor was a woman with skin as black as the ink that filled the inkwell in my school desk. A shadow come to life."[72] Graham loudly insists that the British have machines that do weaving, dismissing Emily's pleas to be quiet by insisting, "She can't understand what I'm saying. . . . They're not civilized. They only understand drums" (5). The "African" woman does not respond to his loud statements and ignores his rude inquiries about the location of the bathroom. Instead, she continues with her performance as though "she'd heard no one speak" (5). Suddenly, Graham, Emily, and Queenie are approached by another "ethnographic spectacle": an African man whom Queenie describes physically in terms much rehearsed in racist discourse—"over-inflated lips," "a nose squashed flat," "blacker than sooty cork," "blinding white teeth," a "monkey man." Emily and Graham, mocking the man's putative ugliness, urge Queenie to kiss him and are dumbfounded when, in "clear English," he says, "Perhaps we could shake hands instead?" (5). After shaking hands with Queenie, the man tactfully directs Graham to the restroom. However, because Graham is unable to find the toilet he resorts to peeing behind a bush, as he thinks "savages" do. Thus, the novel parodies colonialism's demarcations of savagery and civilization.

Encapsulated in this scene are many of the themes that reverberate through any consideration of Sarah Baartman as ethnographic spectacle. Other than the obvious racism, the most striking aspect of British engagement with these black people is the instant consolidation of imperial notions of "us" as civilized and "them" as savage. The lower-class Graham and Emily, who work for Queenie's father as "butcher's boy" and "outside girl," respectively, immediately assume the authority of the empire with the fiction of a white imperial subject eliding their class difference that, hitherto, had been very real. No matter what class position Graham, Emily, and Queenie occupy, they are still "white" and British and hence superior to any African. The prologue ends with Queenie's father, over her mother's protests, insisting that Queenie stand with him on the railway above the exhibit: he shows Queenie the correct vantage point for viewing the empire—with the world at her feet.

European encounters with colonial difference were brought back to Europe itself, commodified and put on display so that the epistemic workings of empire would be inculcated in the citizens at "home" who had little to do with the daily machinations of imperialism. As Veit Erlmann argues, this placing of difference on display was crucial, as "empire is at heart a society of the spectacle . . . The opening of the world as a site for the modeling of Western and African identities and its simultaneous self-enclosure in panoramic superficies go hand in hand."[73] The encounter with difference was staged as black peoples were coercively displayed and forced to "step lively" to authenticate scientific and ethnographic narratives of Western superiority. The African woman at Queenie's exhibit thus does not break her character when confronted by the Western audience but, instead, doggedly continues weaving as if she exists in an Africa beyond time, hearing, and civilization. Whether she was a weaver in Africa is debatable. For the most part, the particulars of these spectacular bodies, such as their geographic origin, occupation, and tribal affiliation, were unimportant. Of more significance, according to Magubane, was their "incorporat[ion] into [Europe's] theatrical machinery," whereby they were rendered as objects to be viewed with condescending pleasure by the so-called civilized world.[74]

A few years before Baartman and her exhibitors arrived in England, a London Missionary Society, attempting to demonstrate the power of Christian conversion, had shown audiences three "civilized" Hottentots: John and Martha van Rooy and Martha Arendse. The novelty of the society's show lay in the construction of difference between "converted Hottentots" and "wild" ones or bushmen. The society manipulated and exploited the space between what audiences expected of Hottentots and the exemplars of Christian modesty and decorum that they encountered instead. Upon arrival in London, Alexander Dunlop approached William Bullock of the Liverpool Natural History Museum, thinking that Bullock would not be able to turn down the proposition of exhibiting a Hottentot woman from the Cape that he described as "an object of great curiosity."[75] Bullock turned down the offer because of the London Missionary Society's previous show and because he wanted to keep away from any subject matter as potentially prurient as a "savage" Hottentot with large buttocks. Dunlop thus had to retool his marketing of Baartman. Needing another angle, as Crais and Scully develop, he chose to diversify his show by combining the more respectable ethnographic spectacle with the freak show, all the while hinting at the "deviant" sexuality of the prostitute, a target of social reform at the time.[76] To lend the performance an aura of the scientific and the authentic, he cobbled together an array of ethnographic props such as the "Hottentot" one-string bow that Baartman occasionally and "reluctantly" played during her exhibition, and he provided a plethora of ethnographic information that audiences could peruse if they wanted to supplement their experience. Thus, the spectacle was legitimized as educational and not just prurient, smart and not just sensational. Even before seeing Baartman's body on-stage, viewers were told how to read her performance via advertisements in the newspaper and broadsheets. As Wiss notes, one of the broadsheets, based on the first of two aquatints by the well-known Frederick Christian Lewis, depicted Baartman not as she would appear but, rather, as the audience should imagine her.[77] Lewis pieces together an iconography from various ethnographic writings on "Hottentots," such as Sir Thomas Herbert's *A Relation of Some Yeares Travaile, Begvunne Anno 1626, into Afrique and the Greater Asia* (1634) and Peter Kolb's *The Present State of the Cape of Good-Hope* (1731). He depicts Baartman as scantily clad, with face painted and walking stick in hand, wearing an altered version of the *kaross* (a sheepskin mantle), smoking a pipe.[78] She also is shown wearing a tortoise-shell necklace that Crais and Scully call "her last, her only, physical connection to a world she had lost."[79] Ultimately however, these ethnographic details were not about understanding the historical and cultural specificity of Africans. Rather, this "educational material" as Strother reminds us, was first and foremost about the production of a knowing self who enacted the gaze.[80] Magubane explains, "First, [the viewing subjects should] be 'curious' about the world in such a way as to 'contemplate' Africa and Africans even as they turned away; they should immerse themselves and yet stand apart.... In other words, the 'characteristic cognitive move of the modern subject' was to transfer onto objects 'the principles of one's relation to [them]' and conceive of them as 'totally intended for cognition alone.'... Individual lives 'appear as no more than stage parts.'"[81] For the most part, then, the performing body did not perform itself but, rather, created the identity of the audience. The ethnographic performance empowered the spectatorial gaze in ways that consolidated the imperial self as knowing subject, who from an elevated vantage point overlooking the scene could consume a world reduced to fungible black bodies demarcating racialized and sexualized Otherness.

Perhaps one of the most important criteria for assessing an ethnographic display lay in the apparent realness of the spectacle. Like the African weaver in Levy's novel, for the performance to be worthy of belief, the performer had to show little to no awareness that she was demonstrating her tribe or race. Certainly, the performer was self-aware to a certain extent, but to ensure the success of the ethnographic show, she was supposed to either "forget" that she was on-stage as the performance unfolded or remain unaware of *what* she was performing.[82] In other words, while Baartman knew that she was on display, the success of her show lay in her enacted ignorance of what was on display and why. This dynamic, as T. Denean Sharpley-Whiting notes, can be seen in the popular *Journal des Dames et des Modes* that reported in February 1815: "The doors of the salon open, and the Hottentot Venus could be seen entering. . . . Candies are given to her to entice her to leap about and sing; she is told that she is the prettiest woman in all society."[83] Z. S. Strother quotes other newspaper reports that Baartman was given insincere compliments and called on to "judge the most affectionate gentlemen in the company."[84] How Baartman could be expected to judge given that her English was still rudimentary at the time remains a mystery. In various newspaper accounts, Baartman is supposedly misled to believe that her performance is one of beauty and desirability instead of a racist enactment of her biological and cultural deviancy and inferiority. Thus, Baartman's supposed belief that the audience is witnessing her great beauty authenticates her sexualized performance as a primitive specimen. Any evidence of the performer's self-awareness of her status as an ethnographic object would detract from the characterization of the spectacle as a demonstration of a "person" in her natural environment. As Coco Fusco argues, representing "the 'reality' of the Other's life . . . [necessitates a] fictional narrative of Western culture 'discovering' the negation of itself in something *authentically* and *radically* distinct."[85]

This preoccupation with authenticity is also demonstrated by the spectators' obsession with the realness of Baartman's body, a fixation that unites the ethnographic spectacle, the freak show, and the slave auction. The audience of the ethnographic spectacle repeatedly took up the invitation to "verify" her steatopygia, and Charles Matthews, a popular theatrical actor of the time, tells of the numerous attempts by the audience to learn whether she was for real: "One pinched her, another walked around her; one gentleman poked her with his cane, and one lady employed her parasol to ascertain that all was, as she called it, '*nattral*.'"[86] As many scholars, including Sharpley-Whiting, Anne Fausto-Sterling, and Barbara Chase-Riboud, have argued, such incidents of phallic poking and prodding draw our attention not only to the obvious eroticization of Baartman's performance, but also to the erotics of ethnography as it sent out various emissaries to "explore" dark continents.[87]

For Baartman to constitute a convincing spectacle, she would have to perform her "naturalness" with regard to her authenticity. This particular difficulty, of the performer supposedly not understanding what she was performing that resulted in a "real" performance of her alterity, alerts us to the coerciveness of these multiple stagings. It also speaks of the inability of the audience to read the self-awareness of Baartman's staging. Many in Baartman's audience could not see the (coerced) performative aspects of her performance. Instead, she is reduced only to the will-less object of their gaze, the racialized and sexualized object of their knowledge production.

To return to the novel *Small Island*, Levy's fictionalization of the ethnographic spectacle forces the reader to think through the question of authenticity via the different responses to Graham's racism by the two performers in the exhibit. The black woman performs her "natural" primitivism flawlessly; she sits on the dirt floor, weaves, and she does not respond to Graham's taunting in any way. Instead, she "just carried on like she'd heard no one speak—pushing her stick through the tangle of threads" (5). While it may be the case that the woman does not speak English, it is improbable that she did not hear Graham shouting at her. Her refusal even to look up highlights her performance of authenticity while also allowing Graham and Emily to maintain the fiction of her savage, brute insensibility. In other words, for reasons that remain illegible, she "chooses" to remain a shadow of the audience's racist projections. In this way, her performance provides an interesting foil to the performance of the African man who refuses to play the authentic savage. Indeed, he resists Queenie's racist reduction of his physicality via his polite, clear English when he suggests a very appropriate handshake instead of a kiss. His assertion of his subjectivity results in Queenie thinking that his hand is warm and sweaty, just "like anyone else's" (5); it also nonplusses Graham, who cannot assimilate it to his notion of authentic black savagery and white civilization rooted in the ethnographic spectacle.

This exhibited African couple presents a pivotal moment to think through the legibility of will. The man's articulateness, his polite handshake, his quiet yet determined undermining of stereotypes are more familiar to those searching for instantiations of resistant will. One assumes that here is a man who skillfully navigates and challenges a racist terrain with strategic instantiations of will. The African woman, by contrast, remains a shadowy figure, seemingly unresponsive to the situation in which she finds herself. One might read her continued weaving as compliance, a surrender of her will to the violence of unfreedom. Another approach would be to attempt to discover more about her to reach some approximation of her agency. Instead, I want to think through the politics of bodily readability that relies on what, in her lovely book *Wandering*, Sara Cervenak describes as the "illusion of a normative body that enjoys and regulates his or her own 'autonomous, self-motivated, endless, spectacular movement.' "[88] The power of the African woman's thoughts can be theorized and felt, not only as a "mutant form of enunciation, articulation, and textuality, but also as an enactment that signals the refusal of all three qualities."[89] In other words, the power of the weaver's will, like Baartman's, lies precisely in its discursive waywardness that "bends away from forces that attempt to translate or read."[90] Rather than attempting to unveil and discover the woman's true intentions, what if we respect and creatively interact with her silence, her bending away? While not trying to decipher her true meaning, I propose an imaginative engagement with her illegibility. Such a methodology accepts her philosophical unavailability even as it critically conjures up the paths that she may or may not have trod.

Private Dances and Freak Shows

The freak show, located at the nexus of capitalism, urbanization, scientific racism, and the growth of a culture of entertainment, forms another coercive performance tradition within which to locate Baartman historically. It is not my intent here to rehearse the well-documented history of freak shows or discussions of their agency.[91] Instead, I would like to think through questions of audience, as well as argue that the freak show's display of "human oddities" was rarely distinct from the ethnological display, with these performance genres operating along a continuum. However, no matter how much they overlapped, there were differences in the ways bodies were read within each tradition, particularly when one looks at the burgeoning transnational discourse of scientific racism. The freak, for the most part, is an individual marked by abnormality, the familiar made strange and Other. Conversely, the figure presented by the ethnographic spectacle is domesticated and made into an Other by which difference is made consumable, easily ingested, and just as quickly forgotten as the imperial self is consolidated. Unlike the freak, this Other of the ethnographic spectacle is not individuated but generalized as a surrogate for an entire ethnic or racialized community. The ethnographic spectacle familiarizes collective difference, while the freak show estranges individual similarity, marking the seemingly familiar as deviant and abnormal. For all of these important differences, however, the freak show and the ethnographic spectacle both map out the boundaries of the self through the marginalization of Otherness. In both performance genealogies, this remapping results in the organization of social relations via oppositional categories not just of normality versus aberration, but also of health versus pathology, whiteness versus blackness, and citizen versus threat to society.

The freak is an example of "embodied deviance," what Jacqueline Urla and Jennifer Terry define as "deviant social behavior (however that is defined) manifest[ing] in the materiality of the body, as a cause or an effect, or perhaps as merely a suggestive trace."[92] Freak shows reveal the centrality of the processes of nation-building in constructing the normate citizen-subject. The display of black bodies posited as belonging to another country or continent distinguishes the foreign and Other even when these bodies were deemed part of the empire. For example, the fame of Chang and Eng, conjoined twins born in Siam (present day Thailand) exhibited in 1829, lay not only in their joined bodies that helped define the classic, symmetrical individuality of the normate but also in their Thai origin. The exoticism implicit in their racialization consolidated the normal, symmetrical body crucially as white. As Wiss writes, "This popular association of physical eccentricity and exotic origin led to a thriving business for London showmen who placed additional value on displaying not just an individual and randomized exhibition of difference, but a systematized radical otherness—the exotic and foreign other as an example of their 'race.' "[93] Like Chang and Eng, Baartman occupied a curious intersection between freak show and ethnographic spectacle. On the one hand, she was not a freak but a "most correct and perfect specimen," what Strother calls a type.[94] Baartman's playing of a Khoikhoi instrument and the broadsheets showing her in traditional face paint with kaross over shoulder, for example, position her as a surrogate for the entirety of the Hottentots under British rule at the Cape Colony. Even as Baartman was thus framed as an ethnographic type, however, she was also advertised as exceptional among her own people. Furthermore, there was some argument in her time about whether her steatopygia was representative of all "Hottentots" or whether she was unique even among her own people. While some sources insist that all Hottentots displayed steatopygia, many did not. For example, Magubane notes that, in *Travels in the Interior of Southern Africa* (1822), William Burchell claims, "It is not a fact that the whole of the Hottentot race is thus formed. Neither is there any particular tribe to which this steatopygia, as it may be called, is peculiar."[95] Thus, Baartman functions as *both* type and individual, ethnographic exhibition and freak.

This dynamic is obviously complicated when considering a black British or African American audience, where the normalcy of the viewer is undercut by his or her racial similarity to the body on display. Of utmost importance is who constituted the audience for Baartman's exhibitions, how their positions affected their understanding of her performances, and within which traditions they located her performances. One should not fail to mention that there was a considerable black presence in Regency London. According to Crais and Scully, by 1810 "the black population of London was between five and ten thousand strong, and overwhelmingly male."[96] Londoners were thus familiar with blacks and could compare and contrast their limited and racist understandings of black bodies with the body of Sarah Baartman. Indeed, as Qureshi points out, "Londoners' experience of blacks was inextricably tied up with performance over a broad range of social situations; black performers ranged from the casual busker in the street to professional musicians. . . . A substantial proportion earned their living as musicians and actors, with some achieving celebrity status," such as the actor Ira Aldridge.[97] Black Londoners also appeared in freak shows, as was the case with Amelia Harlequin, a "white Negress" who performed in 1788 at Bartholomew Fair. This association of blackness with theatricality was further strengthened by the large number of white actors who corked up as blackface minstrels to perform.

The newly freed population of black Londoners would have been familiar with the various spectacular stagings of their racial identities. It is conceivable that blacks attended Baartman's shows, especially after their politicization by the African Association's lawsuit. But how they responded to Baartman remains a matter of speculation. I stress that there would not have been some immediate assumption of mythic commonality between blacks in London and the Khoikhoi Baartman. Such an assumption, as Qureshi writes, "not only ignores the racial heterogeneity of London but also ethnic differences between peoples of the same colour, differences of which the public was not only aware but which showmen capitalized upon" in the ethnographic detail with which they displayed Baartman.[98] Attention to these differences is also important to avoid an ahistorical understanding of the Khoikhoi as representative of all Africans and of all Africans as black.

While we have little information describing black viewers' responses to Baartman's exhibition, we do have an interesting example later in the century of African Americans' protestations of the exhibition of the Central African Ota Benga. The Congolese Ota Benga was displayed from 1860s to 1924, mainly in the Monkey House of the Bronx Zoo. African American leaders recognized the differences between themselves and Africans. Indeed, some of their responses revealed their racism toward Ota Benga, such as their use of the word "boy" to describe the thirty-year-old man and their belief in his mental and moral inferiority. But what African American viewers also saw were the similarities between the display of Ota Benga and the display of black bodies during slavery and in its aftermath. Adams notes that "although [black audiences] did not identify with the Pygmy themselves, they felt sure that zoo visitors would equate the caged African with American blacks."[99] They realized that, given the visual politics that helped racialize the black body on display, white viewers would not make the distinction between themselves and the African. These black audiences thus linked their own treatment with the treatment of Ota Benga. Adams quotes Reverend Gordon, superintendent of the Howard Colored Orphan Asylum, as saying, "You people are on top. We've got to rise.... Why shut a boy [sic] up in a cage with chimpanzees to show that Negroes are akin to apes? Give us opportunities."[100] While black audience members, then, saw Ota Benga as one of them given the racial politics of the spectacle, they also participated in the racist visual economy that consolidated their own civilization and projected savagery onto the racialized African object on display. Finally released into the care of African American clergy, Ota Benga was subjected to their attempts to turn him from savage Pygmy into Christian "gentleman." Adams notes that on March 1916, Ota Benga committed suicide by shooting himself with a stolen revolver in a tangled instantiation of will and coercion.[101]

There can be little doubt that Baartman's performance was also underpinned by something that expensive theater boxes and educational pamphlets attempted to obscure: the stereotype of Hottentot women as oversexed and as possessing unparalleled sexual prowess, marked by their supposed "biological" differences such as elongated labia. Baartman lived in Cape Town for more than ten years before she left for London in the mid-1790s. During this time, as many scholars, including Crais and Scully, report, Cape Town survived on an "economy of maritime masculinity."[102] A center of maritime traffic, the city boomed when soldiers and sailors who had just crossed the Atlantic and Indian oceans arrived with money to spend on lodging, food, drink, and sex. The Dutch East India Company capitalized on these needs by "encouraging" slave women housed at the Slave Lodge on Adderly Street to prostitute themselves. The company reaped large profits while slave women stashed whatever income they could keep to eventually buy their freedom, as well as the freedom of their children. Venereal disease was so common that the Slave Lodge hired its own doctors, one of whom was Alexander Dunlop, a Scottish physician who was often in dire financial straits and who would become one of Baartman's exhibitors.

Many of the sailors and soldiers had sexual fantasies about Hottentot women specifically and sought such women out. This became easier as the numbers of Khoikhoi women in the eastern Cape rose from a handful in the 1790s to a significant number by 1805.[103] By this time, Baartman was living in the home of Hendrik Cesars (Pieter Cesars's brother). Crais and Scully report that the Cesarses were Christian free blacks, descended from slaves in East Asia and South Asia, with a great-grandfather who had originated in Macassar in the Celebes Islands.[104] While not a slave, Hendrik Cesars also was not a citizen because of his race, and he struggled to earn a living in a competitive economy that privileged whites. Baartman soon became a crucial source of income for him and his family. In 1808, he began to show Baartman in various states of undress to hospital patients, many of whom were suffering from venereal diseases and still more who harbored sexual fantasies about the Hottentot. Cesars's wife, Anna (also a free black), insisted that "Sara showed herself to those 'who wished to see her.'"[105] Whether patients also paid for sexual favors, we do not know. Baartman was a woman reduced to racialized sexual object even though she certainly negotiated that objectification the best she could.

Dunlop was struggling to pay his bills, and the impending abolition of the slave trade in 1807 and subsequent closing of the Slave Lodge spelled financial disaster for him. He had offered his services as a physician at various hospitals, and it was perhaps during his rounds at one of them that he encountered Baartman performing for patients and became convinced that this was his path out of economic ruin. Thus began the complicated set of maneuvers between Cesars and Dunlop to travel to London and display Baartman alongside two enslaved black boys. Dunlop, in effect, wanted Baartman to continue the erotic and exotic performance she had already been enacting. Only the audience would supposedly change: instead of Capetonian sailors and soldiers of all hues, it would be London gentlemen, ladies, and perhaps even dukes who would stare at and fondle Baartman's body.

Just before Baartman's trial in 1810, the fourth Duke of Queensberry requested that the Hottentot Venus be brought to his mansion in Piccadilly. The eighty-five-year-old duke—or "Old Q," as he was known—was given to excesses of all kinds, especially when it came to sex, horse racing, and gambling. John Robert Robinson notes in his memoir of Old Q, "With . . . confidence in the Duke's power of perception and diagnosis, a daily paper relates the visit of the then well-known 'Hottentot Venus' to his house, where his grace had 'a select party of amateurs of natural production' to see the black damsel."[106] On the duke's request, Baartman supposedly danced a simple African fandango. The duke was much impressed, going on to carefully examine her bottom.

When considering Baartman's fandango in front of the duke, I am reminded of another scene many years later in Paris, an uncanny echo on February 24, 1926, when Count Harry Kessler asked Josephine Baker to dance for his dinner guests in a cleared space in his library. These two historical moments are surrogations of each other: in both, a white man with considerable social capital invites a famous black female performer to his home for a private showing. In both instances, the black women titillate their audiences by dancing on request, and the women do this no matter how insulting the request may have been or whether or not they dance professionally. Reading the two instances together provides me with a ghostly afterlife that vibrates between the historical moments, allowing me to map a genealogy of black women's diasporic performances. Given the utter illegibility of both women's agency, I use the more detailed descriptions of Baker's performance to critically imagine a possible eruption of her and Baartman's will from within the deep of archival absence.

Kessler's diary mentions that Baker is reluctant to perform naked in front of his female guests because "they are ladies."[107] It is only his promise that he will choreograph a ballet for her set to Strauss's music that supposedly entices Baker from the corner where she has been sitting, according to Kessler, either due to her "not [being] in the mood," her feeling "embarrassed" at her nudity or her "shyness."[108] After describing the ballet he was planning for Baker, not to her but to two other guests, Baker "was as though transformed" and begins a set of "vigorous and vividly grotesque" movements in front of Aristide Maillol's *Crouching Woman*, a sculpture with the classical, flowing lines of a figurative female nude.[109] About Baker's pantomime Kessler writes, "Maillol's creation was obviously much more interesting and real to her than the humans standing about her. Genius (for she is a genius in the matter of grotesque movement) was addressing genius." While Kessler was correct, in spite of himself, about Baker's genius, he missed Baker's biting indictment of her treatment compared with that of the white women in the room. She is naked and pressured to perform, while they are regarded as ladies who might be offended by the sight of her naked blackness. By deliberately copying the sculpture's gestures, by talking to it and resting against it in various "bizarre" poses, Baker acknowledges that she is made and unmade in opposition to Western conceptualizations of the ideal female nude represented by the sculpture. She embodies primitive and grotesque blackness, while the sculpture, like the women in the audience, represents elegant and civilized whiteness. Baker then deforms Maillol's *Crouching Woman* by changing it through her words, unbalancing its symmetry with the addition of her body parts, mocking its frozen inertness through her vivacity.

At this point, Baker suddenly stops "frolicking" with *Crouching Woman* and starts to perform "her negro dances, spicing them with every sort of extravagance."[110] After explicitly showing us *how* she is Othered, she plays her assigned role by dancing her "negro" dances. However, she performs them excessively, with a meaningful extravagance. She gives her audience what they think they want, and then she gives them more. Something important can be located in this "more," in frenzied movements that exceed the form. This frenzy belongs to a woman suffocating and jerking with rage. Her frenzy is not containable, despite Kessler's constant description of her movements as childlike, clownish. When one of Kessler's guests, Fried, attempts somewhat clumsily to join Baker in the dance, she immediately starts to mimic him. Another audience member, Lulu Meien, also attempts a few "delightful and harmonious" movements. In both cases, Baker outperforms them, "extinguishing" their putative grace with a "wonderfully stylist grotesquerie."[111] Not allowing either Fried or Meien to perform "negro" dance moves without interruption, Baker instead caricatures their steps and thereby wrenches control of the impromptu stage back into her very capable hands. Thus, through her mockery, imitation, and caricaturing—first of the Western ideal of body and movement, and then of the white dancers' attempt to appropriate "negro" dance—she signifies on the white privilege that relegates the black female body to will-less spectacle. She embodies her will in her frenetic movement, in her somatic sarcasm, in the "grotesque" throwing around of her limbs.

Baartman, unlike Baker, was not a professional dancer. One can only intuit how accomplished her "savage Fandango" was. But the virtuosity of the performers was really not the point of either of these scenes. Rather, the myth of primitive blackness ensured that both their bodies were spectacularized and objectified. This is why Baker's frenzied movements that exposed the creation and consumption of the Other become so significant. Her flailing limbs, the precision with which she mimicked the other guests, and her interaction with Maillol's sculpture opens a space to imagine how both she and Baartman negotiated the choreography they were forced to enact.

Another way to imagine Baartman's will is to look across the water at slaves for sale. Several contemporary critics have noticed, though not elaborated on, the connections between the slave auctions and Baartman's performance. For example, Ann Nymann asserts that the "image of the naked black woman for sale resonates disturbingly with eighteenth-and nineteenth-century iconography of black female sexuality, such as the 'Hottentot Venus.'"[112] In his study of fantasy and ideology in South African artistic representations of the black body, Okwui Enwezor states, "*Baas* and *massa*; *kaffir* and *nigger*; the Hottentot and the auction block; Jim Crow and apartheid. The uncanny resemblance of these characterizations is not an accident. For they are both founded on blackness as anathema to the discourse of whiteness; whiteness as a resource out of which the trope of nationality and citizenship is constructed, and everything else . . . is negated, defaced, marginalized, colonized."[113] The fragmented black body, as Hartman writes, testifies to the imagined wholeness of whiteness and firmly links performance and blackness through the "spectacularization of black pain."[114] This coupling of blackness with its staging results in a normalization of that display that obscures the violence required to maintain the black body's status as abject. At this nexus, the specter of violence reappears as the black body is rendered as spectacle, displayed to consolidate what Enwezor calls the "ideological fantasy of whiteness."[115]

Herein lies my turn toward descriptions of Baartman's performances onstage as recorded by audiences of the time and my insistence on comparing them to the performances of slaves for sale. The African Association tried to use this comparison as a way to distinguish wage labor from slave labor, free as diametrically opposed to unfree. Using the same comparison, I argue that wage and slave labor both revolve around *the same* false dichotomy of coercion and voluntarism. Capital uses the respective threat and promise of wage labor and slave labor to consolidate power. While being careful not to collapse Baartman's contractual obligation and the slave's commodification, comparing her performances to those of slaves for sale fleshes out the various degrees of coercion and consent implicit in all of these painful performances of subjugation. In these systems of labor, which are more similar than dissimilar, a gesture, a word, a pause, or a sigh can speak volumes about notions of coercion and consent, victim and agent, and the inextricability of black identity from performance. By attuning my ear to these spaces of silence, I argue for eruptions of limited notion of "will."

Buyers of slaves were aware of the numerous tricks of the trade and spent considerable time trying to extract the "truth" from the carefully enacted performances insisted on by the slave trader at the time of auction. Buyers prided themselves on their ability to separate the slave body from these coerced performances. In rituals of mastery, a buyer would question, probe, finger, and grope slaves in an attempt to read the truth of their bodies. Thus, buyers mapped their desires onto the black body as spectacle and thereby imagined blackness into being. An engraving that appeared in *Le Commerce de l'Amerique par Marseille* (Avignon, 1764) entitled "Marche d'Esclave" (Slave Market) depicts an Englishman licking the chin of a slave to determine his age and deduce from the taste of his sweat whether the slave was sick.[116] So important was being a "good judge of slaves" that it became part and parcel of the requirements of a white masculinist social world. As Roach puts it, "In the staging of New Orleans slave auctions, there is a fiercely laminating adhesion of bodies and objects, the individual desire for pleasure and the collective desire to compete for possession. As competitions between men, the auctions seethe with the potential for homosocial violence."[117] Similar fantasies operated around Baartman's body. Audiences pinched, poked, groped, and questioned as they attempted to confirm the veracity of Baartman's sexualized and racialized performance. Through an enactment of this degrading ritual, they consolidated their own mastery and their own fantasy of white superiority and subjectivity. They refused to be fooled by the exhibitor who merely wanted their money; rather, as rational beings, they were able to "correctly" read Baartman's body in ways that structured their own whiteness. However, one must remember that even while black bodies were being packaged, sold, bought, and misread, the Other was potentially always looking back. Urla and Terry write that, even as these black bodies on display constituted semiotic fields onto which "physicians, scientists, and lay people [could] inscribe and project powerful cultural meanings and moral prohibitions," these bodies were also resisting hegemonic readings by pushing against the fantasies and anxieties enacted to create abject spectacles of blackness in the first place.[118] In his groundbreaking history *Soul by Soul*, Walter Johnson notes, "As the traders instructed them in how to represent themselves as salable, the slaves learned about slaveholders' system of slave-buying signs; as the buyers looked them over and asked them questions, the slaves looked back and came to their own conclusion about the prospects held by a given sale."[119] At every opportunity, black bodies were observing, learning, and looking back. In other words, the performative, even as it has the power to make bodies in certain ways, has the ability to unmake those same bodies, and it is with a creative reading of the interstices of performance that I wish to conclude this chapter.

No mechanism of power can foreclose all possibilities of disruption, intervention, and transformation. Power, rather than being an absolute, assumes various guises via historically specific mechanisms. Such variance results in the unevenness of the workings of power, an unevenness often seized on and exploited by resisting subjects. Conditions of oppression shape the performative modes of resistance seized on by the black body, even as they exceeded and disrupted them. Hartman reminds us that these performative modes of resistance are characterized by "the nonautonomy of the field of action; provisional ways of operating within the dominant space; local, multiple, and dispersed sites of resistance that have not been strategically codified or integrated" and a re-working of the discourse of abject (black) body.[120] Thus, while Baartman could not refuse her performance outright, I imagine her disruption of her display in various ways that resist the hegemonic readings of her body as ethnographic spectacle/freak and captive body. For example, her temporary refusal to appear on-stage, while not canceling out her eventual display, slows down the performance; the seamlessness of an unself-conscious performance is disrupted. Instead of viewing an object, the audience is momentarily confronted with troublesome assertions of a denied subjectivity. Perhaps Baartman's "work slowdown" was no accident. Rather, her "reluctance" drew her audience's attention to the complex workings of her will within the cramped space of her coerced performance. Similarly, her reportedly "rude" performance of the one-string bow can be seen as a refusal of virtuosity of an instrument whose playing was supposedly instinctual to her and her tribe.[121] Via her lackluster bow playing, Baartman denaturalizes her performance, using her non-virtuosity to speak against the intentions of the exhibitors. Likewise, her "morose" attitudes, her frequent sighs, and her sullenness all work against the ideological underpinnings of subjugation that insist on the simulation of pleasure and "consent" on the part of the dominated. To paraphrase Judith Halberstam, the "failure" of her performance should be seen as "a refusal of mastery, a critique of intuitive connections between . . . success and profit."[122] Using Hartman's theorization of slave resistance, Baartman's slowness, her "sullenness," and her general reluctance indicated that the "simulation of consent in the context of extreme domination was an orchestration intent upon making the captive body speak the master's truth as well as disproving the suffering of the enslaved."[123] Her failure is both a resistant way to be in the world and an interpretative strategy necessitated by the painful experiences of exclusion and misery. Baartman shows herself suffering and captive, even within the confines of a so-called voluntary exhibition of her body.

Baartman's refusals resonate with slaves' coerced performances of consent that took place during auctions. Johnson argues that, in a New Orleans context, "Ultimately . . . the rites of the market had to be enacted by the slaves. From the time the buyers entered the yard in the morning to the time they left at night, the slaves were expected to enact carefully scripted roles" under threat of beating, deprivation, torture, and inducements.[124] Slaves for sale were forced to perform complex roles. While traders could "feed them up," oil their bodies, provide tallow for their hair, allow their wounds to heal, pluck gray hairs, and dress them up, slaves were still required to "act" as they were advertised. Traders needed slaves to perform the role of human commodities, and to this end the traders forced slaves to claim amazing skills, invent more palatable histories, and pretend to be various ages. In other words, slaves were told to give buyers what they wanted. This small space of performance can be imagined to provide the key for many slaves in resisting and shaping their subjugation. These somatic performances would have been perfect opportunities to undermine their own sale. Johnson documents a Virginia trader in 1850, for example, who wrote to another trader about Coleman, who managed to delay his sale by telling potential buyers that he had lost his hair because he had "cupped," a process utilized by medical practitioners of the time to treat stagnant blood where they drew the skin up by creating a vacuum in a cup using either fire or suction. Another letter from South Carolina states, "James is cutting up. . . . I could sell him like hot cakes if he would talk Right. . . . The boy is trying to make himself unsound. He says he wore a truss in Charleston."[125] Johnson asks us to imagine that slaves manipulated information about themselves to have some limited say over their sale, often presenting themselves as the opposite of whatever the potential buyer was seeking. The slave John Parker, for example, recalled: " 'I made up my mind I was going to select my owner so when anyone came to inspect me I did not like, I answered all questions with a 'yes' and made myself disagreeable."[126] By making himself disagreeable, Parker ripped off the veil of simulated pleasure that covered slavery's consumption of the black body. Through his orneriness, Parker marked out a small terrain of resistance that countered notions of consensual domination, insisting on a form of subjectivity that disrupted the myth of "happy darkies" on plantations. Other slaves cut off fingers and mutilated their bodies to protest the necromancy of a marketplace that reduced them to fungible commodities even as they used its logic of laboring commodity. In such instances, one sees slaves using the internal logic of the marketplace to protest their sale and, in some small way, shape the terms of that sale.

As contemporary theorists, we are desperately searching for signs of resistance to which we have little or no access. Even though this will is not discernible within the archive, we should still attempt to critically imagine it. Doing so is a political act that does not overlook the ultimate illegibility of will or the depressing reality that acts of resistance often do little to alter the structures of domination and exploitation. Death stopped the display of Baartman's body but not her "bad" performances. Her refusal to appear on-stage when called ultimately resulted in a delay of her show, but not its cancellation. No matter how skillful and careful the slave's imagined manipulation of the discourses whereby his or her body was contained, ultimately he or she, in most cases, was still sold and continued to suffer under the brutal regime of slavery. The slave Ednoull comes to mind here: knowing his immense monetary value to his master, Ednoull threatened to kill himself if he was separated from his wife, Sally.[127] Ednoull also cited a promise his master gave him that the marriage bond would not be broken by sale. Ednoull thus invoked not only a grammar of moral obligation and honor but also an economic language of property to attempt to "resist" his sale and separation from his wife. The terrible irony of threatening to end one's life as a form of resistance should not be lost. Ednoull was able to bring about only a delay: records show he was for sale six months later in Baton Rouge.

Since these performative acts of resistance ultimately did not end oppression, one could argue that they are not examples of "will" at all. Instead, one could see them as evidence of the failure of "will" and the success of the processes by which the black body was commodified and dispossessed. Such a reading, then, would lead us to conclude that Baartman was only ever a victim and slave, only ever a commodity. In these historical contexts in which the effects of power appear to be overwhelmingly repressive, bodies are brutally displayed at will as fungible objects, and every glimmer of resistance is met with even harsher punitive measures, it would be easy to dismiss those tiny challenges embodied in the interstices of various performances. It is possible for the inheritors of slavery's legacy to be overwhelmed by the image of the twelve-year-old Monday's broken body beaten by his mistress because his lupus made his nose run on the napkins,[128] of a sick Baartman dying of consumption far from "home." However, critically imagining the possibility of performative instantiations of black will becomes essential if we, as theorists, are not to replicate its archival erasure. Elastic and politically concerned readings of coercion and consent, resistance and victimization work against the foreclosure of agency. They also militate against simplified narratives of retrieval, in which absences are artificially filled instead of acknowledged and engaged. While the performative cannot simply transcend the constraints of domination, it can provide us with a way to denaturalize the abjection and commodification of blackness. In this way, the performative can create a context within which we can imagine the transformation of the spectacle into something more than an expression of the master's will.

"FORCE REFIGURED AS CONSENT"

The Strange Case of Tryntjie of Madagascar

Love had many expressions. . . . Love was the language of dominion,
and its offspring were men and women in chains.
—SAIDIYA HARTMAN, *LOSE YOUR MOTHER*, 62

On March 2, 1713, Tryntjie of Madagascar, a twenty-five-year-old enslaved woman, was sentenced to death. Charges against her included the "godless" treatment of her child that resulted in his death; the attempted poisoning of her mistress, Elizabeth Lingelbach;[1] and adultery with her mistress's husband, Willem Menssink. Tryntjie was taken to a place of public execution, bound to a pole, and strangled to death with a cord. Her body was then fastened to a forked post and left to be eaten by birds and animals until it disintegrated. Her co-conspirators fared better. Gerrit of Tutucorijn stood beneath the gallows with a noose around his neck, forced to contemplate, I suppose, his use of necromancy against his owners and his fragile mortality. He was then placed in chains and sent to Robben Island for twenty-five years, where in all likelihood he died. Isaac of Masulipatam was whipped, branded, shackled, and sent to Robben Island for three years. Carel of Bengal was beaten with rods and made to wear chains for two years while continuing to perform his duties as Lingelbach's slave.[2] I approach Tryntjie's remains cautiously, warily eyeing the birds that, after centuries, still remember the taste of death and that, in turn, watch me without moving until I raise my arms and yell. They scatter. I turn back toward Tryntjie's public performance of death, for it is only this brutal sentencing that has prevented her from sliding into historical obscurity. The execution that ended her life allows us to further unravel slavery in the Cape.

In this chapter, I read Tryntjie's story through what I call the "performative ritual" of the murder trial. Such a reading necessitates a reengagement with the legal archive and an examination of how the law applied to slaves during this period in the Cape. Since slavery was abolished in Holland in the Middle Ages, Dutch slave markets in the colonies had few clear legal precedents or systems of governance. Instead, as Robert Shell writes, Roman Dutch law, along with Indonesian and Indian customs, were forged into a form of common law that consisted of a series of ad hoc ordinances and regulations called *plakkaten*.[3] The highest court in the Cape colony, the Council of Justice, which enforced these plakkaten for enslaved and free alike, kept detailed records. These records allow us to hold in our hands the fragmented afterlives of Tryntjie and her fellow slaves. At the same time, however, these documents do not allow for transparent narratives of retrieval. Trials do not portray the quotidian violence against subjugated bodies that underpinned slavery; rather, they delineate exceptional cases that often cast the slave as the source of transgression and offense. Via the performative ritual of justice, they cement the link between an increasingly racialized slave agency and criminality.

The attempt to ossify these links between black agency and criminality can be seen in laws at the time that regulated slave behavior. John Edwin Mason cites the following decree[4] where "a constable seeing a slave willfully jostle or push against a European, even of the lowest class . . . is obliged, in the absence of the master, immediately to apprehend such slave, and have him punished with flogging."[5] Such laws did not merely distinguish the slave from the European. At a more fundamental level, the slave was defined as a racialized Other whose transgression of the law was both the precondition and the evidence of blackness itself. A similar link between a burgeoning status of enslaved blackness and criminality can be seen in Peter Kolb's *The Present State of the Cape of Good Hope*, originally published Germany in 1731. Kolb describes the slaves at the Cape as criminalized Others who are "the most untractable, revengeful, cruel Wretches that I have ever heard of. 'Tis now and then a most difficult Thing to keep 'em in Order. When Resentment enflames them, whether against the Europeans or one another, they care not what Villanies they commit in order to be reveng'd. And under every Kind of Punishment they are undaunted."[6] After remarking to his readers that the slave who murders a white person is met with a terrible death, he goes on to somewhat cavalierly describe the torture and execution of a specific party of slaves at the Cape who, in their attempt at escape, had murdered a European.[7] In his detailing of limbs breaking under violent blows, splayed bodies on top of a pole and a "half roasted" slave trying to escape the fire set around him even while chained, the slave body's aberrant criminality is literally written onto a body that is broken and remade into the image of a criminal. The criminal begins to function as short-hand for what was then a nascent discourse of biological blackness. Given this history where criminality constitutes the very core of black subjectivity, we have to be cautious of criminal proceedings as a source, reading through them as one would peer through a dark glass.

As Victor Turner argues, performances such as legal trials expose culture's most profound "truths" through their participation in social systems and their embodiment of power relations.[8] While the universal "truths" of these performances are debatable, Turner allows us to think about performance as the ritualistic construction of social reality. Diana Taylor elaborates, writing, "The constructedness of performance signals [not] its artificiality." Rather "the constructed is . . . coterminous with the real. Although . . . a ritual . . . requires bracketing or framing that differentiates it from other social practices surrounding it, this does not imply that the performance is not real or true."[9] By considering Tryntjie's trial as a performance, we can understand the proceedings as a ritual through which communities wrestled with painful social and political issues. Performance gives us structured opportunities to participate in the making of the social with its modes of power. It allows us to depart from a Western privileging of texts and narratives by turning toward what Taylor describes as "meaning-making paradigms that structure social environments, behaviors, and potential outcomes," providing us with a way to understand social and historical systems and events.[10] Because the performance also integrates its audience or spectators into its frame, we as readers are clearly implicated in the political scenes unfolding before us. Tryntjie's trial thus begins and begins again as we hold the past open and bear witness, despite the impossibility of fully doing so.

An Appetite or a Generosity: Gendered Desire in Cape Slavery

To understand the performative aspects of Tryntjie's trial, we need to have insight into how slave women were perceived and treated at the time. In the records of white travelers, slave women's experiences were predominantly characterized both by their absence and by their simultaneous overwhelming presence, to the extent that women's voices are missing, but, as Tony Ballantyne and Antoinette Burton note, these women's bodies abound as "a subject of concern, scrutiny, anxiety, and surveillance."[11] As Suzette Spencer states, the slave woman left "no written body of records, yet her body functions as both the invisible enigma and the open or naked surface upon which historians inscribe multiple narratives."[12] As was the case in most colonial transatlantic slave societies, male slaves greatly outnumbered female slaves. Only in the final years of the Dutch East India Company's rule did the number of female slaves exceed 25 percent of the slave population. When going through the transcripts of trials from the Council of Justice between 1705 and 1794, for instance, one is struck by the scarcity of female slaves as anything other than victims of both their owners and their fellow slaves, such as the cases of Regina van Ternaten and Diana, both of whom I mention in the introduction. What all of these cases highlight is the absence of women's voices alongside the extensive cataloguing and scrutiny of women's bodies as sexual objects. This historical inaudibility, which indexes the construction of black femininity, is not challenged but supported by the spectacular visibility of the injured black bodies scattered throughout the archive's pages.

In addition to the Dutch East India Company's slave barracks being the principal brothel of the region, observers note the ubiquity of sexual violence and coercion that characterized slave life. During one of his journeys into the Cape interior in the 1770s, Anders Sparrman, a Swedish natural scientist who traveled with Captain Cook, described the treatment of slaves in the Cape to support his call for the amelioration of their conditions and the eventual abolition of the trade. From describing how he was awakened one morning by the "horrid shrieks and cries of January and February" being beaten on one farm, to a "lonely" bailiff on another farm whose "mildness and kindness" he praises as the best guarantee of slave's "good behavior," Sparrman's writings show over and over not only the casual disregard for slaves but also the role that sexual coercion plays in the maintenance of power. The "mild and kind" bailiff or overseer, bemoaning the fact that his master did not allow female slaves to reside on the premises, provides Sparrman with a candid sexual ranking: "First the *Madagascar* women, who are the blackest and the best; next to these the *Malabars*, then the *Bugunese* or *Malays*, after these the Hottentots, and last and worst of all, the white Dutch women."[13] Such a devaluation of white femininity was rare, since most white men, at least publicly, believed that whiteness or a light complexion was more sexually attractive than a dark complexion. What this candid list does reveal is that the sexual enjoyment of slaves was ubiquitous. It was widely accepted and in fact, often considered a necessary albeit morally questionable form of controlling and perpetuating slave populations.

For example, Reverend William Wright of Trinity College, Dublin saw the widespread exploitation of the slave's sexual labor as an "incurable evil of slavery." Like Peter Kolb in his indictment of slave criminality, Wright attributed the slave's supposed sexual immorality with their lack of unrestraint. The putative inability, not of Europeans but of slaves, to control their various appetites leads directly to their immorality, evidenced by their promiscuous and adulterous relationships with each other and other "natives." As such, slave women were inherently immoral and the system of slavery could only be blamed for its corruption of the morally vulnerable slave owner who often found himself or herself sinking to the slave's level.

Diarists and travelers to the Cape such as Wright had difficulty grasping the meaning of the behavior they witnessed. Not only did they underestimate the role of violence and coercion in slave women's relationships with white men, but they also overestimated black women's agency as seductresses and willing participants in the seemingly consensual liaisons that are produced by systems of domination. They turned a blind eye to master/slave intimacy, tacitly accepting its utility while railing against the sins accrued and the threat to property posed by such practices and racially hybrid offspring.

Thus on the one hand, Menssink loudly invokes what he insisted was the Cape custom of living by an Old Testament rule that, as Nigel Penn notes, "allowed patriarchal slave owners the right to sleep with their slave women."[14] On the other hand, he threatens Tryntjie with death if she reveals that he is the father of her child. Menssink's anxiety, I argue, focuses on the possible dissolution of his white paternity on which claims of slavery and freedom were based.

The patriarchal household underpinned the social hierarchies at the Cape, providing the basis for the subordination of both free and slave labor through paternalism and brute force. Menssink's separation from his wife might have undercut his patriarchal authority, something he would have regarded as shameful. Perhaps his machinations were attempts to reassert this patriarchal authority so integral to Cape colonial life. Cape mistresses, like slave mistresses everywhere, took serious issue with their husbands' sexual victimization of slaves. One example provided by Mason is that of Samuel Hudson, who writes about a farmer who "frequently had some quarrels with his wife respecting a Slave Maid who unfortunately happened to be more desirable than her Mistress which had caused heart burnings and jealousy and many severe chatisements [*sic*] when ever opertunities [*sic*] offered by the Absence of the Husband."[15] The wife eventually murders the slave woman. The drama among Menssink, Lingelbach, and Tryntjie thus was not uncommon. The sexual exploitation of the slave woman, the punitive actions taken by her mistress, and the struggle between the master and his wife—these dynamics were part and parcel of a system of slavery in which the terrible enjoyment of the slave woman's body was the logical expression of the values inherent in a slave-owning society where black bodies are fungible and completely subject to the master's will. While few of Menssink's contemporaries would have applauded his voracious consumption of slave women, they nevertheless made every legal and moral gesture necessary to support the structures that made it possible.

The presence of white wives in the patriarchal household complicates the heteronormative scene of defiling white fathers and ravished black mothers. While their husbands' and sons' sexual use of slaves troubled white women, they also were deeply complicit. Consider, for example, the writings of the Scottish Lady Anne Barnard, whose careful observations during her five-year stay in the Cape outlines what she felt was Dutch women's acceptance, and even encouragement, of the sexual exploitation of their slaves by their husbands. Barnard remarks that slaves were not allowed to marry, "though there is often constancy from choice. . . . I remember making a Dutch lady stare one day when I said, it must be difficult to preserve so many young Girls *correct*. . . . She did not understand what I meant, and I found that Virtue in a female slave was considered to be a most *unproductive* quality and as such it is discouraged by the Mistress, who boasts of the number of Children her Slaves have and encourages the addresses of those by whom they may be half caste."[16]

What all the various travelers such as Barnard and Wright describe is how the sexual exploitation of slaves was not only the bedrock of domination but also the heart of the patriarchal household. This violence not only created the patriarchal white family; it also threw the very category of desire into what Hortense Spillers has famously described as "unrelieved crisis."[17] Individual sexual preferences, such as those described by Sparrman in his racialized rankings of women, are embedded within a desire and intimacy that takes its meaning from racist culture. Arguing against a particular strain of queer feminist theory in which scholar-activists such as Audre Lorde insist on the "erotic" as a challenge to power, Sharon Holland suggests that desire, instead of existing in a pure space of individual likes and dislikes, "is shaped, like many other emotions, and circumscribed by the racist culture that we live in."[18] Everyday performances of pleasure are ensnared in structures of racialization, seduction and romance, producing desire that is always historically situated. What occurs between Tryntjie and Menssink describes not just their relationship or their colonial context but also speaks volumes as to how we understand the very shape of desire today. This desire can challenge power in its insistence on embodied affect, as Lorde reminds us, but it also crucially bears the weight of the past. Patricia Williams in *The Alchemy of Race and Rights* talks about her great-great-grandmother who, at the age of thirteen, appears in Austin Miller's list of personal assets as "slave, female" with an eight-month-old infant. This eight-month-old infant, like the rest of her great-great-grandmother's children, would grow up as the property of their father though they would never call him this. Williams writes: "I see her shape and his hand in the vast networking of our society, and in the evils and oversights that plague our lives and laws. The control he had over her body. The force he was in her life, in the shape of my life today . . . The choice to breed slaves in his image, to choose her mate and be that mate. In his attempt to own what no man can own, the habit of his power and the absence of her choice. I look for her shape and his hand."[19]

Performances of Sexual Mastery: Court Proceedings

Despite the limitations of the archive, scholars such as John Mason, Robert Ross, Robert Shell, and Nigel Worden have used written records to resurrect the socially dead. Tryntjie in particular has been revived thanks to the publication of H. F. Heese's *Reg en Onreg*, which reproduces her sentencing, and a slim volume by Nigel Penn entitled *Rogues, Rebels and Runaways*, which recreates a gripping narrative of intrigue, necromancy, beer, and what he terms the "socially subversive love for a slave woman."[20] Much of this chapter will focus on analyzing Penn's unique micro-history, which blends narrative and archival documentation to give us an account of Tryntjie and Menssink's relationship. Penn's fascinating and rich work brings Tryntjie to life; we catch glimpses of her desires, her fears, and her possible thoughts. While this chapter is deeply indebted to and respectful of Penn's work, I wish to disrupt the problematic narratives of romance, love, and consent through which he recuperates the "lost" will of slaves. These stories of seduction are what Christina Sharpe calls "monstrous intimacies"—that is, "a series of repetitions of master narratives of violence and forced submission that are read or reinscribed as consent and affection: intimacies that involve shame and trauma and their transgenerational transmission."[21] Exposing fictions of love and consent insists on recognizing the illegibility of will of the subordinated woman buried in the archive. This project requires a critical imaginative poetics based on the "afterlife" of a recurring history.

Tryntjie's story raises a couple of key questions: (1) what is the role of gender in defining the experience of slavery; and (2) how does one theorize a long-standing and habitual sexual relationship between a slave and her master without resorting to simplistic narratives of seduction, reciprocity, and rape that revolve around the legibility of consent? How does one understand the actions of Tryntjie, who, despite being under rigorous control and surveillance by Elizabeth Lingelbach, overcame significant physical obstacles in order to meet with Menssink for sexual encounters over a period of years? As Spillers states, under the conditions of slavery "the customary lexis of sexuality, including 'reproduction,' 'motherhood,' 'pleasure,' [choice,] and 'desire' are thrown into unrelieved crisis."[22] By rethinking enslaved women's subjectivity, I wish to continue the discussion begun in chapter 1 in which I insist that the will of the subjugated black woman, while absolutely present, remains illegible even as we anxiously sift through the past in search of it. The very vocabularies of agency and action available during Tryntjie's life and at this present moment fail us when dealing with the extreme conditions of slavery. Tryntjie's relationship with Menssink needs to be discussed at the crossroads of sex, consent, coercion, and rape, and this discussion requires the invention of new terminology. As Sharpe reminds us, the idiom of freedom "is so bound up with large narratives of emancipation like feminism, Marxism, and nationalism that it is often difficult for us to think outside of their terms of 'self-determination,' 'self-making,' and 'consciousness.'"[23] It becomes almost impossible to articulate the delicate balancing act between "acting and being acted on" that slave women perform each day. In an attempt to forge this new language, this chapter revisits the notion of "consent" that underlies slavery's sexual interactions and exposes the strategies that turn slave owners' brutal enjoyment of slaves' bodies into tales of "socially subversive love."[24]

Tryntjie (b. 1688) was among 115 slaves brought to Table Bay from the Madagascan coast aboard the Dutch slaving frigate *De Soldaat*. She was eight years old. In 1709, Elizabeth Lingelbach bought Tryntjie as a household slave. At the time of this purchase, Lingelbach and Menssink were already separated because of Menssink's sexual exploitation of Lingelbach's female slaves, which continued even after their estrangement. In 1706, for example, Lingelbach, while investigating a noise in the attic, found her husband clad in only a

Japanese robe hiding with the slave Willemijntje in a closet with baskets over their heads. Penn writes that Willemijntje tearfully confessed that Menssink "haar al eenige tijt vleeslijke conversatie had gehoude" (had been having carnal intercourse with her for some time).[25] Lingelbach attempted to elicit Willemijntje's help in trapping Menssink and thereby providing grounds for a rare divorce. However, Lingelbach subsequently sold Willemijntje when she discovered Willemijntje again with Menssink in a rendezvous that was not part of the plan for entrapment. In 1707, Menssink, after being seen entering Lingelbach's yard, was discovered again with his pants down in an "indecent" situation with the slave Flora of Madagascar, who, ironically, replaced Willemijntje. Incensed, Lingelbach approached Jean d'Ableing, acting governor of the Cape, to ask for a divorce. He told her "that she should wait" (38). Tryntjie's relationship with Menssink, while humiliating and painful, therefore should not have come as a surprise to Lingelbach. Rather, she, like us, may have begun to see a pattern of Menssink's sexual enjoyment of slaves and his use of them to manipulate her and gain her wealth. Lingelbach's description of her husband's exploits also presents us with a rare opportunity to study the sexual workings of Cape slavery, offering an overview of master-slave sexual norms and practices. As Sharon Block writes, through Menssink's excesses one can trace the processes by which racial and class identities were forged as white "men's . . . identities largely determined whether they could coerce sex undetected and unpunished, just as [slave] women's identities determined their vulnerability to men's sexual force. Such identities [were] generated through these very sexual interactions."[26] The rest of this section sketches out a reconstructed narrative of Menssink and Tryntjie's relationship using the primary research and narratives of the historians Heese and Penn. The story is convoluted and occasionally borders on the absurd, but it allows me to set the stage for my later discussion about consent, coercion, and the afterlives of slave women. By reading across various fields and literatures, I examine how Penn deploys the archive to encounter the presence and seething absence of black will.

Menssink's initial encounter with Tryntjie occurred two days after her purchase. It was eleven o'clock, and Tryntjie was "linger[ing]" in the darkness at the corner of the street where her mistress lived, waiting for her lover Fredrick ("En elf uuren, op de hoek van de straat daar haar Jufftrouw in woond").[27] The man who eventually approached was not her lover but, rather, Menssink, whose authority over her rested on his marriage to her mistress, as well as on his status as a white man who was one of the Cape's most important brewers of beer. Penn writes that Menssink, "emboldened by his considerable experience in the ungentle art of bending female slaves to his will, . . . had the further advantage of being able to utilise his powerful status as a means of seduction" (9). Tryntjie initially refused his advances but later followed Isaac of Masulipatam, enslaved by Menssink, to Menssink's house, where she "consented" to the master's demands and received four *dubbeltjes* or pence and a glass of corn beer as a reward. Thus began her four-year relationship with Menssink, who would send either Isaac of Masulipatam or Gerrit of Tutucorijn to fetch her. At other times, Penn writes, Tryntjie would go to Menssink "of her own accord" (39). For reasons we can only guess at, the "replaced" lover Fredrick informed the mistress about these liaisons, resulting in Tryntjie's being confined to the house. Since Tryntjie could not go to him, Menssink went to her, overcoming any number of obstacles as he jumped over walls and climbed through windows to make their rendezvous. According to Tryntjie, Menssink gave her a bundled-up cloth containing white and yellow dust that, when placed at the foot of the bed, would cause Lingelbach to remain fast asleep. Later, according to Penn, Lingelbach claimed that this dust was the "ground-up bones of the dead" (40). The powder enabled Menssink to have sex with Tryntjie in his wife's bed while his wife slept, for more than a year. Court proceedings describe numerous other liaisons, such as when Menssink, clad in the Japanese robe with a red scarf on his head, outwitted his wife's various attempts to thwart his access to Tryntjie by hiding in a nearby cellar that was flooded or enlisted Gerrit and Isaac to carry a ladder back and forth that would enable him to climb into his wife's loft.

Lingelbach only realized that her husband still had sexual access to Tryntjie when Tryntjie became pregnant. Lingelbach commanded Tryntjie to ensnare Menssink to gather evidence of his infidelity for divorce proceedings. Instead, Tryntjie informed Menssink that Lingelbach has caught wind of his behavior, which led to her eventual imprisonment in a public jail. Gerrit took presents to Tryntjie while she was in jail and conveyed his master's assurances that if Lingelbach sold Tryntjie, he would buy her. For Penn, this is an indication that Menssink's feelings for Tryntjie were singular: "Menssink had not attempted to buy Willemijntje when she had been sold and his declaration in this instance was an indication of his obsession" (43). A chained Tryntjie eventually returns to her mistress; within two weeks, Lingelbach awakened to see a figure hurrying down her loft ladder. Menssink was again pursuing his passion. Lingelbach also contended that her husband had passed on two bundles containing a mixture of powder and hair that Tryntjie was supposed to place in her mistress's food. Lingelbach's accusation was a powerful one, for the law states that if either spouse attempts murder, the other has grounds for a divorce. By making these allegations, Lingelbach was that much closer to her desired divorce.

The trope of poisoning would have been a familiar one to her audience and activated all sorts of fears. Cape slaves, like female slaves in the Caribbean who prepared their owners' food, for example, had a reputation for being poisoners. Poisoning and the threat of poisoning formed part of the slave's arsenal of resistance to the daily machinations of slavery. The specter of poisoning evoked all sorts of fears in slave owners, particularly regarding the fraught relationship between slavery and familial intimacy. In this respect, the idea of poisoning functioned both metaphorically and literally. The threat of ingesting dangerous foreign bodies resonated with fear around the incorporation of (female) slaves into the domestic space. Poisoning signified the threat posed by enslaved bodies ensconced within the household, whether sleeping at the foot of the owner's bed, nursing the master's children, or cooking food for the family. In other words, the poison was both the slave herself and the substances she would wield against whites if her criminality were not held in check.

Surprisingly, then, Lingelbach did not report this attempted poisoning. Perhaps she was distracted by the birth of Tryntjie's "half-slag" (half-breed) child. Menssink, according to Penn, extorted Tryntjie to remain silent about the child's paternity: "Even if it is the devil's, Menssink urged her, you must not say whose it is. So long as there is no evidence, you must lie to your mistress" (45). Menssink later gave Tryntjie some of his finest beer (which apparently was terrible, as he was a disastrous brewer). He also sent a package of kapok (a lightweight, silky down obtained from kapok seed pods) that he instructed Tryntjie to put in her mistress's food. Tryntjie's mental well-being supposedly deteriorated after the birth of her child. Lingelbach testified that Tryntjie baked the kapok into loaves of bread and cooked it with her spinach and that Tryntjie neglected her baby, leaving him naked on the floor overnight. Later, according to Lingelbach, Tryntjie stuck needles in the baby's head and cut his ears with scissors when he cried. The mistress claimed to have rescued "der mongrul" from the floor and ensured his well-being by giving him a dose of saffron after he was exposed to the cold. Meanwhile, Menssink's alleged attempts to poison his wife intensified. Tryntjie was commanded to prepare all sorts of items for her mistress's consumption and to participate in a particular practice of "black magic," burying the hand of a criminal as close to her mistress's headboard as possible. Under Menssink's orders, Gerrit secured this criminal hand, presumably from a prisoner hanged from a public scaffold as a warning to other criminals. Gerrit then skinned the hand, ground the flesh to powder, and gave the powder to Tryntjie, who fed it to her mistress. After eating the poisoned skin, Lingelbach remarkably remained in good health.

I linger here for a moment to consider the relationship between power and what historical records call "magic," particularly as embodied in the hand that Gerrit procured and that would prove a major factor leading to his imprisonment for life on Robben Island.[28] In *The Politics of Evil*, Clifton Crais refuses to see such instances of "magic" as a native primitivism antithetical to the instrumental rationality of Western rule. Instead, he shows how indigenous peoples combine morality, "magic," social health, and notions of action to understand "life and death; jealousy, hatred and selfishness; agriculture and the rains; the persecutions of the state; the exploits of the powerful and the exploitation of the powerless."[29] Crucially, in the case of Tryntjie magic was a means of understanding both imperial and native governance. It was part and parcel of "imperialism's arsenal" in that colonial officials deployed a destructive magic.[30] But an indigenous grammar of "magic" also responded to this imperial evil by continually reinventing a resistant power anchored in the very diverse and fluid belief systems that constituted the spiritual and political landscape of the eastern Cape. "Magic" thus contradictorily came to stand for both the violent workings of the state and the non-secular political imagination that often exceeded the limits of Western epistemologies; the magical embodied both the terror of imperial governance and native terrorist attempts to overthrow imperial evil and restore the social health of a just society.

Given these multiple registers of magic in the workings of power, the human bones that Gerrit buried outside Lingelbach's bedroom require closer attention. As a source of otherworldly power, these remains resonate throughout the African diaspora. Indeed, in the American South, magical/medicinal bundles or conjure bags are often called "hands." The hand as a source of power can be seen in a wide array of cultural and religious practices. It is probable that the bones Gerrit buried belonged to one of the executed criminals in the Cape, who often had their right hands cut off as part of their sentences. The need for the hand to belong to a criminal relates specifically to "imperialism's arsenal" and "indigenous grammars" of governance at work on the Cape. It is conceivable that the use of the felon's hand puns on the monarch's touch that was supposed to cure sufferers of scrofula in early modern England.[31] The power of the king's hand to heal is referenced and inverted by Gerrit's use of an executed felon's hand.[32] The insistence that this is the hand of someone who was publicly executed reminds us of the entire array of exchanges among colonizers, victims, and audiences in theatrical performances of executions. Such public killings supposedly consolidate the imperial power of the colonizing state; the dead felon is denied a proper burial so that his or her corpse can speak the state's power. But the performance of an execution consists of appropriations and reappropriations of power among audiences with various sympathies, between the enslaved and the free, between whites and Others. Gerrit's granting of power to the executed felon's hand borrows from, or steals from, the semantic authority traditionally granted to the monarch or state, inverting it and claiming it for those who could be considered the most disempowered members of society.

Meanwhile, the drama surrounding Tryntjie escalated as it neared its end. Tryntjie attempted to run away, perhaps to escape Menssink's ever more urgent exhortations that she kill his wife or possibly because Menssink promised to pay her passage out of the Cape should she need it. She hid in a rock shelter at Lion's Head, and later Gerrit and Isaac led her to Menssink's house, where she spent the night. She returned to her rock shelter at dawn and began a four-week period of moving between shelter and a rendezvous spot with Menssink, even though, according to Penn, Isaac warned her of the danger, saying, "Trijntje, waar kom jy toe, weet jy wel wat je doet sal uijtkomen en dan ben je om hals" (Trijntje, where are you going? You know that what you are doing will lead to your death) (50). Unexpectedly and for reasons we can only guess at, Tryntjie turned herself in and returned to Lingelbach's household, where Menssink "coerced" her to feed kapok to their baby. Afraid that Tryntjie would confess the paternity of their child, he hoped to remove any evidence. Tragically, Tryntjie confessed to forcing this kapok down her son's throat, which then swelled up. The boy died two days later and was buried without a postmortem, as his death was thought to be from natural causes.[33] In November, a doctor found traces of human hair and kapok in Lingelbach's stool, sufficient evidence to legally accuse Tryntjie of poisoning her mistress. The slave woman was finally arrested in November 1712, as were Gerrit, Isaac, and Carel.

Menssink was briefly detained, but despite the evidence of letters he wrote to his wife promising to mend his philandering ways and the testimony of the four slaves, he was never called before the court. He was never asked for a statement, interrogated, or cross-examined. He was completely absolved from any criminal proceedings by the Court of Justice, even though, under Roman Dutch law practiced in the eighteenth-century Cape, adultery was a crime that could result in criminal prosecution. Looking at trials for adultery, a pattern becomes clear: adultery practiced by women was more severely punished than adultery practiced by men. As Penn writes, "Male sexual impropriety was treated with greater leniency by the law than female sexual impropriety" (55). If one adds race to the mix, male sexual impropriety practiced not with a white woman but with a slave who belonged to him by way of his wife was not seen as a serious instance of infidelity. Lingelbach did eventually get her divorce, in 1714, which was extremely rare for Dutch couples in the seventeenth and eighteenth centuries, and the recognition of Menssink's behavior as adulterous was essential to her hard-fought victory. But the courts kept the adultery separate from the crimes that the slaves were accused of, probably due to the implications of trying a white master as a co-conspirator with his slaves. The implicit equality suggested by their joint criminality would weaken Cape slave society's attempts to racially mark and thus distinguish white master from black slave. Menssink's reputation as the Cape's primary beer brewer also would have separated him from the lower class of slaves with whom he consorted, thereby shielding him from prosecution. All of the evidence presented by the various slaves was never used against Menssink legally. Instead, Tryntjie bore the brunt of the sentencing for "her "Godless intention" to poison her mistress and the "enormity" of her actions in pursuing that goal. Penn cites the official sentencing, which identifies her "Godless and tyrannical treatment of her innocent offspring," her adultery, and the "horrific" acts accomplished with the help of her three fellow accused as adding up to "matters of evil and dangerous consequence which could not be tolerated in a country where justice was stressed" (58).

The year that Tryntjie was strangled to death was a bad year for the indigenous Khoikhoi and slaves in general. On April 18, 1713, Dutch East India Company slaves displayed the first signs of smallpox, and by May 6, the disease was claiming fragile life after life, spreading farther and farther inland, decimating the Khoikhoi and infecting the inland settlers. The corpses of slaves and Khoikhoi could not be buried fast enough, and the stench lay thick in the air. Only in December did the epidemic abate, leaving a population already devastated by slavery and colonization reeling in its wake. The death of Tryntjie must be placed within this context, in which the living conditions of slaves and indigenous peoples enabled the wildfire spread of the disease and continually reinforced the disposability of certain lives and the valuation of others.

"Spirals of Pleasure and Power": Romancing Bondage

Returning to Block's notion of "force refigured as consent," I wish to examine Nigel Penn's reading of the archival material in his description of Tryntjie's relationship with Menssink (a reading that forms the basis of Andre Brink's novel *The Rights of Desire*). The notion of "love," no matter how qualified, appears repeatedly when scholars describe the fraught relationships between slave women and their owners. While careful to say that Tryntjie's "choice" made her Menssink's captive, Penn nevertheless claims that Menssink was bound "by an emotion so powerful that he would eventually disgrace himself, ruin his fortunes, and cause the death of the woman he *loved*" (10; emphasis added). This rewriting of sexual violence as (reciprocal) desire obfuscates not only the habitual use of sex to control a captive labor force but also the absolute possession of a body definitive of slavery. In her discussion of slave concubinage, Jenny Sharpe speaks of the search "for words to describe a relationship that conventional language cannot name because it breaks with the conventions of slavery and freedom . . . [heteronormative] marriage and morality."[34] As noted in the introduction, words such as "rape," "desire," "love," "coercion," "fatal passion," "seduction," and "romance" cannot even approximate what would make a slave woman agree to force kapok down her own son's throat, causing his death; make her consent to her master's sexual dictates year after year; or enable her to drink the glass of corn beer and spend the four dubbeltjies she received after their first sexual contact. Constitutive of slavery, the yoking together of captive person and property places in crisis our notions of consent, will, and agency. At best we can comprehend situations such as Tryntjie's only by examining the contemporary notions of submission and coercion that anchor our present-day, racially coded understanding of habitual sexual violence.

Theorists often remark on how narratives of seduction were used in the antebellum American South to obscure the habitual sexual violence characteristic of slavery. Based on reciprocated and complicit affective ties of love, caring, passion, and kindness, the trope of seduction erases the extreme conditions of domination and constraint under which the slave woman operated. By making recourse to the bonds not of slavery but of affection, seduction changes the landscape of slavery from one of brutal domination to a kinder, gentler world of secret passions, manipulations by the weak, and forbidden loves. Given the inadequacy of the language we have to describe violence and sexuality in general, it should come as no surprise that the terminology of seduction still permeates the work of scholars today. Spencer cites the lawyer and historian Annette Gordon-Reed's observations with regard to Sally Hemings's exploitation by Thomas Jefferson: "Might not Sally Hemings have thought being the mistress of a slave master a suitable role?... We have to confront the unpleasant notion for many, both black and white, that Sally Hemings may have welcomed any advances that Thomas Jefferson may have made."[35] In Gordon-Reed's interpretation, we can see the yoking together of violence and coercion, with Hemings "welcoming" Jefferson's "advances" and submitting to her role, as demonstrated, presumably, by the number of years of her "service" and her numerous children. Thus, as Saidiya Hartman has argued, an old discourse of seduction keeps being invented anew by the "wedding of intimacy and violent domination as regulatory norms [that] exemplif[y] the logic through which violence is displaced as mutual and reciprocal desire."[36] Perhaps one could recast Gordon-Reed's question to confront the unsettling notion for many, black and white: that we cannot know whether Sally Hemings welcomed Jefferson's advances and that any invitation on her part can be understood only within the terrible constrictions of slavery that blur the lines between coercion and consent.

Despite the great care that Penn takes, his micro-history also reinvents this narrative of seduction. The language used to describe Tryntjie and Menssink's relationship is saturated with romantic terms, from the opening scene when the two first "meet" to the fatal conclusion. We are introduced to Tryntjie as she "linger[s] in the darkness," waiting for a lover, only to meet Menssink, who uses "his status as a means of seduction" (9). This encounter is again described by Penn as a seduction (39), and the pair are called "lovers" on more than one occasion (39–40, 42). The sexual act is described often as "making love" and as "lovers surrender[ing] to their passions" (49), and Menssink's later attempt to help Tryntjie escape stems not only from "mercenary considerations" but also from his "genuine love for Trijntje" (49). This purported love for Tryntjie is reiterated when Penn describes Menssink as a member of the Burgher Council who "was prepared to murder his own wife in order to enjoy the love of a dark-skinned slave woman and inherit his wife's property" (56). Penn concludes by saying that Menssink's "biggest crime was to have loved not wisely but too well, and the government could not countenance the prospect of a prominent free burgher confessing to an unacceptable, all-consuming passion—namely, a socially subversive love for a slave woman" (71). Thus, one sees in his history the great care Penn takes to humanize Menssink, who could have gone down in history as a lecherous, violent, manipulative, and murderous man who made bad beer. Instead, we are left with a portrait of a conflicted Dutch brewer in the grips of a fatal passion for a beautiful slave woman who has captured his imagination, his heart, and his desire. Willing to stop at nothing, Menssink pursues this star-crossed relationship, only to be left tragically alone as his lover hangs rotting on a scaffold. But this sentimental humanization of Menssink comes at a great price: the tremendous sexualized violence of slavery gets elided, and the injury that characterized Tryntjie's life is written over.

Penn does attempt to theorize sex, power, and slavery, and he is careful to say that one cannot guess at Tryntjie's motivations, choosing instead to dwell on Menssink and his desire. Why can we supposedly access only Menssink and not Tryntjie? While I, too, feel that one cannot guess at Tryntjie's motivations, I want to linger on the conditions that produce this illegibility. Penn turns to Michel Foucault and Barbara Bush to argue that sexual power is never only repressive. The keys to interpreting the relationship among white men, white women, and slave women can be found in the ambivalence of this sexual power, Penn states. I quote Penn's argument at length, for in its contours we see the unintentional reinvention of a more contemporary narrative of seduction through the framing of restrictive choice, coercion, and direct threat as romance:

> For white men black women were "forbidden fruit": sexual relations between black and white could create "perpetual spirals of power and pleasure" from which white women were excluded. White women were excluded from the pleasure . . . but not necessarily from the pain of their husband's power. . . . Conversely, in the labyrinthic "spirals of pleasure and power," power relations could be temporarily inverted, and "Black women, too, despite their racial and sexual inferiority could at times manipulate white men to their own advantage." Clearly, there were times when Menssink was not in control of his emotions and was dangerously addicted to Trijntje's sexual charms. Although Menssink's passion temporarily empowered the slave woman it was, in the long run, to prove fatal—if not to Menssink himself, then for Trijntje, and very nearly for Elizabeth too. (42)

This dense paragraph repeats several constructs that need unpacking. First, in his attempt to describe Tryntjie's agency, Penn repeats discourses popular during slavery of the slave ultimately controlling the slave master. Second, while Penn shies away from Tryntjie's motivations, his language of love is predicated on Tryntjie's implicit consent. And third, Penn excludes white women from the economy of pleasure and desire that underpins slavery, positing white femininity as essentially innocent of the workings of power.

Hartman contends that seduction "demands the absolute and 'perfect' submission of the enslaved as the guiding principle of slave relations and yet seeks to mitigate the avowedly necessary brutality of slave relations through the shared affections of owner and captive."[37] Asking how violence gets recast as reciprocal relationships resulting from the manipulations of the dominated, she turns to George Fitzhugh's *Cannibals All! Or, Slaves without Masters* (1857). The pro-slavery Fitzhugh writes that the strength of the weakness upsets the natural balance of patriarchal power within the family and household. Hartman quotes Fitzhugh as saying, "The dependent exercise, because of their dependence, as much control over their superiors, in most things, as those superiors exercise over them. Thus and thus only, can conditions be equalized."[38] Fitzhugh argues that, through various manipulations, the weak—that is, women, slaves, and children—wrest power from the master, who becomes the greatest slave of all. Such theories of reversals of power appear in Penn's history where Menssink's power as a white slaveholder is mitigated and reversed by Tryntjie's power as the slave woman to whom he has allegedly surrendered his power. Whether Tryntjie participates in the exchange out of affection or sexual desire or self-interest, Penn depicts Tryntjie as a black woman manipulating a white man to her own advantage. This manipulation results in perceptions of Tryntjie and Menssink as equal participants in the "perpetual spirals of power and pleasure." Through her exercise of her power, albeit of the weak, the reader is left with a sense of Tryntjie's complicity and willful submission in the equalizing power play that is seduction. Power itself becomes a province of the weak rather than of crushing systems of inequity and exploitation. Rather than evoking the unilateral subjugation of slavery, power comes to stand for the severely curtailed negotiations of slaves as they attempt to survive.

This is not to suggest that Tryntjie did not manipulate the limited access to power that Menssink's attention gave her. We can imagine her disruptive assertions in the fleeting instances of her performance. Like Sarah Baartman who played her instrument "rudely," perhaps the only way for us to catch a glimpse of Tryntjie's approximations of agency, her acts that are "akin to freedom," lies in the reading of her performative gestures. Tryntjie's attempt to run away, as did so many slaves before and after her, provides us with an opportunity to do this. Records indicate that she expected Menssink to put her aboard a ship for England when she ran away, but no such ship materialized. Instead, she traveled back and forth between Lion's Head and Menssink's house until she returned herself to Lingelbach. By reading Tryntjie's performative gestures, one could argue that she convinced Menssink to help end her status as a slave by helping her to leave the Cape. By not securing her departure while maintaining his sexual access to her, Menssink may have ensured her eventual return to Lingelbach's household. What such a possibility indicates is not so much that Tryntjie derived power from her condition of subjugated dependence. Rather, Menssink's possible role in impeding her escape illustrates that the very parameters of resistance are shaped by the discourses of power that necessitate resistance in the first place. Consider how Tryntjie negotiates her "value" with Menssink and Lingelbach by stealing and returning herself during her escape attempt. Here we see her implicit understanding of her fungibility and her assessment of her differing value as property to her two owners. With each escape and return, Tryntjie reinscribes her status as property in the hopes of ultimately freeing herself from the status of chattel. This is not the weak manipulating power through seduction but rather the weak navigating a terrain and performing liberatory strategies where there are almost no spaces free from subjugation and its effects. Tryntjie does not and cannot achieve equality or freedom through her dealings with Menssink and Lingelbach—the best she can hope for are minute, often temporarily gains within the context of domination. These gains occasionally come at the expense of other slaves and can work to reinforce the very systems of subjugation that the slave is attempting to alleviate. Thus one can see in Tryntjie's sexual behavior what Sharpe calls the "contradictory practice of slave women subjecting themselves to sexual exploitation in order to remove themselves (if only provisionally) from the threat of rape or the control of their owners" (xviii). And while these performative disruptions might have provided some respite, they also reinforced the systemic sexual violence attendant to slavery. These advantages within the context of subjugation are described in 1861 by Linda Brent in her *Incidents in the Life of a Slave Girl* as "something akin to freedom."[39] Brent's sexual "choices," which she recognizes all too clearly as only approximating freedom, draw attention to the severe constraints under which she operates as a slave woman. Brent's and Tryntjie's conditions, then, place notions of consent, volition, will, and indeed desire itself in crisis.

In the face of this crisis, how do we understand Tryntjie's participation in the Foucauldian "spirals of power and pleasure"? Put simply, given the crisis of choice under conditions of slavery, what would Tryntjie's "no" sound like to Menssink? Or, alternatively, what would her "yes" sound like? The infamous Jamaican overseer Thomas Thistlewood, who recorded in meticulous detail his 1,774 separate sexual acts with 109 different slave women, gave the women a small sum of money if they complied. If they refused, he made them comply. If the slave woman's "yes" and "no" result in similar consequences, if her coerced submission and her consent amount to the same action, then her consent, like her non-consent, becomes illegible unless criminalized. And if Tryntjie did say "yes," what was she saying "yes" to?

The language of consent is based on the notion of contract, but the coercive alchemy at work in the transformation of human beings into property pressures this language.[40] Slavery is indeed a social contract but exclusively among free whites and not between whites and the slaves, despite all attempts to cast it as such through the language of paternalism, duty, love, and sentimentalism. Slaves, as Spencer notes, are not "free and equal" guardians of their own consent even though dominant discourses such as seduction attributed to them "'free' agency (romance) unmediated by force."[41] The exclusion of slaves from the social contract renders "consent" absurd within the context of slavery. After documenting how Menssink sent various slaves to "fetch" Tryntjie, Penn says that "sometimes, however, she went of her own accord" (39). Such an individualized notion of consent fails to fully describe the unequal distribution of power that existed before Tryntjie's negotiation took place. Her "choice" becomes an isolated moment, divorced from the larger societal structures characterized by disparity and coercion. One cannot speak of the slave woman's "own accord" under structural conditions that render the slave incapable of choice. Indeed, as Hartman has observed, consent "is unseemly in a context in which the very notion of subjectivity is predicated upon the negation of will. The impossibility of an absolute dissociation of choice and compulsion and the inability to escape the entanglements of will-lessness and willfulness constitutive of the subject of slave law condition the ambiguous representation of sexual violence . . . and culminate in the displacement of rape as seduction."[42]

Block relates the story of the white servant Rebecca McCarter, who in 1789, during cross-examination in her rape case, said, "He struggled with me . . . and left me so that I could scarcely lift my arm to my head. . . . I consented to the connection with Def[endant]. . . . I struggled each time—but consented at last."[43] Although the differences between McCarter and Tryntjie are numerous, both cases necessitate a juxtaposition of violent coercive acts and a choice to consent. In contemporary understandings of sexual violence, the criterion for determining rape often tends to be physical injury. As J. A. Scutt writes, for sexual acts to be considered nonconsensual, the "showing of physical damage beyond the simple evidence of penetration has, almost, the status of a legal standard."[44] However, as Block points out, current expectations of physical injury as an indicator of sexual non-consent were not as widely accepted in the early modern period, when consensual sex could be painfully violent and sexual violation could occur without overt physical force and resistance to it. Thus, McCarter's having been thrown about and injured so severely that she was unable to raise her arm over her head was dismissed as "at best performative, and, at worst, irrelevant."[45] Her physical injury was understood as part of the sexual overpowering that led to her consent; as the Southern planter William Byrd says in his diaries about another incident, she "wou'd certainly have been ravish't, if her timely consent had not prevented the Violence."[46]

Just as McCarter's injuries were subsumed into her supposed consent, so, too, were black women's injuries, but for different reasons. A black woman's lack of consent could not be proved via the legibility of physical wounds because the status of injury for the slave was normalized, unseen, and unmarked because violence constituted a socially acceptable use of one's property. Often in instances of rape, injury done to the body is evidence of a nonconsensual sexual act. However, in a situation based on the non-recognition of slave women's will, physical injury cannot index violation. Rather, physical injury reflects, first and foremost, the institution of slavery and the creation of the slave body. Thus, the lack of physical injury cannot be used to prove consent, just as the presence of physical injury cannot prove any force other than the coercion of slavery itself. The normalization of black injury, the slippage between consent and coerced submission, and the criminalization of slave agency contributed to the immense difficulty of theorizing the experience of Tryntjie and of black will more generally.

Critically imagine for a moment the violence that slaves experienced during the course of a day in the Lingelbach-Menssink household. According to Penn's account, prior to Tryntjie's arrival, Lingelbach had discovered Menssink sexually violating the slave girl Susanna and attempted to normalize the situation by pretending to hit Susanna. Lingelbach then seized the girl and dragged her by her hair. This behavior painfully echoes incidents in Lingelbach's marriage in which Menssink dragged her by the hair across a room, beat her with a *sjambok*, and sat on her chest, among a long list of other abuses. If such incidents were in fact quotidian, how does one distinguish the injury of routine violence from the injury of non-consent? And is the injury of non-consent not actually another instance of routine violence? Here is yet another aspect of the slave woman's experience that becomes invisible due to the normalization of wounding that is constitutive of slavery. As Block argues in another context, in the sexual attacks on Tryntjie, "Social and economic power underwrote sexual power, not only in the ability to evade legal punishment but also through the very commission of sexual coercion. The porous boundaries between consensual and coercive sexual relations allowed some men to confuse sexual force with the appearance of consent."[47] Thus, part and parcel of the prerogative of mastery was the ability to create extreme situations of domination in which a slave woman's power to refuse or consent was eroded to the point of meaninglessness.

The ability to redefine force as tacit consent indelibly links coerced and consensual sex in a constitutive dialectic. If we acknowledge that a slave woman's refusal is masterfully folded into consent, then all consent, including the presumed consent of white wives, must be reexamined. Racialized systems of exploitation in marriage cannot be uncoupled from gendered sexual violation under slavery. Thus, Lingelbach and Tryntjie are bound to each other through various gendered and racialized systems that assume their sexual consent to white patriarchal authority. Penn astutely realizes this when he includes white women in the "spirals of pleasure and power" that characterize slavery. However, I find curious and heterosexist his qualification that white women are "excluded from the pleasure, but not necessarily from the pain" of their husbands' power. The social power of slavery derives much of its potency through the pleasurable enjoyment of property. Property was used and abused by master and mistress alike. Taking full advantage of their privilege, white women developed intimate relations with the slaves in their household while also participating fully in slavery and its benefits. Thus, while patriarchy regarded slaves and women as childlike and subordinate, married women of the slaveholding class were not on the same level as slaves.

However, Marli Weiner argues in her study of mistresses and slave women in South Carolina, "Women's potential to identify common ground across racial lines offered the possibility of transcending slavery and viewing one another as individuals."[48] Perhaps we see such a potentially radical moment when Lingelbach picks up Tryntjie's crying son, who has been left in a doorway, or in her appeals to Tryntjie to help her get free of Menssink. Yet at the same time, the possibility for bonds of sympathy and understanding are severely limited by Lingelbach's inability to imagine a world without the privileges of slavery. The slave mistress, no matter what common ground she may have found with her slaves, still remained highly invested in the pleasures of property. White women were not passive observers in the daily running of a slave household; they trained slaves in domestic tasks, enjoyed the benefits of spared labor, and, according to Mason, implemented what Cape slaveholders called "domestic correction."[49] Through both brutal and sympathetic actions, slave mistresses upheld slavery often by collaborating with slave masters in maintaining the racial and class structures that enabled white supremacy.

I would argue that Lingelbach does not wish to stop Tryntjie's sexual abuse as much as she wishes to exploit that sexual abuse in her struggle against her husband, whose repeated acts of "adultery" probably caused her tremendous anguish. Instead of finding sympathy or common ground with Tryntjie over their shared mistreatment by Menssink, Lingelbach uses Tryntjie as a pawn in her struggle with her husband for control over herself. She attempts to determine the terms of Tryntjie's use as property and to define the meaning of the sexual acts that were integral to the management of slave labor. As Block writes, "Control over the public terms of the sexual acts became a three-way contest as mistresses tried to redefine their husbands's and laborers's sexual relations."[50] It is no coincidence that Tryntjie is Lingelbach's slave. Menssink consistently chooses slaves who not only belong to his wife, but who are essential to the running of her household. Thus, both Menssink and Lingelbach use Tryntjie's body as the violated terrain on which to stage their family drama. Control over the meaning of Tryntjie's spectacular performances by the couple allowed them to recast her will to serve both their individual agendas and their shared privilege.

One of the most striking features of this case is Menssink's repeated use of Tryntjie to assert his sexual dominance over his wife. Instead of stealing Tryntjie away when she is forced to sleep at the foot of her mistress's bed, Menssink gives Tryntjie a powder to make Lingelbach sleep through the night so that the sex act occurs in his wife's physical presence. Not content with this, Menssink later moves his activities to the bed *next to his wife* after drugging her. His wife's courtyard, her attic, her front room, her bedroom, her bed: the places Menssink chose for his encounters with Tryntjie reassert his eroded patriarchal authority by claiming as his the places and people owned by his wife. In addition, the frequency with which he is caught, while perhaps indicating that he was as incompetent at subterfuge as he was at beer brewing, also speaks to his desire to control Lingelbach through the sexual use of her property. There were many slave women to whom Menssink would have had easier sexual access than his wife's slaves. Penn states that Menssink's choices of slaves were part of his demonstration "to the slave woman, to his wife, and to himself—that he remained the master despite a humiliating separation, which signaled to Cape Society that his wife rejected him" (37). I would argue that Menssink's various performances of (sexual) mastery were not just about the separation from his wife but also part of the everyday performances of sexual violence that underpinned the slave owner's domination of both his wife and slaves.

But what should not be overlooked is Lingelbach's competing performance of (sexual) mastery.[51] While she is definitely a victim of exploitation by her husband, she also uses the sexualized body of Tryntjie and other slave women to claim her authority as a white woman. Consider Menssink's relationship with Lingelbach's slave Willemijntje. After discovering Menssink in his Japanese robe with Willemijntje, Lingelbach asserted her claims of ownership by asking the slave to help trap her husband. When Willemijntje "failed" to do this, Lingelbach sold her *buijten* (outside) to rural areas, where the work was physically more strenuous and the slaves were more isolated. She thus wanted her slave's sexuality to be used to her advantage, not Menssink's. She repeatedly attempted to use slaves as sexual bait to entrap Menssink. Lingelbach's sexual mastery is more similar to Menssink's than we might think if we accept that sexual violation does not express desire or lust but, instead, functions as a tool that dominates and exploits racialized and gendered subjects. If, as Pamela Scully argues, "White men . . . perceived relations of power operating through a complex racial and sexual economy premised on the subordination and sexual availability of black women," so did white women.[52] While there are definitely moments in which white women attempted to make tentative alliances with black women against the various forces of patriarchy, I would argue that this was not Lingelbach's primary motivation. Lingelbach appeared to be far more concerned with gaining the upper hand over her husband through the sexual mastery of her slaves than with identifying with black women by virtue of their misuse at the hands of slave masters. The prerogatives of mastery are not limited to actual acts of sexual violation. They also include the very conditions that enable, define, and perpetuate sexual abuse in the first place.

I conclude this chapter with a discussion of another startling textual appearance of Tryntjie: the Afrikaner writer Andre Brink's novel *The Rights of Desire* imaginatively exhumes Tryntjie's body.[53] Using Penn's micro-history as his source, Brink introduces the ghost of Tryntjie to his story about Ruben Olivier, an aging white man who is struggling to adjust to a postapartheid South Africa and to his recent retirement. Concerned for his safety in the wake of violent attacks in the neighborhood, Olivier's children want him either to leave South Africa or take a lodger, despite his insistence that he is already being looked after by his housekeeper, Magrieta, and the ghost of Antje of Bengal, who is a fictionalization of Tryntjie. Olivier relents and takes a lodger, twenty-nine-year-old Tessa Butler, who turns his life inside out as he contemplates both his sexual desire for her and her sexual refusal of him.

Like many of Brink's novels, *The Rights of Desire* is concerned with the relationship between history and fiction. In his essay "Interrogating Silence," Brink states that "history provides one of the most fertile silences to be revisited by South African writers: not because no voices have traversed it before, but because the dominant discourse of white historiography (as well as temptations to replace it by a new dominant discourse of black historiography) has inevitably silenced, for so long, so many other possibilities."[54] Engaging with this silence in imaginative ways necessitates Brink's turn toward what he terms "magic," a word that, for him, constitutes "an awareness of more things in heaven and earth than have been dreamt of in our philosophy, a free interaction between the worlds of the living and the dead, a rich oneiric stratum; also of ancestral-historical-commitment."[55] The term "magic" resonates in complicated ways, particularly given the indictments against Tryntjie's supposed use of black magic and the rumors I discuss in an earlier chapter about Sarah Baartman's body being used for muti. Brink's evocation of the magical acknowledges that South Africa, like the Americas, is haunted by the ghosts of slavery. The novel begins by declaring, "The house is haunted. . . . Two fixtures came with the house. The ghost of Antje of Bengal. And the housekeeper, Magrieta Daniels" (3). As a contemporary "Colored" woman in South Africa, Magrieta can be seen as the descendant of Antje and other slaves brought to the Cape. Both Magrieta and Olivier are well aware of this. The stories Magrieta repeats about her family go all the way back to "an ancestor first brought from East India as a slave. In the course of many retellings this matriarch became, predictably, a contemporary of Antje of Bengal. Her name was not known" (214). Magrieta and Olivier are unable to "fill out any details from archives or books," even though they both are intimately aware of her presence (214). Magrieta's connection to Antje is based not just on lineage but also on the historical link between domestic labor and slavery. The violence of slavery and colonization experienced by Magrieta's ancestors reverberates into the present through her body. Magrieta "harbour[s] some-where inside her global body the violence and rage, the raping and the killing and burning of her everyday world, its poverty, its meekness and patience and suffering, its anger and rebellion and despair. . . . in her ears still the shouting of a lynching mob, the screams of a victim; on her retinas the imprint of a hacked-off head; in her nostrils a smell of smoke and blood" (142). Olivier realizes that this history of violence separates him and Magrieta so completely that, even though she has worked for him for almost forty years, at times she is as "unreal to [him] as any ghost" (142). She becomes obscured by her his-tory of erasure and marginalization, and there are many moments in which, despite his good intentions, he is unable to see her. This is how Brink portrays the house of South Africa: haunted not only by slavery but also by its legacies that continue to disenfranchise the descendants of slaves, men and women like Magrieta.

Sharpe states, "Slavery continues to haunt the present because its stories, particularly those of slave women, have been improperly buried. But an im-proper burial does not mean that they are irretrievably lost."[56] Brink makes this metaphor literal by describing the haunting of his house by Antje, who wanders through his rooms, sometimes with her severed head tucked under her arm. While Olivier never actually sees her until the end of the novel, he feels her presence and hears about her from Magrieta, who has almost daily conversations with her, and from Tessa, who catches occasional glimpses of the specter. Antje's wandering ends only when Olivier finds her lost body in his cellar. He immediately reburies her in a redressive act that reconnects her severed head to her body. This reassembling of her body resonates with Toni Morrison's notion of a literary archaeology in which the novelist excavates and pieces together the fragments and silences of the archive. However, I would argue that the illusion of Antje finally made whole and put to rest is simply that: an illusion. Magic, no matter how powerful, cannot put broken bodies back together; it can only provide us with a glimpse of otherworldly possibilities. Like Beloved, who returns, still hungry, to the watery grave from which she comes, or Baartman's possibly empty grave in Hankey, Antje of

Bengal as the fictional representation of Tryntjie of Madagascar cannot really lie in peace until the current inequities that continue slavery's regimes in its various forms are addressed and until the social conditions of Magrieta's life are ameliorated. Until then, ghosts will continue to rattle their chains.

At times, Brink's fictional text directly mimics historical writing as he gestures to absences in the archive. Thus, Olivier explains Antje's presence to both Tessa and us using a historical tone as the text dramatically switches from an affective, introspective first-person narrative to a seemingly more objective third-person narrative complete with bibliographic citations. The personal ramblings of Olivier are abruptly interrupted by a narration that informs us that the fullest and most recent published account of Antje's life appears in "Geoffrey Dugmore's *A Sparrow for Two Farthings: Slavery at the Cape, 1657–1795* (Juta, Cape Town)" (40). Following this made-up reference is a citation of Nigel Penn's work as the history that the text mimics:

> Certainly the "spirals of power and pleasure" cited by Nigel Penn in a different but comparable account ("The Fatal Passion of Brewer Menssink" in *Rogues, Rebels and Runaways*, David Philip, Cape Town) were much in evidence in the relationship between Willem Mostert and Antje of Bengal.... Among the items later listed at the murder trial were delicacies like "a powder and hair mixture," "ground-up bones of the dead" ... an unholy assortment collectively described by one historian as "perhaps, primarily, a magical substance whose power derived less from pharmacology than necromancy" (Dugmore, page 114). (42, 45)

In the movement between fact and fiction, Brink not only critically imagines Antje's story; he also alerts us to the limitations of the archive itself that, while supposedly giving us hard material evidence, also re-creates politicized silences and absences. Fact and fiction blur into each other almost seamlessly as Penn's statement about the use of the dead felon's hand becomes the voice of the imaginary historian Dugmore writing about the love between Willem Mostert and Antje of Bengal. As if to emphasize both the meagerness and tenuousness of our knowledge concerning Antje/Tryntjie, Brink alters Penn's history in ways that can both obscure and cast light on Tryntjie. Instead of getting her divorce, Mostert's wife, Susara (the fictional analogue for Lingelbach), eventually dies from poisoning amid the frenzied and incessant coupling of the "lovers." Susara's death instantly changes Mostert, who withdraws in grief, waving Antje away when "she came to him [as h]is lust ... had perished with the last breath of his wife" (47). Willem is not allowed to suffer in solitude; instead, the numerous slaves to whom he made promises come to collect on them. After brutally beating one of the slaves who sought him out for her promised freedom, the matter of Susara's murder comes to the attention of the Court of Justice. The trial then proceeds which mirrors the prosecution of Tryntjie, but again, with a difference. Two days after Antje's execution, "under the cover of darkness, Willem managed to retrieve the dismembered parts of the broken, once beloved body, and returned to his home in Papenboom" (48). This statement is followed by the suicide of Mostert, who hangs himself from an oak tree. Antje's material body disappears as rumors of her ghost surface. And "that, at least, in the absence of hard evidence, is the consensus among the few historians who have shown interest in the sad affair" (48). The sentimentality of this initial retelling of the story of Willem and Antje is deliberately cloying. Whereas Penn (despite his sliding into narratives of romance) says accurately that we have no way to know how Menssink responded to Tryntjie's torture and hanging, Brink's initial story provides the reader with a romantic ending as the devastated lover collects the broken body of his beloved under cover of night. Mostert commits suicide, although we are not quite sure why. Is he devastated by his wife's death that also killed his lust? Or is he traumatized by Antje's death, for without her his life has no meaning? The story once again appears to be not a tragedy of coercion, resistance, and slavery, but a romance of a flawed man who loved somebody too well.

However, immediately after retelling Antje's story in a third-person voice that blends imaginative fiction with imaginative history, Olivier returns the reader to the intimate setting of his study, where he and Tessa drink wine before a fire. He becomes conscious of "wet branches scraping against a window, a sound in the chimney. Something from Mrs. Radcliffe. Or *Wuthering Heights*" (50). In this overt reference to the Gothic romance, Brink shows how we have inherited the popular vocabulary of the nineteenth century where anxieties about race were expressed through ghosts and other "magical" elements. According to H. L. Malchow, certain elements of Gothic fiction gave "meaning to a flood of experience[s] and information" that felt like an assault on one's domestic way of life.[57] Patrick Brantlinger suggests something similar when he states that imperialism's "link with occultism is especially symptomatic of the anxieties that attended the climax of the British Empire."[58] These concerns also relate to the demise of the apartheid state and the rise of black nationalism for Olivier, an old Afrikaner who has been made to retire to make way for the dangerous and modern black South Africa. In the silence that follows

Olivier's "history" of Antje, one becomes aware of the epistemic, cultural, and social crisis he faces in postapartheid South Africa, where he struggles to find a new way to be in the face of a vicious history. Thus, the initial sentimental retelling of Antje's story gets dismembered by the events of the narrative and by Brink's reflections on the nature of desire itself.

Tessa's voice cuts through the Gothic gloom. After the retelling of the story, she says, "It's a terrible story. . . . I guess all those historians were men?" When asked why she thinks so, she points out, "It's supposed to be Antje's story, but she hardly features in it" (51). Using Tessa's voice, Brink points out how absences and silences in the historical record, along with racial and gender biases, shape Penn's micro-history of Tryntjie. Thus, Olivier's inability to actually see the ghost of Antje becomes important thematically. His historical position as a male Afrikaner mediates and obscures his knowledge of her. Just as the historian sees Antje only through fragments of documents and historical silences, Olivier can see Antje only through Magrieta and Tessa. But he does feel her absent presence. "I suppose I can say I've been aware of her presence. . . . In a sense, to me at least, Antje's absence was more real than anything around us, visible in the half-dark study. Like an obscure moon illuminating our darkness from somewhere very far away, very long ago" (50–51). The phrase "obscure moon" recalls the novel's epigraph, a line from Wallace Stevens's "The Motive for Metaphor": "The obscure moon lighting an obscure world / Of things that would never be quite expressed, / Where you yourself were never quite yourself / And did not want nor have to be."[59] While Stevens contemplates what it means *not* to want under an obscure moon, Brink asks us what it means to desire under the light of a traumatic history of slavery and sexual coercion. Antje illuminates Olivier's dark explorations into desire, possession, and history. The catalyst for these explorations, however, is not the slave woman, as in Menssink's or Mostert's case, but Tessa, who will not have sex with him. Tessa brings home lover after lover as Olivier watches, contemplating the nature of his possessiveness and the rights of his desire. Olivier is not the only one watching. Magrieta and Antje are watching Tessa and Olivier, as well, and their various interventions deliver crucial lessons about ownership of women's bodies, labor, and storytelling.

The Rights of Desire takes its title from a line in J. M. Coetzee's *Disgrace*, which Brink quotes as the novel's other epigraph: "I rest my case on the rights of desire. . . . On the god who makes even the small birds quiver." When the protagonist of *Disgrace*, David Lurie, states that his "case rests on the rights of desire,"[60] he is talking to his daughter Lucy about the accusation against him for sexually harassing a student at Cape Technical University. Consider his troubling description of his last sexual encounter with the student: "[She] does not resist. All she does is avert herself: avert her lips, avert her eyes. . . . Not rape, not quite that, but undesired nevertheless, undesired to the core."[61] His defense against this charge of sexual harassment is his right to feel desire for his student, despite her lack of desire. To his insistence that an animal cannot be punished for following its instincts, Lucy responds, "So males must be allowed to follow their instincts unchecked? Is that the moral?"[62] Lurie insists that, although the consequences of desire can be subject to discipline, one should never regret desire itself or one will grow to hate one's own nature. This conversation occurs while he and Lucy walk her dogs. When they return from their walk, they are confronted by three men, who lock Lurie in the bathroom, set fire to him, and gang rape his daughter. Although Lucy's rape is never described in the text, Lurie's notion of the rights of desire comes full circle. One cannot help but gasp when one sees, in the trembling body of Lucy, the result of three men who exercise their "rights" by unleashing their desire as a terrorizing form of discipline.

In many ways, Brink's Olivier is a tribute to Lurie. Both are aging white intellectuals struggling to understand and express their sexuality in a world haunted by gender and racial inequity. As the inheritors of Menssink's legacy, both are compelled to map out new ways to be that do not repeat sexist and racist modes of sexual consumption, and both fail to chart this new, post-apartheid existence. But whereas "nothing will stop" Lurie from actualizing his desire, not even his student's aversion to what he insists is not "quite" rape, Olivier does not have sex with Tessa, even though he wants to. He accepts her refusal, albeit reluctantly. In his acceptance that the right of desire coexists with the right of refusal, Olivier comes to realize that desire is not a right at all. In a "Note on the Rites of Desire" that immediately follows Olivier's first sighting of Antje after forty years of living with her, he writes:

> If I desire, I may well claim the "right" to desire. But once a right is acknowledged, how does one demarcate its territory, define a content and a consequence? It "has" no territory as it is constantly on the move; it can have no content, because the moment it contains something, that implies the possibility of fulfillment—and fulfillment is the end of desire, attainment its self-immolation. . . . If I claim desire as my right and its nature lies in motion, its motion towards the other, does not my right to desire invoke the right of the other to refuse me? And does that not make a mockery of

"right," as much as of "desire"? The most I can claim for desire is the right to be frustrated, to be denied, otherwise it self-destructs. If there are rights, yes, then I suppose desire has a right to be. But that does not give me the right to demand rights for desire. I desire, ergo I am? But only if "I am," in this equation, becomes wholly conditional upon "You are." And where does that leave desire? (154)

This note dismantles the notion of desire as a right and instead posits desire as a movement that requires another, whether for its fulfillment or for its frustration. As such, desire is above all relational and not located in an autonomous right-bearing body.

Understanding contemporary (legal) formulations of the body casts light on how we interpret Tessa's and Antje's story. Within legal discourse, Alan Hyde rethinks the construction of the body as a "privacy interest" or "zone." He shows that the "private body," with its desires, is seen as a right, yet this right cannot be absolute.[63] In the visualization of rights as spaces—or, as Brink puts it, "territories on the move"—the private body as a right is always "weighed against other interests and therefore not absolute; it is, therefore, public and social. . . . [Rights] exist on an infinite and perhaps darkling plain, along with innumerable other rights and interests."[64] In his claim of his inviolate right to desire, Lurie immolates the rights of his student, erasing her ability to consent or to refuse him. His right to desire, instead of being negotiated or balanced with his student's rights of privacy or bodily autonomy, overrides hers in his coercive assertion of his privacy rights.

In a world of competing rights, whose rights take precedence? Whose will is subsumed in the encounter between Menssink and Tryntjie or of their fictional counterparts, Mostert and Antje? The answer historically has been that white men of a specific class exert their rights over others. The reason for this lies partly in the notion of the right to privacy in the first place. Hyde suggests that the privacy interests often rest on the idea of a man or woman owning his or her body or being in possession of himself or herself. This notion of self-ownership on which privacy rights rests allows for the sale of blood or sperm or the renting of one's uterus.

A similar logic persists today. According to Hyde, during the presidential election of 1992, Admiral James B. Stockdale, a candidate on Ross Perot's ticket, supported abortion rights by stating, "I believe that a woman owns her body and what she does with it is her own business, period."[65] This statement resonates with Frederick Douglass's much earlier description of his escape from slavery as a theft of "this head," "these arms," "these legs." Douglass, in an ultimate paradox, claims himself using the master's language of property, a language that marks him as a criminal even as he erupts out of the category of slave.[66] While its strategic necessity could be argued, ownership of one's body reiterates notions of bodily property central to slavery. These abstract rights of self-ownership, instead of contesting the commodity form, actually support it by creating the body as a fungible, discrete property that can be owned, albeit by oneself. Rather than being able to criticize and contest the terms of economic regulation that dominate our society, we are reduced, as Foucault argued, to the language of abstract political rights that Hyde argues "grants autonomy to the holder by privileging him or her to ignore the needs of others."[67]

The free market does not replace slavery but leaves the same systems of oppression intact, substituting more liberatory imaginings of freedom with the putative freedom of contract and of rights. Tessa provides us with a perfect example of this notion of a woman owning her body to do with it as she sees fit. By parading her string of lovers through the house even as she consistently refuses to have sex with Olivier, Tessa celebrates and flaunts her ownership of her own body, a self-possession that she feels redresses traditional patriarchal ownership of women's bodies and sexuality. However, this privatization of sexuality results not only in the individualization of redress but also in an obfuscation of public structural inequities. In other words, Tessa's feeling that she owns herself and her sexuality limits her critique of patriarchy to her individual choice of whom to have sex with. Patriarchy is no longer seen as a large system. Instead, it is seen as a consequence of individual choices. It is therefore no accident that each time Tessa brings a lover home, she encounters Antje either in the passage or in the bed. Once Tessa even feels Antje between her shoulder blades as she straddles her lover. Antje's spectral presence makes overt the linkages between Tessa and herself in that both of their bodies are being regarded as property. In this way, the haunting refuses Tessa's individualized resistance to patriarchy.

While there is significant difference between self-ownership and being owned by a slave master, the former is a direct legacy of the latter in which bodies are reduced to fungible, autonomous objects to be bought and sold in a market economy. Tessa's putative (sexual) self-ownership thus does not free her from but, instead, reentangles her in, the structures of domination that slaves struggled so desperately against. Her parading of her lovers under Olivier's nose leads her to ask about Antje, "Suppose it wasn't he who dragged her into his bedroom, into his bed, to make love under the eyes of his wife? . . . Suppose it was she? Suppose that was the condition she set; that she'd only make love if his wife was present" (249)? Tessa imagines that she is similar to Antje in terms of individual actions but fails to understand a more fundamental, structural correspondence. Instead of realizing the dangers of bodily fungibility, Tessa attributes an agency to Antje that completely contradicts the historical structure of slavery. The result is disastrous as she imagines Antje "forcing" herself on Mostert; Antje dictating the terms of sexual interaction with her slave master; Antje welcoming the court proceedings against her because the "only way she felt she could have some kind of justice done [for the murder of Mostert's wife] was to pay for it with her own life" (250). Some of these suggestions stick in my throat in their underestimation of the violence of slavery and overestimation of the possibilities of agency within conditions of extreme domination. But more than that, in her commodification of the body Tessa repeats the very structures of domination that keep women and racial Others subjugated. There is a direct relationship between law's "continuing readiness to treat the body as the property of its owner and law's former readiness to take the next step and treat that property as capable of ownership by another."[68] One's body is not the property of the person inside it, or the property of the person who desires it, or the property of the slave master, for in all of these formulations the body and its desire are reduced to fungible, repeatable forms that reproduce the gross inequities inherent in the exchange of commodities.

The novel ends with two major events: the finding and reburial of Antje's body that I have already discussed and the attempted rape of Tessa by five strangers. In a direct rewriting of the rape scene in Coetzee's *Disgrace*, Olivier and Tessa go for a walk and are attacked and robbed by a group of men. One of them holds a knife to Olivier's throat while the others hold Tessa to the ground and attempt to remove her clothes as she kicks and fights them. Despite their warnings to keep silent, Tessa fights back, screaming loudly, overwhelming Olivier, who thinks that they are raping her. But Tessa's screams are preemptive, and they alert a group of hikers passing by. The hikers' arrival causes the men to run off, leaving Tessa partially undressed and still screaming.

Unlike the rape of Lucy in *Disgrace* and the sexual violation of Tryntjie/Antje, Tessa's rape is aborted. The men's brutal sweeping aside of Tessa's ability to consent or refuse them is mediated by people who simply and honestly answer a call for help. This results in an epiphany for Olivier as he realizes the fictiveness of private, self-sufficient individuals. His goal, like Tessa's, to be an autonomous rights-bearing individual is replaced by the ideal of concerned communal actors who answer the call of clamoring voices. Instead of retreating into a world of individualized desire, Olivier realizes, he must engage in the chaos of a world reeling from slavery and imperialism in all of its forms. Olivier's realization that retreat is no longer a viable option is accompanied by Magrieta's retirement. She refuses to be his servant any longer; it is time, she tells him, marking a crucial shift in the power dynamics to which he had become accustomed. In addition, Tessa asks Olivier, "Will you please tell me to go?" (305). The true marker of Olivier's ethics is that he is finally able to reply with honesty, "Then go, my love" (305). The book ends, then, with the freedom of Magrieta and Tessa. Both are gone before the week is out. Only Antje of Bengal remains reburied in the basement, metaphorically providing the foundation for the rebuilding of a post-slavery society. It is around the statement "Go, my love" that we need to rethink the story of Tryntjie of Madagascar in all her incarnations. As long as Tryntjie and her descendants are enslaved, any conceptualization of romantic love between master and slave is impossible.

For Brink, desire is antithetical to a discourse of rights that rests on notions of individualized and autonomous bodies. Rather, desire provides him with a mode of interaction that retreats from the contractual realm haunted by self-interested formulations of bodily property. Desire exists only in its oscillation between "I am" and "You are," in a move away from self-interested contractual individualism toward more relational, altruistic communalism. However, given the importance of freedom "granted" (no matter how incompletely) in the legal contract, I hesitate to simply embrace Brink's retreat toward an altruistic relationality that relies on ethical, moral people answering the call for help. After all, ethical and moral people throughout history have had tremendous difficulty in hearing, for example, the screams of slaves. I place the call for caring, ethical communities alongside Carl Stychin's revised notion of contract and rights that legally ensures the freedom of everyone. As Stychin develops, this *relational contracting* adjusts over time, "opening up a potentially wider set of values to draw upon in understanding a relationship as contractual."[69] By being historically and contextually specific, "relational contracting" avoids static gendered oppositions that mark the private as feminine, familial, and selfless and the public as masculine, contractual, and self-interested. Relational contracting crucially could enable us to rethink the principle of self-gain inherent in classic contract. Thus, true love in the instance of Menssink and Tryntjie would demand not just Menssink's acting in a caring way toward Tryntjie but also the official emancipation not just of Tryntjie herself but also of all the slaves in the Cape. Such an intimate, relational contractual obligation would work against Menssink's self-interest; he would lose wealth, social status, and so on. But such a wedding of his contractual obligation with a sense of ethical engagement allows us a vision of an alternative politics of love that as Stychin develops, troubles "liberal notions of public and private; ... delink[s] the private familial realm from the sexual realm; provide[s] greater recognition of changing dynamics and roles within relationships; [and] shift[s] away from the dyadic model of 'coupledom.'"[70] This form of relationality would insist on equitable, non-coercive contracts of liberation among ethical, caring, and equal actors. It points us toward a radical kinship (elaborated on in chapter 5) based on a shared physical and social vulnerability that can be both imaginatively and politically generative.

Miss Huíla, Paulina Vadi. From "Miss Landmine Angola 2008," by Morten Traavik. Photograph by Gorm K. Gaare.

PERFORMING DEBILITY

Joice Heth and Miss Landmine Angola

Miss Huíla, Paulina Vadi, is twenty-five years old. She has three children and loves the color blue. Her dream job is "whatever." She is posed seductively on top of an antique blue safe in the Hotel Panorama, Ilha do Cabo, wearing a matching blue dress by American Apparel. The shy radiance of her smile and the dollar bills she holds in her hand like a fan arrest the viewer's gaze. Only on the second or maybe third glance does the viewer notices that Vadi has only one leg. The clichéd glamour shot morphs into an image haunted by Vadi's missing limb and its replacement with a military prosthetic, a Russian-made landmine. This landmine, we learn, costs 14 pounds or approximately 20 dollars to make, less than half the cost of Vadi's blue dress.

Paulina Vadi is one of eleven contestants in the Miss Landmine Angola 2008 beauty pageant, the brainchild of the Norwegian theater director and performer Morten Traavik.[1] In a blog on Fans of Reality TV, Traavik recounts that during his first visit to Angola in 2003, two things made a profound impression on him: the tragedy and potential of Angola's numerous landmine victims and the passion that Angolans had for beauty pageants. Describing landmine survivors, Traavik says, "I saw dignified and completely normal people, who have had bad luck—but who are often treated like retards by the local community." After attending a pageant organized by street kids on New Year's Eve, he was struck by how "different [it was] from all the sleaze and the commercialism and the sexism that we, in our Western culture, associate with those kinds of pageants. . . . It was very inclusive and a much more heartwarming experience that was less based on physical perfection."[2] Using his training as a performance artist, Traavik fused these two aspects of his experience in Angola to create the Miss Landmine Angola 2008 beauty pageant and website. He sardonically states, "I'm a slightly guilt-ridden white European wanting to do something significant and save the world a little bit. Bob Geldof syndrome, I guess."[3]

Unlike in other beauty pageants, Miss Landmine has two winners—one voted in by a jury, and the other voted in by visitors to the website. The winner of the jury's vote was Augusta Hurica from Luanda, while voters from more than thirty countries crowned Maria Restino Manuel from the Cuanza Sul Province. The prize for both women was a specially cast prosthetic leg. Manuel, whose leg was blown off when she was fourteen or fifteen years old, was unable to attend the crowning in Luanda because she was pregnant, but her prosthetic limb was presented to her in a separate ceremony in her home village later that week. The winner of the jury's vote, Hurica, is the opening image on the website's home page. A huge bouquet of flowers obscures her red winner's sash, worn across a floor-length yellow gown. A lopsided crown frames her beautiful face. Interestingly, there is no evidence of Hurica's missing limb. Unlike the other contestants, whose attire does little to hide the violence inflicted on their bodies, Hurica's status as winner appears to consolidate her able-bodiedness. As one of the other contestants observes, Hurica has "got the advantage of an artificial limb, and her amputation is not that bad. She lost her foot. People who have never met her wouldn't think she was disabled. She walks really well."[4] Raising awareness about landmines appears to take a back seat to the project's goal of "celebrating true beauty" defined as attractiveness in spite of, rather than because of, disability.

Rather than attempting an ethnography of the contestants, I am interested in how we understand the beauty pageant as a performative *spectacle*. The Internet and YouTube are increasingly being recognized as important archives of popular performance, raising the question of how to read this new kind of archive for black will. I look at the overt framing of black women's agency by the website's designers and pageant organizers. How online sites are put together to represent these Angolan women is essential if we want to understand the current ways history continues to represent black women. By examining images, video, and website construction, I attempt to work through the difficult task of reading Angolan women's embodied agency within an online archive that continues to privilege certain voices and relegate others to the margins.

It would be too reductive either to simply dismiss Miss Landmine Angola as a grotesque parody in which a white European places African women on display as freakish beauties or to claim, à la Traavik, that Miss Landmine Angola subverts hegemonic paradigms of beauty, disability, and race while raising political awareness about landmines. There can be no simple understanding of the "will" of the women and their "choice" to participate in the pageant. My central argument is not that these women have no "will" within these contexts of domination but, rather, that this will is largely illegible within traditional structures of representation and history making. Given the impossibility of discerning the agency of these contestants, what is required to account for this agency is an alternative envisioning, a critical imagination attuned to moments in which agency could reside alongside seemingly totalized discourses of power. While not necessarily true in an empirically verifiable sense, this critical imaginative approach to history provides an avenue for thinking through the power of (historicized) fiction. This approach allows us to break out of the closed circuit in which our histories can only ever repeat the dominant discourses we are supposedly historicizing. This chapter will sketch out these tensions between an (un)readable will and the power of domination, between coercion and consent, between two poles of a political field that resemble each other and are often impossible to distinguish. In the sketching out of the tensions between the impossibility of reading coercion or consent, we assemble a complex genealogy that links the Miss Landmine Angola contestants to an imperial history of embodiment, disability, and blackness. Just as Sarah Baartman's exhibition contains echoes of the performances of slave auctions, this genealogy of black disability reverberates diasporically, crisscrossing the Atlantic and Indian oceans with the restlessness of hurricanes. Miss Landmine Angola is haunted by numerous performances that continually return as if for the first time—twice-restored behavior.

Genealogical Echoes: Joice Heth, "Dark Daughter of Madagascar," and Beauty Pageants

In 1835, a new-to-show-business twenty-five-year-old named P. T. Barnum went on the road with "The Greatest Natural and National Curiosity in the World." This curiosity was Joice Heth, who, Barnum claimed, was the 161-year-old former mammy of George Washington. While her recollections of raising Washington were no doubt part of her theatrical draw, it

Miss Landmine Angola 2008, Augusta Hurica. From "Miss Landmine Angola 2008," by Morten Traavik. Photograph by Gorm K. Gaare.

was her injured body that audiences came to see and touch. Benjamin Reiss quotes Barnum's description of Heth, who supposedly weighed only forty-six pounds, when her age and sickness apparently rendered her "unable to change her position; in fact, although she could move one of her arms at will, her lower limbs were fixed in their position, and could not be straightened. She was totally blind. . . . Her left arm lay across her breast, and she had no power to remove it. The fingers of her left hand were drawn down so as nearly to close it, and remained fixed and immovable. The nails upon that

Miss Landmine Angola holding prize prosthetic leg. From "Miss Landmine Angola 2008," by Morten Traavik. Photograph by Gorm K. Gaare.

hand were about four inches in length, and extended above her wrists."[5] This representation of her largely immobile body was all the more striking when juxtaposed with the usual simulated images of spry, limber, muscular, leaping and tumbling slaves put up for auction. The hyper-physicality of the ideal slave contrasted sharply with Heth's debility. After a public autopsy, in which more than a thousand paying spectators watched the surgeon David L. Rogers carve up her body, her age of 161 years was shown to be fraudulent. She was estimated to have died at a mere eighty years old, no small accomplishment for a black woman living in America in the late eighteenth century and early nineteenth century.

While much time has been spent assessing whether P. T. Barnum intentionally committed fraud or not, I am more interested in how Heth's coerced performance, like the performances of Miss Landmine Angola participants, consolidated not just the white patriarchal power structure of the nation but also the normate whiteness and mastery of the stager. Heth's fame rested on the connections between her "familial relations" with George Washington; the severity of her debility that exalted and idealized Washington's body as father of the nation. Framing her as reliant on white men for subsistence even as she supposedly nursed and coddled them, her performance of injured blackness created a disembodied whiteness curiously independent of white mothers but deeply indebted to black women's labor. Heth was put on display to embody the myth of the founding father. But what her surrogation also illustrated was the foundational status of slave labor in all social, economic, and political realms and the reduction of this labor to caricature, freak show, blackface performance (a racist repertoire of behavior coded as black), and a profound silence. As a performer in a freak show, Heth did not represent herself as an individual (we know next to nothing about her own history). Instead, in her role as grotesque, disabled, black body, she functioned as a surrogate in a critical genealogy of black women's performances. While seen as exceptional in her disfiguration, she was also cast as representative, typical of black women everywhere. Her both exceptional and representative performance, as Joseph Roach writes, unraveled "the putative seamlessness of origins" by highlighting "the historical transmission and dissemination of cultural practices through collective representations."[6] Instead of simply reiterating foundational origin myths that imagined American citizenship springing sui generis from the loins of the white father—namely, George Washington—Heth's performance enacted the violent processes of surrogation that make up the Atlantic world.

These performances then take part in a tradition that Uri McMillan perceptively calls "staging longevity." In their obsession with genealogies, ancestry, and origin stories, white audiences needed the performances of ancient negresses to contextualize and dramatize a linearly progressive American past.[7] Women such as Heth, and later Joice Heth's Grandmother and Mother Boston, embodied what McMillan calls "mammy-memory," the reiteration of the subjugation implicit in a black motherhood that derived its contours from slavery and its privileging of white sons.[8] A sort of performative conduit, the ugliness and horror of the freakish black crone, enabled white spectators to celebrate not just their own superior beauty but also the grandeur of a masculinist American history marching inexorably toward progress. Barnum actively played on his audience's desire for narratives of progressive American history, for stagings of black subservience through images of disabled black mothering of white sons, and for a framework that undercut the humanity of formally freed black bodies.

The cluster of issues of coercion and agency that revolve around Sarah Baartman's display in London and Tryntjie of Madagascar's sexual interactions (discussed in previous chapters) also saturate Heth's historical presence. Early in his career, Barnum had no qualms about describing his supposed reduction of Heth to little more than a puppet. As Reiss writes, "His absolute mastery of her—his negation of her will, and his ability to fashion her into whatever audiences would pay him to see—is virtually the entire point" of his early autobiographical writings.[9] Barnum strips Heth of any agency, instead claiming himself as sole author of her performance, which without him would have no meaning. Her debilitated body was the tabula rasa on which he wrote himself.

It is therefore no coincidence that responses to Heth's performance included a debate about whether she was a human being or an automaton—a remotely operated collection of metal springs and gears housed within a mummy of India rubber and whalebone. Heth's performance reminded audiences of one of the most famous automata of the time: The Turk, or the Automaton Chess Player, constructed by Wolfgang von Kempelen. After decades of touring almost every major European city, The Turk was brought to the United States and displayed in 1826 by Johan Maelzel, who was then its owner. Audiences watched, wondered, and played chess against the automaton in an effort to beat what was promoted as a thinking, breathing "intelligent machine" but what turned out to be a fancy box remotely operated by a trained chess player.[10] This evocation of the automaton as audience members stared at Heth's disabled body is significant, and not just because of doubts regarding black people's status as human. As James Cook argues, the automaton illustrates the fundamental reorganization of craft professions and changing class politics of the 1820s and 1830s. To increase production, many crafts were being de-skilled, and artisans' jobs were either lost to machines or reduced to mind-numbing, repetitive tasks.[11] For the emerging middle class dealing with the crisis of labor in the wake of the official end of slavery, these changes were welcomed because they connoted a different, more modern worker who was docile, obedient, and efficient—a kind of automaton without individual will, controlled through the implementation of new disciplinary techniques and investments. Michel Foucault explicates the link between "celebrated automata," such as those that belonged to Frederick II, and the new worker, arguing that automata functioned to illustrate the workings of the docile body.[12] He argues that constant and uninterrupted coercion monitored not the end product but the processes of the active body, reducing it to the level of a mechanism that was both useful and obedient:

> What was . . . being formed was a policy of coercions that act upon the body, a calculated manipulation of its elements, its gestures, its behavior. The human body was entering a machinery of power that explores it, breaks it down, and rearranges it. A "political anatomy" which was also a "mechanics of power" was being born; it defined how one may have a hold over others' bodies, not only so that they may do what one wishes, but so that they may operate as one wishes, with the techniques, the speed, and the efficiency that one determine.[13]

In the public's speculation that Heth was not human but an automaton one sees a white population haunted by the specter of "uncontrollable" angry freed slaves struggling to imagine a postbellum labor force exorcised of these vengeful specters. Lower-class whites were fearful of being forced to compete for jobs with blacks, while middle-class whites were worried about protecting their property and status. The combination of these fears and anxieties resulted in deep, conflicted desires. White people longed for a simpler, happier time when foolish, smiling black women supposedly suckled white patriarchs, but they also dreamed of a more modern time, when all workers, white and black, knew their place.

Little wonder that Barnum delighted in such a controversy. He actively fanned the flames of doubt with anonymous letters to local newspapers as to whether Heth was flesh and blood or merely a grotesque automaton engineered and operated by its creator. Ticket sales surged. Later, in the 1869 version of his autobiography, *Struggles and Triumphs*, Barnum does an about-face. Instead of suggesting that Heth was his automaton, he recasts her, according to Reiss, as a mysterious "dark subject" who compelled *his* "agency."[14] She becomes the one wielding the power, dictating the terms of her performance, and she does this at Barnum's expense. Denying his authorship of her backstory, Barnum claimed instead that Heth had manufactured false narratives about her age and her connection to George Washington. Reiss quotes Barnum as saying that "the question naturally arises, if Joice Heth was an imposter, who taught her these things? And how happened it that she was so familiar, not only with ancient psalmody, but also with the minute details of the Washington family? . . . I taught her none of these things. . . . She taught me many facts . . . with which I was not before acquainted."[15]

Clearly, Barnum was desperate to distance himself from the multiple instances of fraud discovered in Heth's marketing and performances. It is conceivable that he genuinely believed that Heth was Washington's mammy and that the severity of her disabilities was commensurate with those of an older woman and not the experiences of an eighty-year-old former slave. But even if he was ignorant of these biographical details, it is clear that he had to exert considerable effort and skill to remain so. It is more likely that, as a shrewd businessman, Barnum protected his financial interests and reputation by suggesting that he was not the exploiter but, instead, the exploited victim. He made easy recourse to paternalist narratives of white victimization where the manipulations by the "weak" slaves result in the enslavement of the master. Supposedly, Heth compelled his individual agency, not the other way around. Considerable debate rages as to whether Barnum legally owned Heth's person,[16] a debate that Barnum attempted to answer through Heth's performance. Edward Dixon, a medical doctor of the time, recollects that during her performance, a "well-smoked and antique-looking bill of sale . . . was hung upon the wall" behind Heth,[17] not only to verify her age, but also to quiet abolitionists' fears that Heth was not simply following her master's orders but was acting in a way that was "true" to herself. Whether or not he owned her, Barnum recast his enjoyment of Heth as his enslavement, not hers.[18] He portrayed himself as the ultimate victim/slave of a cunning former slave who pulled the wool over his eyes and over the eyes of the American public for her own gain. He recast Heth's debility and fictive narrative as cunning strategies that shackled him to his wily charge.

I am not denying that, for various reasons, Heth manipulated her performances of debility. She actively took on the persona of George Washington's nursemaid, intertwining it with a narrative that located her "origin" outside the United States in Madagascar, the island where Tryntjie was born. She thus claimed both a quintessential Americanness through her mothering of Washington and a quintessential foreignness by virtue of her connection to Madagascar (which exported very few slaves directly to North America). Situated both inside and outside the West, her performance of longevity bore witness to a century of changes in the African diasporic world. But it would be deeply problematic to make Heth the sole author of a performance that primarily benefited Barnum and reinforced her raced and gendered subjugation. If she was compelled to do Barnum's bidding, one could ask, why did her amiable and lively appearances seem to have contained no moments of resistant dis-identification with the spectacle of her body? The success of the show rested not only on her disabled embodiment of blackness but also on how well she performed during the question-and-answer period in which she was called on to construct a believable and verified biography while also retelling a quintes-sential American history.

The difficulty of accurately historicizing Heth lies, as I argue throughout the book, in the illegibility of her consent or opposition to her performance. Given that Heth has left little record of her personal history, and, conversely, Barnum has a comparatively immense historical voice, having written and revised his autobiography, as well as manipulated the media as part of his show, one can only rudely approximate Heth's motivations. For example, Reiss tells us about an incident reported in the *Providence Daily Journal* in 1835 that describes Heth's supposed comic arrogance. During a performance at Masonic Hall, she supposedly objected to a bottle of cologne water carried by an audience member. An article published in the *Journal* on September 2, 1835, tells us that Heth called for the audience member's removal, saying, "Clear out with your muskrat, don't bring such stuff about me."[19] While the *Providence Daily Journal* used this example to suggest Heth's "comic" claim-ing of an authority significantly beyond her social status, perhaps one could use the anecdote as an opportunity to read her agency between the lines. This story exemplifies an olfactory racism that helped to consolidate black inferiority. As Mark Smith notes, "Stereotypes concerning black scent per-colated so deeply into colonial society that they crop up in even the driest documents. . . . To J. F. D. Smyth's British nose and ears, the slave South in the 1780s was a place . . . where 'Negroes' gave off a 'rank offensive smell . . . extremely disagreeable and disgustful to Europeans.' The stereotype had wide purchase throughout the colonies and was by no means limited to the South. As one Philadelphia resident . . . wrote in 1769, 'The negroes . . . stink damna-bly.'"[20] This nauseous smell was thought to be innate to black people and not produced by environmental factors such as diet or hard physical labor. The audience member's use of cologne at a performance by a black woman there-fore was no accident; the cologne was imagined to mitigate Heth's stench. Heth's objection to the cologne therefore probably has less to do with her not liking the particular smell than with her taking offense at racist stereotyping. Her insistence on not bringing "that stuff around her" can be read as what

Saidiya Hartman terms an "instance of possibility,"[21] in which she uses the idiom of her performance as uppity "Lady Washington" to object to racist configurations of her body.

But in the quiet hours I ask myself whether I am conflating will with resistance and searching for the possibility of will to avoid the show's despair-invoking pathologization of black women's longevity and the reinforcement of black fungibility. As Walter Johnson writes, the term "'agency' smuggles a notion of the universality of a liberal notion of selfhood, with its emphasis on independence and choice, right into the middle of a conversation about slavery against which that supposedly natural (at least for white men) condition was originally defined."[22] My desire to attribute resistant will to Heth could be read as an attempt by a present-day scholar to give back stolen agency, returning it to its rightful owners in the past through redressive accounts. Hartman writes about her attempt to negotiate the archive by reassembling, from a few words in the archive, the life of a slave girl who died aboard the slave ship *Recovery*: "I too am trying to save the girl, not from death . . . but from oblivion. Yet I am unsure if it is possible to salvage an existence from a handful of words. . . . Hers is a life impossible to reconstruct, not even her name survived."[23] But whereas Hartman carefully and painfully insists that the slave girl's "existence" cannot be reclaimed, I would argue otherwise. Perhaps we should not underestimate the instance of possibility offered in imaginative, performative readings of agency (such as my story of Heth and cologne) whose *veracity, but not politics*,[24] remains in doubt. Hartman's acts of narrative conjuring animate the people recorded in the Dead Book, a record of black people who died during passage, including the slave girl on whom the narrative focuses. Such creative acts shift notions of agency away from discussions of individual self-determination and choice toward an understanding of the lives of black folk as forged by, though not reducible to, their enslavement and colonization. Inventing clandestine, tactical, and elastic moments of possibility tethered to history can help construct a transatlantic genealogy of gendered, raced performances, embodying a past anchored in the experiences of enslaved peoples across the globe. These performative genealogical moments show how individual and collective acts operate on a continuum that expands liberal notions of agency beyond traditional boundaries of the individual. Thus, Heth's agency should be seen not only in imaginative readings of her behavior but, crucially, in the repetition of her twice-restored behavior as it recurs across time and space. Hartman reprises her argument in *Venus in Two Acts*, thinking further about how to expose the impossibility of representing the lives of subjugated peoples even while telling a story about them that strains against the limits of the archive. She turns toward a writing practice that she calls "critical fabulation,"[25] writing:

> By playing with and rearranging the basic elements of the story, by re-presenting the sequence of stories and from contested points of view, I have attempted to jeopardize the status of the event, to displace the received or authorized account, and to imagine what might have happened or might have been said or might have been done. . . . The intent of this practice is not to give voice to the slave, but rather to imagine what cannot be verified, a realm of experience which is situated between two zones of death—social and corporeal death—and to reckon with the precarious lives which are visible only in the moment of their disappearance.[26]

Considering Heth's agency through the modality of the performative allows us to imagine moments that might be true, not only about Heth, but also about the historical moment as it unfolds through time and space. It allows for the emergence of a genealogy of performance even while acknowledging the impossibility (and importance) of ever truly knowing the will of these historical actors. It thus becomes crucial to look at various performance genres more closely, to think about the need to perform/write the impossible. What can the genre of performance tell us about the struggles various historical actors faced concerning their existence as archival trace or archival silence? It is for this reason that I turn to the beauty pageant.

Lovely Freaks

To further elaborate the connections between disability and the construction of the normate that occurs in Miss Landmine Angola, we need to historicize the beauty pageant as a performance genre. Just as Barnum constructed the able-bodied normalcy of white men through displays of painfully embodied blackness, so, too, did he imagine white women's beauty in contradistinction to the grotesqueness of his sideshow freaks. In 1854, he attempted to stage a "beauty contest" in which women paraded in front of a group of judges. The beauty pageant apparently was an idea before its time, as Barnum was unable to convince "respectable" women to participate and, in their absence, substituted their daguerreotypes. Thus, the photographic beauty contest was born. According to Colleen Ballerino Cohen and her colleagues, this event was so popular at exhibitions and "dime museums" that newspapers "later adopted Barnum's idea, and by the end of the century, almost every newspaper held photographic beauty contests."[27] The transition of beauty contests from photographic images to bodies on-stage occurred when public bathing was no longer the sole province of the elite in spas but was adopted by white middle-class women as part of a regime of health and beauty. The first recorded beauty contest, Miss United States, was held in 1880 in Rehoboth, Delaware, to promote tourism. Organizers, like Barnum earlier, were aware that the event could be legitimated only by the respectability of the participants. Pageants, as Robert Lavenda notes, translated the eroticism and overt sexuality of events such as the bathing suit competition into a language of health, flexibility, and physical well-being.[28] The importance of the participant's virtue and of the pageant as a stage for middle-class respectability and morality could be seen in the prize awarded to the winner of the 1880 pageant: a bridal trousseau.[29] This emphasis on the putative respectability of contestants continues in today's beauty pageants, which unsuccessfully attempt to desexualize contestants through recourse to an idealized pure femininity and romanticized heterosexuality. Miss USA contestants, for example, cannot be married, reinforcing notions of authentic womanhood as being either virginal or mothering. Beauty queens also continue to have no real earning power. The modeling contracts and scholarships offered to contestants are tokens, at best, often amounting to less than the cost of competing. In this way, pageant winners supposedly operate outside a market economy, using their cultural capital to advance humanitarian, regional, and national concerns.

But why use the beauty pageant at a platform to advance these concerns at all? As Mary Moran asks in her study of Liberian beauty contests and rallies, "What is it about the privileging of a particular kind of female physical appearance that serves as such a highly charged point of articulation between local and national discourses?"[30] Of course, beauty contests are inextricable from the performance of normative gender, but in the so-called Third World, they also embody discourses of progress and development. Local assimilation of the pageant form occasionally results in local aesthetics' influencing and at least partially replacing homogenized Western standards of beauty. By drawing attention to regional, largely rural constituencies, beauty pageants can actively counter postcolonial nationalist projects that typically have neglected rural areas and marginal citizens such as the disabled or the unemployed. In some senses, the community-organized beauty pageant that Traavik tells Robyn Stubbs he encountered on his initial visit to Angola "that street kids in the back alley had put together on New Year's Eve" could be seen as resisting postcolonial development politics that simultaneously interpellate and neglect certain "backward" populations. Traavik describes the pageant to Stubbs as "a feel-good experience; it was more like a street party with the whole neighborhood attending. The kids organized everything themselves, with girls from seven to 17 parading through all the regular motions of a beauty contest with earnestness and dedication."[31] The condescension implied, for instance, by Traavik's use of the words "kids" does not diminish the resistance that is possibly suggested by such a pageant. These street performances appropriate public space, transforming back alleys and sidewalks into runways, stages, and audience seats. Such cross-cultural interventions in the genre of the pageant both borrow from and rescript normative gender initiation, consumption, and beauty. The beauty pageant parodies and subverts a rigid Western aesthetic that has excluded many black people.

Unlike this back alley celebration of local community, Miss Landmine Angola operates nationally as a state-sanctioned event. It also functions, according to Moran "internationally and cross-culturally within a discourse of evolutionary changes that includes a hierarchical understanding of the relationship between center and periphery."[32] By exposing the participants to national and global aesthetic and cultural practices, the pageant supposedly offers these contestants a chance to incorporate more recognizable "modern" or "advanced" ideas about their role as black consumers, budding feminists, and human rights activists. To wit, Quartim Matongueiro, one of the Miss Landmine Angola judges, insists that the pageant allows the Angolan government to see that disabled people are key to *developing* Angola.[33]

Beauty pageants thus are profoundly ambivalent spaces of performance. Their conservative articulations of masculinist discourses conflate national and women's bodies. However, no singular performance of femininity and nationhood can perfectly and seamlessly embody the ideal. Especially in these contexts of Angolan street pageants or Miss Landmine Angola, the participants' poverty and their blatant embodiment of the injuries of colonialism and war belie the myth of progress and refuse transparent notions of the nation-state predicated on the normatively gendered individual. Miss Landmine Angola participants insist on the hybridization of femininity that includes differently abled bodies even while reinforcing the notion of the civilized normate body. Sarah Banet-Weiser astutely argues that the beauty pageant represents a complicated arrangement of claims and embodies a variety of nationalist expressions: it is a civic ritual, a place where a particular public can "tell stories to themselves about themselves," and it is a mass-mediated spectacle firmly embedded within commodity culture, in a historical moment where almost all forms of social participation and social meaning are determined by a continuous interplay between representation and consumption. It is also a highly visible performance of gender, where the disciplinary practices that construct women are palpable, on display. . . . It is a profoundly political arena, in the sense that the presentation and reinvention of femininity [and sexuality] that takes place on stage produces political subjects.[34]

Beauty pageants as civic rituals flesh out the interplay of nation, race, and gender, as well as the inextricability of these rituals from capitalism and its modes of consumption. These performances stage the unattainable ideal against the specter of the aberrant. The aberrant body has to be continually reanimated to lend shape to the ideal, and vice versa. The inextricability of both bodies thus sutures together the performance traditions of beauty pageant and freak show; these various spectacles acquire meaning only in relation to each other as they construct a transatlantic arena of shared symbols and aesthetics that drive consumptive practices. Within these performative circuits, beauty pageants are haunted by freak shows, and freak shows parody, disrupt, and prop up beauty pageants.

The development of a gendered and raced vocabulary of beauty and ugliness enabled audiences to construct an aesthetic continuum of normalcy, familiarity, and symmetry with women like Heth on one end and the pure white beauty queen on the other. These polarized bodies were seen as simultaneously exceptional and representative. The freak represented black, lower-class, deviant bodies in general, even while her embodiment of those categories was exceptional; likewise, as Lavenda argues, the beauty queen was supposed to be "Everywoman—or Everygirl . . . represent[ing] a golden mean of accomplishment that appears accessible to all respectable girls of her class in her town and other similar small towns."[35] At the same time, this Everywoman, the beauty queen, represented an ideal of long-limbed, glossy-haired perfection toward which every little girl was supposed to aspire. In this way, freak show and beauty pageant blur into each other, each functioning as ritual in the shaping of gendered narratives of exceptionalism and representation, of everyone and no one, of beauty and the lovely freak.

This blurring is even more pronounced in the case of Miss Landmine Angola, where the "freakish" war-ravaged black body is removed from one stage and asked to perform on another. In an interview with CNN, Traavik recalled that several nongovernmental organizations denied funding for his brainchild, with one "labeling his idea a 'freak show.'"[36] What happens when Angolan amputees (located firmly in the genealogy of the freak show) are placed in a beauty pageant that purports to celebrate their amputated limbs and their non-normate beauty? Are the oppositions of freak and beauty undercut by the forced amalgamation of positionalities, or is the dichotomy reinforced? Does Miss Landmine Angola provide greater opportunities for the expression of black women's agency? As in the instance of the performance in which Baartman was required to judge who her most ardent suitor was,[37] is the joke on the performer or on the audience? Is the audience "playing along" with the sincere but ignorant participants who do not know that they are being humored? Is the performer hoodwinking the audience? Or should this be understood as a joke at all? Is this instead a sincere reappraisal of increasingly standardized and imperial standards of beauty? Or is this their reinforcement?

To tease out answers to these questions, we must return to the civic function of both the beauty pageant and the freak show. Traditionally in the American context, as Banet-Weiser argues, "One of the tasks of nationalist rituals and discourses is to demonstrate the ability to contain disruption, to subvert potential crises, and to incorporate disjunctures into smoother, less conflicted landscapes."[38] As civic rituals, both freak shows and beauty pageants are important sites for the articulation, assimilation, and possible intervention in crises of citizenship and belonging that revolve around the material and cultural conditions of a post-slavery global economy. In the case of Heth, audiences struggling with the changing national landscape felt "menaced" by freed slaves and workers displaced by increasing industrialization and mechanization. The sentimental maternal servitude evoked by Heth's performance as George Washington's nanny contained the inherent threat of "free" black labor, while her apparent fragility ameliorated the menace of a hyper-embodied blackness. What is more, conversations about whether she was a human or an automaton displaced debates about the humanity of freed slaves. Simultaneously, her alleged longevity provided the backdrop for pedagogical narratives of national progress. Similarly, today's beauty pageants operate on a global terrain where gender roles and other traditional identities are in crisis. The interplay of spectacle, gender, and consumption manages these crises by incorporating difference without substantively addressing inequities. Contained within the pageant form, the crises are buried, silenced, and translated rather than addressed.

As opposition to the pageant's history of celebrating a universalized white standard of beauty became increasingly vocal after the Civil Rights Movement, pageant organizations scrambled to respond to demands for the inclusion of racial and ethnic diversity. Instead of the black body merely being the freakish specter haunting ideal beauty, pageants were asked to include women of color as contestants in a civic ritual designed to exclude them. Pageant organizers attempted to contain the crises of a nation that was facing louder calls for gender equality and racial inclusion. They responded in numerous ways, one of which was to crown the first black Miss America, Vanessa Williams, in 1983. After her crowning, Williams received numerous death threats and angry racist mail, suggesting that her victory had struck a nerve.[39] These hostile responses targeted both her blackness and the "inauthenticity" of her blackness, which supposedly failed to make her a true representative of black people. (Williams is light-skinned with green eyes.) Like the nation, Miss America dealt with demands for diversity by including a few exceptional women of color as representative. Such palliative gestures commodified diversity, the purchase of which allowed white consumers to leave their white privilege intact while demonstrating their progressive largesse ("Look how far we've come"). The inclusion of black contestants made no changes to underlying criteria of beauty or to pageants' organizational structures (whose "lower" echelons such as the janitorial services were staffed by women of color) or to the larger forces of racial bias and socioeconomic inequity ravaging the nation. As Richard Iton writes, "The engagement with and interpellation via cultural representations of black life by (white) American citizens historically has been quite compatible with the marginalization and disenfranchisement of African Americans as political subjects and potential [community] members."[40] The protests around the Miss America pageant in 1968 are often seen as having ushered in second-wave feminism in the United States. Symbolic demonstrations during these protests, such as the disposal of bras, high-heeled shoes, and other "instruments of torture" into a "Freedom Trash Can," further consolidated what would become second-wave feminism, and pageant organizers scrambled to respond. Some of the responses, as Banet-Weiser states, included a greater emphasis on the talent and interview portions of the competition; a shift in language away from beauty toward "health" and "fitness";[41] the stressing of women's empowerment achieved by looking one's best; and a repeated emphasis on the contestant's "consent" to compete. In response to feminist protests, contestants repeatedly stated that their participation in the pageant was not a sign of victimization but, rather, an example of their self-agency as free, democratic citizens. In an appropriation of mainstream feminist discourse, contestants stressed how looking good made them feel better about themselves, enabling them to excel in whatever they "chose" to do. Perhaps the reason for the seeming stalemate between second-wave feminists and pageant contestants lies in their use of similar liberal notions of individually rooted agency. While one group talked of victimization and the other stressed free will, both privileged notions of volitional subject formation. The tossing of one's bra into a "Freedom Trash Can" was predicated on a similar notion of subjectivity as the choice to wear confidence-boosting high-heeled shoes.

The organizers and contestants in Miss America and Miss Landmine Angola face similar problems around representation, gender, and subjectivity. In attempting to manage Angola's political and historical anxieties, Miss Landmine Angola demonstrates the inherent instability of a nation that is in fact, a diasporic space—a complex amalgamation of the living legacies of slavery and colonialism, as well as the failure of postcolonialism in all but the formal sense. Despite being the second-largest petroleum and diamond producer in sub-Saharan Africa, Angola has one of the lowest life expectancies and highest infant mortality rates. It also ranked third in the world for the number of landmines planted. The period of Portuguese rule in Angola began late in the fifteenth century with the trade in slaves (mainly to Brazil), raw materials, and exchanged goods. The selling of slaves continued into the first half of the nineteenth century, leading eventually to Portuguese administrative control at the start of the twentieth century. It was only in January 1975 that a transitional government, made up of the three main guerrilla groups—the Popular Movement for the Liberation of Angola (MPLA), founded in 1956 and headed by Agostinho Neto; the National Front for the Liberation of Angola (FNLA), founded in 1961; and the National Union for the Total Independence of Angola (UNITA), founded in 1966 and headed by Jonas Savimbi—was established. Civil war broke out almost immediately among the three groups and was facilitated and exacerbated by the United States and South Africa, which backed the FNLA and UNITA financially and politically against the Russian- and Cuban-supported MPLA. Despite a cease-fire in 1988, after the largest battle in the history of sub-Saharan Africa, Savimbi continued the war, financed by the sale of "conflict diamonds," until he was killed by Cuban and Angolan government troops in February 2002. The UNITA military finally agreed to a cease-fire with the MPLA, but not before the twenty-seven years of civil war had killed 1.5 million people and displaced 4 million more. These numbers do not include the countless Angolans captured into slavery or killed during official and unofficial Portuguese rule. If the nation were a body, it would have countless missing parts and broken limbs. It would be hungry, as the years of war left its fields lying fallow; it would be hurt and neglected by forces that considered it a pawn in Cold War and nationalist games of power; it would be a global citizen dressed in the tatters of African (post)colonialism. If the Angolan nation were a body, it would be fighting and losing a battle against the cancer of six million to twenty million landmines still embedded in its fleshy soil.

Landmines are designed to maim, not necessarily to kill. According to Physicians against Land Mines, one out of every 334 Angolans has lost a limb as a result of landmine detonation, with children representing 49 percent of all landmine casualties. There is an undeniable necessity to raise awareness about the plight of Angolans living in a country that is so heavily mined. Traavik carefully lists the Miss Landmine Angola contest's primary aims as including "global and local landmine awareness and information," as well as attempts to instill self-worth and pride into landmine amputees. Yet the question becomes whether Miss Landmine Angola is a useful way to turn "victims" into survivors and increase global awareness of the consequences of war or whether, instead, the awareness generated by the images is overshadowed by the pageant's complex use of surrogated performance traditions, liberal ideology, and well-meaning racism.

The Privilege of Objectification: Digital Media

What are some of the strategies deployed by Traavik on the website, and how successful are they? Let us turn to the mechanics of the website itself, which opens with an animated scene. As blue curtains pull back to reveal a starry night sky with shooting stars, Eumir Deodato's fusion jazz version of "Thus Spoke Zarathustra" begins to play. In the distance are the outlines of palm trees and an orange sign with a skull and crossbones that warns us about some lurking danger. The sky starts to move, and rays of a cartoon sun appear. As the sun gets higher in the sky, a white stick figure wearing a dress, a crown, and a dark sash emerges from the horizon, drifting toward the center of the screen. One leg appears to be amputated at the knee. She reaches the center of the image as the music reaches the end of its famous progression, and below her words appear: "Miss Landmine. Everyone has the right to be beautiful." Below are two links, one to Miss Landmine Angola 2008 and another to Miss Landmine Cambodia 2009. Clicking on a link takes the user to the website for that particular pageant, which are roughly the same except the background of the Miss Cambodia Landmine site is pink and purple site and the Miss Landmine Angola site's background is blue and white.

The home page of Miss Landmine Angola is headed by a snapshot of the animation, with the crowned stick figure on the left, while the right side of the screen displays a T-shirt icon labeled "Buy a Tshirt Click Here." The link no longer works; there are no T-shirts to be purchased. Below the heading, a slideshow of photographs of the contestants loops continuously. One cannot pause on any single image; one can only watch them flicker past. This is not a very sophisticated website technologically or artistically. In some ways, Traavik's later satirical website "Pimp My Aid Worker," which parodies liberal humanitarian projects such as Bob Geldof's "We are the World" and "Do They Know It's Christmas?" is more convincing as a media platform for social activism, with, for instance, its music video and interactive game in which the visitor can choose the aid worker's attire. Both sites demonstrate (although in different ways) the extent to which social movements recognize the centrality of digital media and "image politics." As Meg McLagan writes, "The explosion of rights-oriented digital media in the second half of the 1990s represents an expansion of this kind of mass mediated activism, with human rights groups self-consciously deploying publicity strategies and visual rhetoric borrowed from advertising. . . . Today activists of all stripes recognize the necessity of having a presence online—well-designed websites are now assumed to be key 'portals' of entry into activism, especially by members of the younger generation."[42] Web-based activism designs flash graphics, downloadable files, interactive maps, branding logos, and animation to arrest the website visitor visually and inspire participation and donations. For example, the branding logo for Amnesty International USA, a candle wrapped in barbed wire, provides instant visual recognition. Likewise, the Miss Landmine organization's logo takes the form of a glaringly white stick figure that is similar to those used to segregate public restrooms based on biological gender. A crown and sash are added, half a leg is removed, and, voilà, the branding begins. Similarly, animation has become key to certain social activist groups' marketing strategies. The more sophisticated the animation, the more convincing the human rights claims of certain groups appears. Bridging the gap between computer technology and global capitalism, animation often creates what Teri Silvio calls "the uncanny 'illusion of life'" as it projects the "qualities perceived as human—life, power, agency, will, personality, and so on—outside the self, and into the sensory environment, through acts of creation, perception, and interaction."[43] Miss Landmine's opening animated montage, however, does none of that. On the contrary, the overwhelming generic quality of the animated opening, with its stereotypical palm trees, perfectly round yellow sun with triangular rays, and odd choice of music, dashes any illusion of life. This stilted and basic animation flattens out the scene, resulting in a conventionalized montage evacuated of any trace of life, agency, and will. The opening scene directly references the opening of Stanley Kubrick's *2001: A Space Odyssey*, where the sun rises over the Earth to Strauss's famous composition "Also Sprach Zarathustra." The interplay between the pageant website, the film, and music signals some sort of break with conventional moral and aesthetic categories that results in the creation of new forms. It gestures toward a futurity free of traditional political, moral, or aesthetic constraints; the "dawn" of new forms of embodiment and beauty. But while *2001: A Space Odyssey* earned Kubrick an Academy Award for Best Visual Effects in 1968, the lack of technical sophistication on the Miss Landmine site undercuts the futurity promised by the music. While this could be attributed to funding issues, it may also be an ironic point and counterpoint of the visual and the sonic to move away from a seamless aestheticization of political issues. In other words, through this lack of design sophistication the website draws attention to its own artifice, increasing the distance between viewer and subject matter rather than drawing them closer. Whether or not this was Traavik's intention, this distance can be read as a critique of human rights advocates' commercialization of their concerns.

Digital media can enable innovative ways to tell the stories of subjugated groups. Missing from the website, however, is a reciprocal or collaborative ethnography, which might be facilitated by web-based platforms in which "informants" shape the final project by contributing to the selection and presentation of subject matter, interpretations of meaning, and frames of representation. Natalie Underberg issues a warning that in the scramble to digitize human rights issues we lose sight of the basic fact that, in the digital realm, information has become a commodity, and those "'who reap the benefits of this environment are those who control this commodity.'"[44] The website reduces the women to posed images with brief captions that undermine any assumption of their agency by not even gesturing toward its existence.

ℳiss ℒandmine

Miss Landmine logo. From "Miss Landmine Angola 2008,"
by Morten Traavik. Photograph by Gorm K. Gaare.

The website contains no interviews, no video clips, not even quotes that go beyond the two to three words that answer questions on the biography page: "Miss Benguela: unemployed, sells tomatoes in the street when she can get hold of any." In other words, the website's construction de-emphasizes the women's thoughts and feelings about the pageant and their participation in it. It does not even incorporate how the women feel about their disabilities or about landmines as strategies of (civil) war. Traavik's documentary, while not significantly better in representing the various women, does include the voices of three of the contestants: Augusta Hurica, Luisa Miguel, and Maria Antonio. The documentary depicts, for example, Maria Antonio's assessment about what winning the competition could mean for her. While bathing her little boy, one of seven children, she says to the camera, "This competition could really change my life. I might find work. If I had a proper job, I wouldn't have to depend so much on my husband, and I'd be helping support my children." Financial independence seems to be foremost among her reasons for participating, whereas the right to be beautiful does not seem to be that important. Whether she was considered attractive was important earlier in her life, just after the accident, she tells us, when she was afraid she would not be able to find a boyfriend or a husband who would help her achieve a better standard of living. But after seven children and a husband who is becoming increasingly unreliable, beauty is less important to Antonio than the ability to support her family independently. Such nuanced motivations showing that the pageant's goals are not shared by all of the women and that the women's priorities change over time are absent from the website. Instead, the contestants' bodies have become commodified bits of information that Traavik deems important, whose dissemination plays out without them.

The amateurish quality of the website contrasts with the gorgeous photographs of each of the contestants. Beautifully staged in elaborate settings, the photographs radiate light from mirrors, polished floors, and other reflective surfaces. One can almost see one's image in the polished tiled floor, the sheen of straightened hair, or the blue metal of the safe. As Krista Thompson writes, "Light has the power to bring geographic transcendence and social ascendance."[45] As glaring light emanates from commodities, it visually produces notions of wealth by stressing the link between being "modern" and capitalist patterns of consumption, in which buying the latest and "shiniest" thing equates with success (at least until another shiny thing comes along). Sheen visualizes the excessive value of the commodity, the objectification of the body as something to be consumed. Rather than illustrating alternative forms of beauty, the photographs place on display familiar forms of aspirational capital. Not only are the women interpolated into the world of the commodity, but they themselves become part and parcel of the array of commodities on display. In answer to certain criticisms of the pageant, Traavik has said, "In our [sic] part of the world . . . some of the criticisms on beauty pageants is that they are objectifying. And for some of these women it is a privilege to be objectified because that means that you are being seen and heard for the first time. Although I would more call it 'subjectified' in this context because they are really made persons."[46] Thus, these women supposedly need Traavik's pageant to be made into persons via the process of objectification and commodification. Prior to his intervention, they were not capable even of being objectified, a seemingly crucial step in entering the market.

But can these photographs, despite their commodification of the contestants, generate substantive political movements or even significant changes in the popular consciousness that would lead to the end of (post)colonial violence? This equating of increased visibility with increased political awareness is a common one. However, such assumptions must be questioned, given that, historically, the all-too-numerous spectacles of black abjection have led to a reinforcement of repressive regimes rather than to their demise. One cannot automatically assume that mere exposure will lead to progressive politics because sentimental visual appeals, in their encouragement of the viewer's substitution of her own body for that of the sufferer, often allow for a reinvestment of the boundaries between the historically empowered and the subjugated. The mechanism of sentimental identification ("I feel your pain") can displace the amputee, rendering her *less*, not more, visible. The viewer who takes the amputee's place as "authentic" sufferer is then able to consume images of deeply wounded black people without actually recognizing these people as living, sensate beings. What is more, certain representations of suffering, such as photographs of lynching, whipping, and public auctions, actually have the capacity to titillate audiences and give them pleasure. Given that the exposure of injured black bodies throughout the diaspora has not necessarily resulted in a call to end violence but, instead, has often perpetuated violence, the act of witnessing remains inextricable from how and why one witnesses. As part of this diasporic tradition, the familiarity of these pageant images enables consumers to indulge in certain fantasies of empowerment and uplift, which paradoxically leaves intact the very power dynamics that such images are supposed to resist.

The images accrue meaning as surrogates in a genealogy of diasporic performance as these dynamics proliferate within a visual economy. The Miss Landmine Angola images are thus haunted by "forgotten but not gone" surrogations that refer to the spectacular embodiment of blackness, savagery, and suffering, present and past.[47] A passing perusal of recent newsmagazines, for example, shows contemporary Africa as riddled by power-hungry dictators, cut-throat pirates, and armed black soldiers. In a reiteration of the "heart of darkness" trope, today's Africa, at least as represented by the Western media, is depicted as a continent of lawlessness as black people turn against one another with a shocking pre-political savagery, and the children starve as a result. Miss Landmine Angola's photographs of injured bodies are readily subsumed into this performative economy of excessive, "tribal," black-on-black violence. Lacking in this global circulation of imagery is any contextualization of this violence—

specifically, the historical role of slavery, colonialism, Western-aided postcolonial conflicts, the extraction of raw materials, and the continued exploitation of African labor in a global economy. It therefore comes as no surprise that the increased availability of images of violated black bodies may not result in progressive political action or even in the reeducation of viewers. Banet-Weiser quotes Robyn Weigman as saying that, instead, these images can represent a "deft appropriation of the liberationist demand to make 'visible' the subjectivities and histories of the cultural margins, as consumer culture harnesse[s] ethnic, racial and national specificities for its expanding global purposes."[48] Thus, rendering black injury visible need not result in a liberatory politics. On the contrary, such spectacles can increase black disenfranchisement and the stereotypical association of blackness with abjection. I would be remiss if I were to dismiss the role that exposure of horrible injustices has played in fueling successful activist movements. However, it is crucial to develop a nuanced theorization of the performative circuits through which images of Angolan amputees travel.

The photographs of the participants in the Miss Landmine Angola pageant evoke strong responses in viewers via a juxtaposition of three phenomena: the elite white body of a normative pageant contestant; the nontraditional, marginalized black woman whose body conforms to very few traditional criteria of beauty; and the indicators of disability such as the amputated limb or crutch/prosthetic limb. For Rosemary Garland Thomson, introducing disability "into the conventional composition of an upscale fashion photo forces the viewer to reconfigure assumptions about what constitutes the attractive and the desirable."[49] Response after response left at the website for Miss Landmine Angola speaks specifically to the beauty of the images. For example, a comment by Trisha Baptie posted to Stubbs's op-ed about the pageant states, "While I am in no way a supporter of 'traditional' beauty pageants, can I just say how much I loved the photo of the beautiful pregnant amputee[?] To me she just exudes strength and hope, how can it be wrong to capture those two traits in a photo[?]"[50] The photograph of Maria da Fatima Conceicao, Miss Moxico, lying poolside in an aqua dress allows Baptie and other viewers to reconsider not only the feminist value of "traditional" beauty pageants but also the value of an unemployed, unmarried nineteen-year-old expecting her first child. One has to look twice to notice the missing leg, which becomes secondary to the overall normativity of Conceicao and the glamour of her surroundings: pool, sunglasses on the floor beside her, sparkling tiara on her head. The muting of her disability and the disability of several of the other

Miss Moxico, Maria da Fatima Conceicao. From "Miss Landmine Angola 2008," by Morten Traavik. Photograph by Gorm K. Gaare.

participants strike me as significant in a contest that foregrounds the damage caused by landmines. This amputation rendered routine and glamorous is an exotic and sentimental variation of imagery that appeals to a liberal audience's commonplace notions of success. The amputation becomes another fetish detached from all of its history. The erasure of history within the glamour of the commodity begins also to erase the political history contained in the injured body. The business of beauty becomes a way to obfuscate history. In many ways, the Miss Landmine Angola images incorporate the women into socioeconomic spheres from which they have been excluded. However, as Garland-Thomson argues, this sort of inclusion assimilates difference to normative notions of beauty rather than facilitating a challenge to these norms. As Garland-Thomson explains, "This both troubling and empowering form of entry into democratic capitalism produces a kind of instrumental form of equality: the freedom to be appropriated by consumer culture. In a democracy, to reject this paradoxical liberty is one thing; not to be granted it is another."[51] Like the opening up of Western beauty pageants to black women as contestants discussed earlier, the inclusion of non-normate bodies allows for a liberal, sentimental consumption that does not necessarily contest—but, instead, may actually reinscribe—the racial power dynamics of the status quo.

Disability theorists argue that notions of disability rest on artificial boundaries between the biological and the social. Because aspects of biological life such as childbirth, aging, and menstruation are integrated into social relations that lend them cultural meaning, they are not constructed as diseases or disabilities. In other words, the parameters of normative embodiment mark the difference between disability and the normate biological struggle that is called living. This separation between disabled and normate serves many purposes. As Julie Livingston notes, one such purpose is to buttress capital's demand for bodily fitness. Changes in types of work have led to changes in definitions of fitness/able-bodiedness. Thus, Livingston tells us how, in response to capital's need for mining labor, notions of able-bodiedness in Botswana shifted from the wisdom of age to youthful energy and large lung capacity. Prior notions of fitness (skill based on age and experience) were challenged by new criteria of youth, weight, and stamina, determined during physical exams in which colonial rulers decided who was fit to work in the mines.[52] This shift in criteria resulted in aging becoming a narrative of increasing inability to produce instead of increasing ability to navigate social realms. The impact of capital on the definitions of able-bodiedness forces us to ask questions about the Miss Landmine Angola contestants' relationship to African/Angolan cosmologies with regard to sickness, the body, personhood, and care. How do historicized African configurations of the body and disease intersect with imperial definitions of normality and fitness?

Livingston makes a convincing case that the language of human rights discourse, fused with a Christian paternalism, has imposed the categories of the "primitive" and "traditional" on recent and old African practices with certain behavior, such as familial caregiving and limited public exposure in which disabled family members are sequestered. Nongovernmental organizations such as the Red Cross have mobilized to relocate disabled people from "hidden" positions within homes and compounds to more "modern" locations, where African disabled people are afforded the human rights denied to them via entry into the public realm. The Miss Landmine Angola Manifesto's goal of "disabled pride and empowerment" illustrates the push of the international disability rights movement to empower disabled people socially, politically, and economically by stressing their entrance into public society. This focus on personal empowerment rests on the misguided assumption that disabled people in Third World countries suffer greater marginalization and abuse than those of the First World. This agenda is further reinforced by rehabilitation programs that stress the desire and need for individual autonomy as the sine qua non for modern citizenship. And as Livingston articulates, "This autonomous self is, in turn, predicated upon an unquestioned biological model of an individually bounded body."[53] This independent, self-reliant, private body (implied in the manifesto's desire to replace the passive "victim" with the active "survivor") can be seen as the goal of rehabilitation.

The complicated notion of rehabilitation is key to understanding the genealogy of black disability erupting from the Miss Landmine Angola pageant and to thinking through coercion, consent, and agency. In *Crip Theory: Cultural Signs of Queerness and Disability*, Robert McRuer insists that we interrogate the common-sense benevolence implied by the term "rehabilitation." The discourse of rehabilitation, particularly when used to discuss the use of prosthetics, developed out of shock and outrage as injured veterans returned home after the First World War. The injured soldier who was originally considered the epitome of masculinity was unable to assimilate back into the capitalist workforce. His fall from status of public hero to feminized burden on society resulted in several recuperative projects that attempted to fold amputees back into society, to make them whole men again.[54] McRuer writes, "If the proud 'grade, rank, or status' of returning soldiers was somehow endangered by war injuries, rehabilitation promised a restoration of rank, honors, and 'true function.' . . . Rehabilitation increased esteem and repute; rehabilitation ensured desirability and . . . salability."[55] Or, as Livingston puts it, the "set of practices termed 'rehabilitation' . . . incorporated the development of physical, emotional, cognitive, and socioeconomic skills into a single paradigm aimed to make disabled persons more independent."[56] Rehabilitation for marginalized and stigmatized men (and women) can be a laudable goal. However, its logic is implicated in concepts of uplift, the raising up of downtrodden individual men and women to the status of the normal.

African American historians are no strangers to ideologies of "uplift." While connoting a group struggle toward freedom during the antebellum period, with the advent of Jim Crow regimes, "uplift," according to Kevin Gaines, morphed into a type of "bourgeois evolutionism," with black elites promoting a doctrine of self-help that supposedly would elevate the masses to a status of black citizenship.[57] While I do not intend to conflate the African American discourse of uplift with that of rehabilitation, their obvious resonances suggest that the two might work together. McRuer argues that "the perceived failures of the black family or of black communities" both justified and reinforced rehabilitation initiatives.[58] Just as black poverty and segregation were seen as a result of individual (black) pathology and not as a consequence of systemic inequity, so, too, is disability seen as an individual failing and not as a product of culturally determined notions of the normate body. Discourses of uplift and rehabilitation are linked in their desire to make all bodies identical by erasing the (racial/diseased) difference that is both the cause and the result of national crises of citizenship and personhood. Uplift requires that the morally degraded black masses improve themselves through institutions such as education and religion to qualify as citizen-subjects. Similarly, compliance with rehabilitation mandates an acceptance of the idea that the disabled body and mind should be disciplined to fit into society's structures. Thus, to be integrated into society, rehabilitation and uplift require an implicit acceptance of that society, with its norms as the goal toward which we should strive.

But making them identical is not the same as making citizens equal before the law. To integrate the amputee into society by insisting she look and act as if she is not disabled only constructs a false equivalence between the differently embodied and the commodity fetish. According to Garland-Thomson, the women's disability is "muted to the level of gesture, subordinated to the overall normativity of the model's appearance. Thus, commercial visual media cast disabled consumers as simply one of the many variations that compose the market to which they appeal."[59] In several of Traavik's photographs, it takes a second look to see that the model is an amputee. Body positions, props, and camera angles all mute disability in favor of a vision of what a normal society should look like. Just what does this look like for Miss Landmine Angola? How does her rehabilitation challenge what the website's manifesto states is the "inferiority and/or guilt complexes that hinder creativity—historical, cultural, social, personal, African, European" claimed by the pageant's organizers?

The staged scenes within which the women are artfully placed conjures up a life of opulence and wealth—not wealth based on ownership of cattle, land, children, or a family home but, rather, wealth as a Westerner's fantasy of consumption. Petra Kuppers argues that the "disabled performer [is] a point in modernity when extraordinary bodies have a currency as lifestyle accessories, when any shock or alienation value is eroded by the ubiquity of difference that is consumed and packaged."[60] The settings of the photographs and manners in which the women are posed exemplify this consumption and packaging of difference. One woman reclines next to a sparkling blue swimming pool;

another talks on a cell phone next to a sign that says business center; and yet another sits on a stool at an empty bar in front of a tropical drink. Paulina Vadi, who lost her limb while fleeing soldiers attacking her village, coyly holds a fan made of green bills in front of her face. The irony of the unemployed Maria de Fatima Conceicao, who was injured tending fields, now photographed lying next to a swimming pool is overwhelming. The images evoke the grand age of colonialism overlaid with contemporary global tourism: the luxurious hotels with cool lobbies, sunny skies, and attractively displayed women are designed to draw the Western eye (and dollar/euro). The societal conditions that enable such visions of imperial grandeur are what produced the battle-stricken and subjugated conditions of these women's lives in the first place. Thus, these women's participation in the pageant and the ensuing rehabilitation may, in Traavik's parlance, "empower" them individually or make them more physically and financially independent. But it does little to disrupt the political economy that has pockmarked Angola with landmines or the colonial attempts to create docile bodies in compliance with the assumed, prior normal state. I am not fully convinced that the majority of the contestants lack employment due only to their disability. Perhaps the lack of adequately paying work reflects not only the crisis of their disability but also the crisis of the postcolonial nation-state ravaged by war.

The pageant does perform some socially valuable labor. Garland-Thomson reminds us that the entrance of these images into the public realm can challenge our perceptions of normality, beauty, and desire.[61] The putative movement of images of disabled people from sentimental charity, freak show, and medicalized portraits to a global capitalistic public is a major accomplishment of advocacy groups in their drive toward universal rights.[62] Through "beautiful" images, differentially embodied people traditionally labeled outcasts, misfits, and burdens are shown to be just as much a part of a global economy as normate bodies. Yet representations of "glamorous" amputees, as Garland-Thomson reminds us, are "inadvertent activism without any legitimate agency for positive social change. . . . This both troubling and empowering form of entry into democratic capitalism produces a kind of instrumental form of equality: the freedom to be appropriated by consumer culture. In a democracy, to reject this paradoxical liberty is one thing; not to be granted it is another."[63] The public "beauty shots" perform this integration, even as the society that the contestants are being integrated into remains unequal and the conditions of integration revolve around conformity to this inequality.

The pageant form itself need not necessarily reiterate this hegemonic process of integration through conformity, as the form of the beauty contest has been locally assimilated to such an extent that urban Angolan aesthetics shape and possibly replace racialized, normate Western standards of beauty. This could be claimed, to a limited extent, about the beauty contest run by enterprising Angolan youth that Traavik saw in a back alley. But Miss Landmine Angola has to attempt to fulfill the agenda of its sponsors—the European Union, Norway's Art Council, the Angolan government's de-mining commission, and a charity headed by Angola's First Lady Ana Paula dos Santos. Via the Internet, the pageant strives for an international audience who shape the contest by selecting a separate winner from the one locally chosen. Thus, Miss Landmine Angola enacts national aspirations for Angolans to enter the international stage as something other than victims of their failure to self-govern. The real competition, in some senses, occurs between different classes, sponsors, political factions, and national politics. Instead of the women only reappropriating the beauty pageant and making it a hybrid vernacular with which to express their plight within imperial webs, the contest, as Moran suggests, in many ways strives to "modernize" and "standardize"—indeed, "uplift" and "rehabilitate"—African aesthetics, cultural play, and notions of gender.[64]

Furthermore, these women choosing to comply or not rests on a culturally specific, biologically discrete and atomized individual. Assuming each woman's individual compliance to rehabilitation via Miss Landmine Angola overlooks the discourse of community and care where such decisions cannot be individual. Notions of identity based on village, region, gender, and kinship shape understandings of sickness, personhood, and care. Such notions do not replicate the atomized, biomedical body that is individually capable (of making decisions) and individually disabled; that is, as Tobin Siebers reminds us, isolated as defective and in need of cure.[65] Missing from Traavik's celebration of the pageant contestants and from our assumption of their consent as "only" theirs is any mention of the role played by their families, communities, and villages. The women are mainly photographed alone; group portraits are only with other contestants. While the bio section lists the number of children the women have, we do not know those children's names or who helps raise them or even where they are raised. The bios tell us about marital status and region of "origin," but any other information about partners and friends is excluded from the website. We do not hear from any of these groups about how they understand the differential embodiment of the women and participate in the daily responsibilities of survival. Instead, we are left to assume that families and communities find caretaking and the women's dependence onerous and desire the move toward individual autonomy based on compliance to the norm. The language of development merges with an older Christian paternalism to condemn certain social practices deemed "traditional" and to posit the women's agency as constituted via individual acts of consent or noncompliance. The reality, however, is more nuanced, given the intersections between indigenous and global understandings of the body and caregiving, as well as the contradictions between goals of social connectivity and individual autonomy.

Given all of these variables, the contestants' performances reside at crossroads of what Terri Kapsalis terms "the transgressive act of exposure and the submissive act of resignation."[66] Attempting to distinguish between transgressive and submissive acts, however, leads us back to my argument concerning the illegibility of the women's consent. What does it mean to reject the Angolan marginalization of mine victims when the "choice" to be included reinforces the mechanisms of exclusion? Conversely, if the unemployed women refuse to participate in the pageant, their absence from the show may only contribute to their exclusion. Their noncompliance to rehabilitation results in their continued relegation to what Talmadge Wright calls "refuse spaces"—that is, "spaces in which one is refused—refused services, refused dignity . . . refused the basics of food, clothing, and shelter and refused medical care . . . [Those] who live in such spaces, such as the homeless, are then treated by association as equivalent to human 'refuse.' "[67] The beauty contestants' compliance or noncompliance affects not just their participation in a political cultural form but also their occupation of certain social spaces. If an unemployed woman says "no" when asked to participate in Miss Landmine Angola, she and her children may continue to be relegated to "refuse spaces." But saying "yes" does little to change those "refuse spaces"; it merely changes the inhabitants, leaving the geography of exclusion uncontested, or even reinforced. How do we read noncompliance if those women who refused to participate, if they exist, do not appear in the pageant? As McRuer writes, "If agency is part and parcel of identity and integration . . . then—within the frame or narrative structure of the [beauty pageant]—it is difficult to access or represent traces of agency, or agency effects, tied to spaces of disintegration."[68] And if the women chose to participate, what are the possibilities of noncompliance within the formal confines of the pageant and its website?

It is necessary to work with the concept of the fetish if we want to think through the interplay among capitalism, the erotics of disability, and the pageant. The best way to talk about the fetish is not to talk about the fetish. Suffice it to say that the three modalities of fetishism that emerged out of the intercultural moments of capital and slavery—the anthropological, the Marxian, and the Freudian—all revolve around what Marquard Smith calls "a disavowal, a displacement, a replacement of or a compensation for *something else*, a substitute or surrogate for *other things*, now lost, that are magical, mysterious, horrific."[69] The metropolitan subject's (sexual) desire for fungible objects such as the amputee's stump or prosthetic limb replaces what Alfred Binet once referred to as the "adoration of the savage or negro for fish bones or shiny pebbles."[70] Thus, the sexual "perversions" of the subject come to be understood as an encounter with that savage so taken with fish bones. To perpetuate the subject's "perversions," the savage must consistently be disavowed, even as she becomes the object of desire. This, then, is the erotics of empire: reveal, conceal, recognize, overlook, desire, and repudiate/Other the desired object.

To conceal and pleasurably reveal, the amputee's stump is subject not to the erotic gaze, as might be expected, but instead to the medical visualization and penetration of the (pseudo) clinical gaze. Framed as a medical image, the body is crucially defined as nonsexual. Kapsalis describes how representations of feminine genitalia enter the public as art, pornography, or medicine. Whereas art metaphorizes and idealizes genitalia by aestheticizing their representation through the removal of pubic hair, for example, pornographic and medical images expose and spectacularize hidden vulvas. One of the key distinctions between the pornographic and the medical, Kapsalis argues, is the idea of a discoverable pathology that codes the body as suitable for clinical intervention. The display of pathology marks the difference between the clinical gaze and the erotic gaze, the medical object and the sex object. However, the slippages between the pornographic and the medical are numerous: porn's extensive use of medical tropes being a case in point. Moreover, fetishism marks a point of convergence between these two registers. Kapsalis explains that in "pornography, fetish objects may take the form of stockings, slips, and high-heeled shoes" but asks, "Is it possible that *pathology* becomes the fetish in the medical context, that it becomes the visible object on which the male physician may concentrate in order to disavow the missing penis?"[71] Consider the infamous J.

Marion Sims, who conducted surgical experiments on slave women in Montgomery, Alabama, between 1845 and 1849. As one of his biographers noted, "Sims had a great love for the theater and everything dramatic, and he was fascinated by P. T. Barnum's combination of master showmanship (for which he himself had a not inconsiderable gift).' "[72] Early in Sims's career, his audience of physicians gathered to watch him expose the pathologies of slave women in his backyard hospital/theater. Kapsalis argues that Sims's invention of the speculum enabled him to see "what no man had seen before"; to conquer the previously uncharted territory, not just of the slave woman's body, but also of her pathology, the now exposed vesico-vaginal fistula.[73] His exposure of the fetish of the pathological spectacle consolidated Sims's mastery, titillating surgeons with the erotic reveal and concealment of the fistula and the sight of an "obedient" black body, unable to resist. Sims went on to perform for larger and larger audiences; amphitheaters, hospitals, and private rooms of wealthy surgeons replaced his backyard hospital. He helped to establish the theater of pathology as fetish, borrowing performance strategies from showmen and ringmasters such as P. T. Barnum even while influencing those men of the spectacle. Thus, before Joice Heth died, Barnum promised Dr. David L. Rogers first dibs on dissecting her cadaver, provided she died under Barnum's "care" and that he be allowed to manage the staging of her autopsy. The Miss Landmine Angola contestants are clearly part of this genealogy of the freak show, medical display, and spectacular erotics. Normate beauty queens are not usually subject to medical desires. Rather, they are interpolated by the sexual gaze that constructs them as appropriate objects of sexual desire. But the landmine victims display an obvious pathology or medical truth, necessitating medicalized prosthetic intervention even while embodying a sexually desirable "beauty." The pageant thus implicates the diagnostic in the erotic, and vice versa.

In the movie *Kandahar* (2001), by Mohsen Makhmalbaf, a female journalist played by Niloufar Pazira travels from Iran to Kandahar, Afghanistan, to rescue her sister. The relevant scene begins with a shot of a man with two prosthetic feet between his feet. As the shot lingers, we learn that the limbs are for his wife who is looking for a pair to fit her wedding sandals. The connection between heteronormative marital performance and its need for normalcy should not be overlooked. Before we can fully absorb the irony of looking for feet to fit shoes instead of shoes to fit feet, we hear the sound of Red Cross helicopters in the air. In the next shot, Afghan men run toward the sound of the helicopter, which mixes with slow, lyrical instrumental music, as prosthetic legs attached to parachutes fall the ground, like candy bursting from a piñata. Frenzy ensues as the men grab at various limbs, eventually tucking them under their arms and hurrying away. The prosthetic limbs that rain from the sky insist on the material embodied consequences of the thousands of landmines left by Soviet soldiers and mujahidin in postcolonial and factionalist struggles.[74] This surreal image demands that studies of disability account for global bodies and global desires; it also foregrounds the way in which capital enforces normative embodiments even while fracturing those very bodies that serve the interests of production and accumulation. For the Red Cross to prioritize prosthetic limbs in a region where the consequences of war have been so devastating articulates the need to mute the differences and temper the witnessing that these damaged bodies perform.

Similarly, Traavik's rewarding of the pageant winner with a custom-made prosthetic limb from Norway's leading designer speaks volumes about notions of bodily integrity and desirability and the tensions between non-normative embodiments and "passing" for whole. To consider a prosthesis a priority for unemployed women and their children who have been massively dislocated from rural areas and wounded not just by landmines but also by the tactics of soldiers waging various wars seems to indicate a motivation other than mere medical reparation. Marquard Smith argues that the prosthesis turns on an axis of visibility and invisibility that allows or disallows disabled people to "pass" as able-bodied.[75] The rationale for prosthetic technology oscillates between "curative therapeutics, a pragmatic episteme of how medicine and technology come together with a shared compassion . . . to turn the *dis*-abled into the *able*-bodied" and a "frantic effort [fueled by revulsion and desire] to conceal missing body parts, [and] loss itself."[76] The sentimental desire to help by making the same, whether as part of an effort to improve the fit between the environment and the body or as a prescriptive ideal of the normate, underpins the need for "passing" bodies. The success of the prosthesis beyond its facilitation of certain kinds of physical labor thus rests on making the person seem able-bodied (and supposedly desirable) to the casual observer. When the prosthesis is revealed, as it is in campaigns to collect funds for wounded veterans, the goal is an invocation of sentimentalized emotional responses such as an eroticized guilt and pathos that lead to the expenditure of capital.

The images of the Miss Landmine Angola contestants thus alternate between concealment and revelation. The images that artfully conceal the missing limb by placing the women in carefully posed positions ask us to believe that we can pass by these women as they "pass" for able-bodied. Other images that foreground the missing limb intensify appeals for economic assistance. For example, photographs of contestants on the beach holding metal crutches (which at times resembles rifles) focus the eye on the stump to signify loss, trauma, and the need for Traavik's intervention. Only one image shows a contestant using a prosthetic: that of Severina Cuhiela (Miss Cunene), a street vendor who may have been the only woman with a prosthetic leg in the contest. It would have been easy for Cuhiela to "pass" but for certain elements of the photograph. Dressed in a peach dress with a flower in her hair, she leans against a white wall at an angle that foregrounds with her racially "appropriate" prosthetic leg. Her dress, which could have covered her knee, instead ends just above it, emphasizing these women's need for prosthetic technology to function adequately in an able-bodied world. In other words, Cuhiela's prosthesis plays peek-a-boo with her audience; she could pass as able-bodied, but she does not pass because we are shown the artificiality of the leg and are thereby asked to desire the loss to ensure donations to Traavik's organization. The photograph displays the brutality of the injury even while preserving the conventions of a pageant, with its insistence on "beauty." Smith's comments when looking through catalogues by Gillingham of Chard in the 1800s (one of the foremost manufacturers of prostheses) could be applied to the pageant photographs. To advertise their prosthetic limbs, Smith writes, the female models "expose their arms, the napes of their neck[s], the tops of their thighs, the shadow effected by the point at which the tops of their thighs and buttocks meet, revealing skin that has been trussed up by the confines of straps, (garter) belts, and buckles. Skin is squeezed and molded by the bondaged tautness of its restricted lacing, the back-straightening contraptions have a sadistic edge, and the hints of undergarment" invite our fetishistic gaze.[77] What this passage reveals, other than Smith's obvious arousal, is that the prosthetic leg stands in for that other piece of merchandise for sale: the women's bodies. Their bodies are held open to be exposed to a gaze that combines the force of the commodity, the erotic, and the anthropological. Cuhiela's display of her prosthesis thus holds her open to our gaze. Her dress is coyly raised, the mechanics of the knee are the center of attention; we read her beauty and desirability via a displacement of our desire onto that flesh-colored leg.[78] See her beauty revealed, see her disability concealed, see her as a medical . . . no, see her as an erotic subject. Reveal and conceal, stump and prosthesis, reveal and conceal—in this delicate dance we see the emergence of the fetish.

Miss Cunene, Severina Cuhiela. From "Miss Landmine Angola 2008," by Morten Traavik. Photograph by Gorm K. Gaare.

Outside the Conventions of Liberal Agency

The picture I have painted of the pageant may appear overly critical. However, this criticism reflects my realization that the only subject position the site posits, for viewers or for contestants, is one that is utterly subordinated to the politico-aesthetic alternatives provided by global capitalism. Either we condemn the women as "exploited" by Traavik or give them back their "agency" by affirming that everyone has the right to be seen (as beautiful). But this is a false choice, and Walter Johnson deftly identifies the liberal ideology that underlies such false oppositions. As he points out, "The term 'agency' smuggles . . . the universality of a liberal notion of selfhood, with its emphasis on independence and choice, right into the middle of a conversation about slavery against which that supposed natural (at least for white men) condition was originally defined. By applying the jargon of self-determination and choice to the historical condition of civil objectification and choicelessness, [theorists] have . . . ended up in a mess."[79] I find the language of self-determination and choice occasionally useful, but I do agree that it is often used carelessly to conflate agency with resistance and to ignore acts of submission as forms of agency. Considerations of humanness lived outside the conventions of liberal agency are not followed up on: the body becomes individually atomized, coherent, and distanced from engagement with the dominant order on various scales. Thus, the best that the pageant contestants can hope for is a negotiation of the various ways in which they are used by the nation, global capital, humanitarian groups, and other groups. Perhaps this is what Jose Muñoz means when he talks about a strategy of disidentification, a term "meant to be descriptive of the survival strategies the minority subject practices in order to negotiate a phobic majoritarian public sphere that continuously elides or punishes the existence of subjects who do not conform to the phantasm of normative citizenship."[80] Muñoz also crucially adds that disidentification is not always an adequate strategy. Some contexts necessitate overt resistance, while others demand conformity. To a certain extent, the Miss Landmine Angola website literalizes a teleological politics of beauty that begins with mutilated, disabled bodies injured in decontextualized wars and ends with those same bodies miraculously healed/made beautiful via Western liberal models of self-empowerment. This desire to give slaves and others "back their agency" posits a unidirectional claim of the past on the present. Theorists and performance artists supposedly answer this claim by returning a stolen agency to its rightful owners. But this mode of redress rests on a linear, progressive temporality that denies the processes of surrogation (which I discussed earlier) in which different moments repeat with difference, forming global genealogies of performance. Surrogation asks us what a new way to write history would look like without the individual subject at its center and through an acknowledgment that collective and individual subjectivities operate on a continuum. How do we move away from considering the performances of these various landmine survivors only as isolated instrumentalized spectacles advancing liberal calls for human rights? How do we ensure that the suffering of these women does not simply get folded into liberal appeals for recognition from the (global) state?

Alexander Weheliye suggests that political violence "activates a fleshy surplus that simultaneously sustains and disfigures said brutality."[81] This flesh, he goes on to argue, "excavates the social (after)life of [the socially dead], represent[ing] racializing assemblages of subjection that can never annihilate the lines of flight, freedom dreams, practices of liberation, and possibilities of other worlds."[82] To conceptualize the possibility for such "lines of flight," then, we might approach the pageant from a different critical vantage point. Instead of assuming that the women in the pageant are either complicit or resistant to spectacularized violence, perhaps we can see their participation as a construction of temporary community, as a tactical and elastic moment of possibility. This relationally grounded moment of possibility disrupts the equation of the human with white Western masculinity by constructing an African diasporic genealogy of gendered, raced performances that embody the past's and present's claims on each other. Tied to a specific cultural and material history, the critical imagination at work in the pageant might bend and mold space to constitute new black geographies. Performance asks us what a fresh way to embody history would look like without the individual subject at its center and with the acknowledgment that collective and individual subjectivities operate on a continuum. Johnson writes that history "after 'agency' might be written around a 'Copernican revolution' of memory, an intellectual inversion of the relation between the past and the present, by focusing on the present-life of the past, on what elements of the past are drawn upon at any given moment in history and the power-structured processes through which they are selected and enforced."[83] This Copernican revolution, or twice-repeated behavior, moves away from models of volitional subjects acting on their individual choices toward re-membered performances of racialization and disability that call out and respond to each other. Performance remakes space and remakes the body so that human variation is not incidental but, rather, constitutes an essential aspect of reimagining the human. Through these women sharing a stage, finding one another across the applause of an audience (virtual and real), even if only to reject one another, and in their sounding of one another's amputations, the very definition of what it means to be human is fundamentally altered.

SLOW DEATH

"Indian" Performances of Indenture and Slavery

Prologue: Finding Oneself in the Cane Fields

Aziz Hassim's novel *Revenge of Kali*, a four-generation family saga of South African indentured labor, begins with a contemporary preoccupation about genealogy. Where does the protagonist Thiru belong in postapartheid South Africa? What claims of legitimacy can he mobilize to justify his inclusion into a postapartheid nation trying to reconcile itself to past and present racial injustices and entrenched social inequities? Both the prologue and part one of *Revenge of Kali*, entitled "The Canefields," dwell on the difficulties faced by a certain class of poor "Indians" in South Africa. This population confronted different modes of discrimination from an elite Hindu merchant class (stereotyped as oppressive traders), as well as from native Africans who overlooked class distinctions for a simplified animosity toward all "Indians." Many Hindu merchants, in an attempt to negotiate colonial hierarchies, reinforced their supposed superiority to native Africans, while some native Africans rejected all "Indians" as an extension of foreign domination. This historical animosity between two groups of people, both of whom were subjugated by imperial rule, though in different ways, results in Thiru feeling alienated from the South Africa he regards as home. He exclaims, "I'm through apologising for sins that my ancestors were never guilty of. This new war cry: 'Go back where you came from,' what does it mean? Back to the Canefields? The Duchene? India? If I don't belong here, does the so-called Negro, the descendants of slaves, belong in America?"[1]

Through this evocation of the "Negro" slave, Hassim locates Indian claims of belonging in the performance of coerced labor. Rather than reductive origin stories that would locate Indian South Africans as always belonging elsewhere, he attempts, through the figure of the slave, to secure a South African identity for the descendants of Indian indentured servants anchored in the blood, sweat, and tears they expended on the plantation. Just as the "Negro" slave belongs to the New World by virtue of her labor, so does the "coolie" belong to South Africa. Indentured servitude in Natal on the sugarcane plantations becomes transatlantic slavery by another name in another place as "The Canefields" unfolds in what Meg Samuelson calls an "Atlantic register." Samuelson writes that, to distinguish South African Indians with various histories from the stereotype of Hindus as "oppressive traders" and thus work through African Indian historical antagonisms, this "Atlantic register" figures indenture as a form of slavery.[2]

The Revenge of Kali, specifically the section called "The Canefields," in order to assert this Atlantic register appropriates the narrative techniques of African American neo-slave narratives such as the collapsing of the past and the present. The section begins with Thiru arguing with his wife. He explains to both her and the reader that he has to find something more of his ancestors than fragments of documents. He has to return to the cane fields, where he hears their "magnetic" call: "Come, *kanna*. What took you so long?" (15). That night, his experience in the cane fields includes the sound of spectral voices and the agonized urgency of someone running in another time. Time collapses as the past saturates the present and we palimpsestically experience the plantation life of Ellapen, Thiru's great-grandfather. This strategy of folding past and present generations together perpetuates the "Atlantic register" found in African American neo-slave narratives that, according to Ashraf Rushdy, are likewise "structured around a partially hidden family secret that allows the authors to explore the role of generational memory in transmitting and repressing that secret and the function of the nation-state in creating and re-creating the ideologies of family and race that promoted the conditions for the formation of that secret."[3]

The individual family and the nation share the same secret: slavery itself. The secret that Thiru uncovers in his journey into the past is the enslavement of his great-grandfather Ellapen. After a blow to the head, Ellapen awakens aboard the *Truro* and describes his passage in terms that are almost identical to many depictions of the Middle Passage. When he arrives, Ellapen encounters a scene familiar in sentimental depictions of the depravity of slavery:

the separation of kin. The beatific slave Chaureamma and her two angelic daughters, who were also kidnapped from the streets of Madras, are ripped apart as the daughters are sold to different buyers: "Those children, they were devastated. They were screaming, reaching out to each other, the tears pouring down their cheeks. It was a scene out of hell" (53). Straight out of abolitionist literature, this scene of a family torn apart by captivity and forced labor collapses the distinctions between indenture and Atlantic slavery while also suggesting that the family or "multiracial" nation might be put back together by the re-membering of the trauma of enslavement. The suffering of Indian bondage, once remembered, enables Thiru to lay his ancestors to rest and to strengthen familial bonds in the present. The section ends with a downpour that washes clean the blood-soaked earth as truth and reconciliation triumph over the retributive justice of the titular goddess Kali. The exposure of the family secret, then, unites black Africans and Indian Africans.

However, the link between the transatlantic enslavement of black South Africans and the indentured labor of Indians in South Africa, no matter how politically strategic, rests on certain historical generalizations, oversights, and misperceptions that this chapter will attempt to unpack. South Africans, "black" and "Indian," were enslaved as well as indentured in ways that are difficult to grasp if our work remains in an "Atlantic register." Working with the specificity of other slave and coerced labor routes in mind, we move away from Hassim's recuperative depictions of indenture as chattel slavery, but *not* to argue that indenture was a form of free labor. Nor is it to fetishize slavery as the ultimate form of belonging through suffering. Rather, the rest of the chapter attempts a more nuanced discussion of free and unfree labor that centers on questions of will. This discussion of will allows an examination of the processes by which historians read this particular archive of "Indian" indenture.

Overview

In 2010, South Africa was given a world stage as the host of the FIFA World Cup. National leaders and organizations used this stage to articulate national pride and celebrate reintegration into the "modern" world, the country supposedly having shed the atavistic skin of apartheid. As part of a new nationalism, 2010 was also designated the one hundred fiftieth anniversary of the arrival of the first Indian indentured servants in Natal in what has become the de facto origin story of Indians in South Africa. As with all origin stories, this narrative simplifies a very complex landscape where indigenous Khoi

San worked as indentured laborers alongside slaves in the Cape, where Mozambican slaves were freed on their way to Madagascar and put to work as indentured laborers in Durban (the so-called Zanzibaris), and where slaves included "Indians" from Goa and Bengal. This chapter asks what happens if we take account of the slave trade from India and Southeast Asia to various points around the Indian Ocean basin, thinking through the possible links between this trafficking and the mid-nineteenth-century development of indentured labor flows that included both Indians and Africans. How do we conceptualize the "will" of these various coerced laborers without resorting to simplistic binaries of "free" labor and enslavement?

Traditional histories have tended to reinforce the separation of Indian and black diasporas under the signs of either Indian indenture or black enslavement. But what happens when we place these histories side by side? Instead of reifying black or Indian identity, Antoinette Burton asks, can we think of imperial diasporas of the Atlantic and Indian Oceans as "simultaneously travers[ing] racial categories and excavat[ing] the different sites of their reproduction?"[4] Linking the histories of the Atlantic and Indian oceans, and thus histories of Indian and African diasporas, requires a more nuanced understanding of imperial labor schemes. Rather than maintain the traditional racialized binary between slavery and indenture, which revolves around the fetish of the contract, I wish to show how slave trafficking and indentured servitude are inextricable due to their similar use of liberal Enlightenment notions of free will and will-lessness. Such notions underestimate the bondage of slavery and overestimate the freedom of indenture. They also posit a false teleological progression from slavery to freedom. More "civilized" models of voluntary contractual work do not gradually replace the institution of slavery, which is then seen as a primitive vestige of premodernity. Instead, slavery works hand in hand with systems of (un)free labor that perpetuate the systemic violence of plantation life.

By bringing together imperial webs of labor in the Atlantic and Indian ocean worlds, I hope to show how the historiographies of the Cape and Natal have interacted across space and time to shape South Africa's sense of itself as a nation. Very few histories incorporate both Indian Ocean and Atlantic diasporas, Indian and African peoples, Cape slavery and Natal indenture. The tip of Africa seems to mark the boundary between scholars of these diasporas, who seldom follow the ships and human cargo past the place where Indian and Atlantic waters supposedly meet. The southern tip of Africa marks a historiographical region that is strangely uncircumnavigable, a fluid space suspended between bodies of water and systems of signification. Yet it is precisely these liminal qualities, as Isabel Hofmeyr argues, "that can query and throw into doubt all systems of totalization and absorption," enabling us to reimagine our inherited racialized, ethnocentric narratives of diaspora.[5]

Richard Allen points out that more than twenty years ago, historians such as Herbert Gerbeau were already noting that the central difficulty in writing a history of slavery that included the Indian Ocean basin was "coming to terms with a huge, ill-defined, and exceptionally diverse human and geographical domain."[6] The heterogeneity of the South African slave population and their present-day descendants remind us that chattel labor could flow both toward and away from the African continent, combining African and Asian continental legacies. To contextualize debates about the "Indian" indentured laborer's relative freedom, this chapter gives a brief overview of "Indian" slavery and the supposed "free labor" of the Khoi San and so-called Bastaard Hottentots who worked alongside slaves. The presence or absence of a contract is paramount in distinguishing between Indian indenture and slavery. However, the assumption that the presence of labor contracts signifies the indentured worker's agency proves just as problematic as the assumption that the lack of a contract indicates the slave's lack of will. In both cases, reading the contract as an indicator of will presumes an individual subject's ability to choose and the reader's/historian's ability to access that choice within the archive. As I continually argue, while the will of slaves and indentured servants obviously exists, it remains largely illegible within the imperial archive and thus necessitates a critically imaginative poetics that insists on the embodied, material "afterlife" of history.[7]

The hanging body of the suicide victim provides an unlikely doorway into this critically imaginative exploration of will and its lack. I anchor my genealogy of performance to this uncanny instantiation of the politics of will not so much to give voice to the silenced as to imagine the possibilities of their agency. By reading death and self-harm as painfully embodied performances of the politics of coercion and consent, I show how framings of suicide rest on models of individual agency. Suicide either becomes the ultimate example of will-less victimization or a sentimental, voluntaristic story of romantic heroes fighting the good fight by undermining the plantation through the depletion of labor. But what if we think about suicide as a performance that is similar to Lauren Berlant's idea of "slow death," the unglamorous quotidian wearing down of life necessitated by capital. Instead of suicide being reduced to a spectacle of racialized ethnic suffering or heroic liberal individualism, might it demonstrate the processes of surrogation and routine violence constitutive of the plantation? Instead of remaining transfixed by the pained body of the victimized or heroic Other, can we turn toward a brutality obscured by this spectacular body: the violence of capital, which overestimates the differences between enslavement and free labor?

Enslaved Indians and Indentured Africans: Inboekstelsel and Other Death Worlds

> No one . . . can bind himself by a contract to the kind of dependency through which he ceases to be a person, for he can make a contract only insofar as he is a person.
> —IMMANUEL KANT, *THE METAPHYSICAL ELEMENTS OF JUSTICE*, 98

Despite popular and official narratives that have the first "Indians" arriving on southern African shores beginning with the *Truro* in 1860, "Indians" actually were present in South Africa in the seventeenth century. These earlier "Indians" were slaves predominantly owned by the Dutch East India Company (VOC), a fact elided in romantic, contemporary understandings of the identitarian category of "Indian," which was used to obscure the complex reality of a heterogeneous population. As Nigel Worden documents, in 1690 there were some 350 privately owned slaves in the Cape. By the end of the VOC's rule in 1795, official figures put the number at 16,839, along with some 300–600 slaves owned by the VOC itself.[8] Worden writes of Cape slavery that "a *surprising factor* is the relatively high proportion of Indians" from the west coast of Malabar (popular with Dutch traders) and Bengal (a source for British traders during the early eighteenth century).[9] Some slaves whose names indicate Indian origin may also have been brought to the Cape from Batavia after a series of sales throughout southern Asia, culminating in the voyage to the Cape. The VOC's use of Indian slaves stemmed from the company's familiarity with indigenous Asian slave systems, its development of Portuguese slave links, and its use of Asian slaves for public works in Batavia and some spice-producing islands.[10] The VOC's extensive use of Indian slaves at the Cape makes sense, so perhaps Worden's surprise at this situation seems a bit curious. The only reason that these Asian slaves would be surprising is if one expected them to be black.

The population of slaves at the Cape encompassed a large variety of languages, cultures, religions, and even phenotypes. Indeed, some historians argue that this diversity prevented the establishment of any kind of comprehensive unified slave culture or community. Among owners and traders, much was made of the differences among slaves, in particular as it related to their suitability to labor. Similar to North America, where the (often fictive) ethnic identities of slaves functioned as shorthand for personality traits, work ethic, and know-how, at the Cape much seems to have been made of the distinction between "black" and Eastern slaves. Consider Robert Semple, a merchant and shop-keeper who published the book *Walks and Sketches at the Cape of Good Hope* in 1803, wherein he distinguishes among four different types of slaves: Mozambicans, Malays, Malabars, and Hottentots (even though the Khoikhoi were not legally enslaved).[11] Semple's description of Malays, for example, reinforces stereotypical distinctions between racialized groups: "Even at a distance his upright form, his nervous make, his free step announces the Malay, or native of the Island of Java, the king of slaves. As he approaches, mark his long, coal black hair which hangs half down his back, his yellow complexion, his glancing and jealous eye, which looks askance upon slavery. He knows well that from his class are formed the house-painters, the musicians, the ingenious workmen of the Cape."[12]

Such arbitrary distinctions between Asian and black slaves dominated the writing of observers. Semple's description of the Malay having a "free step" ties into popular belief that the yoke of slavery did not sit well on Asian shoulders.[13] Asian slaves, with their supposed cunning, vindictiveness, and vengefulness, were more likely to resist enslavement than black slaves who, on the other hand, were seen as either passive, patient, and long-suffering or treacherous and sullen. Black slaves were thus supposedly better suited for manual labor on the farms, while Asian slaves putatively excelled at skilled craftsmanship. However, there is little evidence that fieldwork was exclusively reserved for Mozambicans and other "black" slaves. While there were certainly greater numbers of Eastern craftsmen in Cape Town due to the city's demand for certain types of skilled labor, fieldwork in the hinterlands was done by Indian, Indonesian, Madagascan, and Mozambican slaves alike. The makeup of this agricultural labor force largely depended on which slaves were captured and traded during a particular period.

Despite their diversity, these people, who worked alongside the dismally treated Khoikhoi on Dutch-owned and British-policed farms developed a sense of themselves as a laboring class in opposition to a relatively homogenous white slave-owning class who (greatly aided by intermarriage that kept the inheritance of wealth within closed circuits) gradually consolidated their power around the idea of the superiority of their whiteness. Class structure became more and more intertwined with racial categories that consolidated a multiplicity of slave origin into naturalized positions of racial Otherness.[14] These divisions in turn influenced the proletarization of Cape workers that occurred during the 1800s, a century before the rest of the country. What's more, as Worden reminds us, this process of racialization also impacted the development of "racial capitalism of modern South Africa as a whole," a legacy obscured by the violence of the apartheid regime.[15] The slave-based economy influenced the organization of social class after manumission. The homogeneity of the slave-owning class developed into a bourgeois class that cohered around their putative whiteness. Performances of nascent whiteness supported the continuation of the logic of social stratification inherited from slavery, and the rest of South Africa followed in the wake of the Western Cape's early proletarianization.

The tremendous cultural and ethnic diversity of the slaves in the Cape accurately represents what happens when slaves arrive via both indigenous and national slave routes. As foreign-born slaves procreated with one another, as well as with the Khoikhoi, the San, and slave owners, phenotype and skin color became even more unreliable markers of identity. The conversion of many slaves to Islam;[16] the development of language systems that enabled slaves to communicate across languages, dialects, and accents; and the development of an identity loosely based on their subordinated status meant that the kind of distinctions that Semple so confidently articulated became increasingly difficult to delineate. Performances of state violence both during slavery and after manumission overwrote the slave body to create categories of Otherness that gradually began to congeal into the putative certainty of race. These pedagogical narratives erase the diversity of the slave body, naturalizing slavery as black and "forgetting" those Asians whose presence in South Africa predated "coolie" indenture.

To complicate the labor politics of the plantation even further, slaves were not the only people working there. Nigel Worden's and Robert Shell's exceptional work draws attention to many Asian slaves and to the other "unusual" factor of Cape slavery: the presence of Khoikhoi workers on plantations. Despite the company's initial ban on Khoikhoi laborers and the colonial insistence on an increasing numbers of slaves to replace indigenous populations that refused to "work," a large number of Khoikhoi worked side by side with slaves. What planters called a "shortage of slaves" and what others describe as the unwillingness of sullen slaves to work led to the Khoikhois' gradual entry into the plantation economy. Frontier settlers in particular relied heavily on the skill and knowledge of Khoikhoi to maintain livestock and carry out other agricultural labor. By the end of the seventeenth century, the erosion of the material, legal, and social independence of Khoikhoi chiefdoms caused some Khoikhoi to enter into the plantation labor system. However, it was the colonial appropriation of grazing land in the east during the late eighteenth century that forced large numbers of starving and displaced Khoikhoi into the plantation economy, and by 1806 indigenous workers were found on almost half of all farms. These workers, as Worden writes, entered into a "social structure already conditioned by the slave system and, although nominally free, became subject to similar means of coercion and control which were later to be applied in a modified form to Bantu-speaking laborers."[17]

The status of these Khoikhoi furthers my argument about free and unfree labor. The distinctions between slave and indentured labor became increasingly blurred, especially given that indenture contracts for the most part were oral and often broken by all of the parties involved. Nigel Penn points out that the terms of indenture were recorded only when either contractor or indentured worker complained to VOC officials about a breach of contract. In the early half of the eighteenth century, most of the complainants were from Khoikhoi regarding the planters' withholding of wages. The first documented case of this occurred in 1717, although the details are unknown. In 1726, an unnamed Khoi laborer complained that Corporal Jacob Titus had withheld a payment of sheep. Titus justified his actions by claiming that the worker had left nine months early, in breach of contract, but the worker explained he was forced to leave because of mistreatment by a soldier. As Penn documents, the company found in favor of the worker, warning Titus that "no further engagement shall be entered into with that people, rather leaving them to depart with their cattle wither soever they like."[18]

The company initially did try to maintain the legal distinction between slave and indentured servant, but these distinctions were increasingly eroded, not least because the material working conditions of the Khoikhoi and slaves became increasingly similar as the number of Khoikhoi working on the plantations began to increase. According to Worden, the "Khoikhoi might have had nominal rights in the legal code but by the end of the Company period 'they could no longer exercise them.'"[19] By the end of the eighteenth century, the Cape courts were condoning the seizure of Khoi livestock. Khoi testimony needed the backing of a settler to be admissible, and a system of indenture, or *inboekstelsel*, formally approved in 1775, placed the tenuous notion of free labor under further crisis.

The legislation around inboekstelsel, euphemistically known as "apprenticeship," targeted the labor of children whose mothers were Khoi and whose father were enslaved. These (male) children, disparagingly named "Bastard Hottentots," were forced into a period of indenture that putatively ended when they turned twenty-five. Consider then the plight of the "free" Khoi mothers who, to remain with their children, had to remain on the farms. By twenty-five, the Bastard Hottentots were often parents themselves and thus were further indebted to whites. By the late eighteenth century, settler commando raids kidnapped and indentured those children "abandoned" by their frequently murdered parents. Such was the inboekstelsel system. For those children raised under inboekstelsel, the likelihood of independence from white settlers became increasingly low, especially, as Worden reminds us, with the implementation of the Caledon Code of 1809, which "institutional[ized] the servile status of the colonial Khoi and San, while extending the rule of law at the Cape" and rendering these populations "aliens in their own land."[20]

Much can be said about these bonded workers. I wish to focus on their imbrication in an exploitative wage economy and the relationship of that economy to slave labor. As in the case of indentured Indians later, the distinction of Khoikhoi labor as free and slave labor as "unfree" proved impossible to sustain. Nor is it accurate simply to equate the unfreedoms of the contractually "free" market with the bondage of slavery. I argue that one did not replace the other but, rather, that all labor relations at various moments combine aspects of freedom and unfreedom. Slavery and indenture repeat the same performance on the same plantations across time and space; both systems, in their deployment of similar narratives of race, consent, and force, function as surrogates for imperial capital.

Neither Victim nor Opportunist: Middle-Passaged Guests
Some Hundred Years Later

> Middle-passaged
>   Passing
> Beneath the colouring of desire
>   In the enemy's eye
> A scatter of worlds and broken wishes
>   In Shiva's unending dance.[21]

On the coast of KwaZulu, Natal, there were other South African plantations in need of free or underpaid labor. Although separated chronologically and on opposite coasts, the regimes of coercive plantation labor at the Cape and in Natal were instantiations of each other, generating similar myths of national origin.[22] Between 1860 and 1911, approximately 152,184 apprenticed servants, hailing predominantly from Tamil- and Telugu-speaking areas of southern India, arrived in KwaZulu-Natal. For the most part, these servants worked the sugarcane plantations, but to a more limited extent they also labored in coal mines and built railroads. This particular form of apprenticeship was called "indenture," the term, according to Véronique Bragard, referring specifically to the two or more copies of a contract that "all ha[d] their tops and edges correspondingly indented or separated for identification and security . . . so that when brought together again at any time, the two edges exactly tallied and showed they were parts of one and the same original document."[23]

Historians have approached indentured labor in South Africa in ways that can be divided roughly into two categories. The first approach, which I call the "free choice model," insists on the conscious and rational decision to leave India and contractually commit to working on South African plantations. Given environmental, social, political, and socioeconomic motives, this historiographic approach insists that "coolies" voluntarily traveled to South Africa to rationally maximize the opportunities of indenture, subsuming Indian indenture within the category of labor migration rather than imperial labor reallocation. According to this theory, Indians migrated to fill post-emancipation labor shortages caused by a newly liberated group of black people who were supposedly eager to avoid work.[24] As what Madhavi Kale describes as "mobile, deployable units—carriers—of differentially valorized cultures/bundles of cultural resources,"[25] indentured Indians were distinguished from the enslaved on the basis of a general willingness to work. Complaints about kidnapping or abuse were regarded as anomalous. The Indian Law Commissioners reiterated this notion of free will in a ruling from 1836 cited by Marina Carter and Khal Torabully: "It does not appear that any complaint of ill-treatment has been received. . . . [S]uch emigrants go voluntarily and with a knowledge of the conditions to which they subscribe."[26] Representatives of Kolkata (then Calcutta) firms, for example, refused to consider suspending the operation of the free market, claiming that cases of kidnapping and deception were random instances perpetuated by a few scrupulous individuals. This free choice model where "Indians" maximized their opportunity traditionally has been contrasted with Hugh Tinker's understanding of indenture as "a new form of slavery."[27] According to Tinker's model, the abolition of the slave trade did not put an end to plantation slavery. Instead, following abolition, sugar planters looked to indentured labor to replace former plantation slaves who purportedly were disinclined to work after emancipation. The proximity between indenture and slavery was noted at the time.

In the same year as the Indian Law Commissioners' 1836 ruling, according to Carter and Torabully, an article entitled "The Kidnapping Coolie Trade Revived" appeared in a Kolkata newspaper insisting that men and women were being abducted and sold as slaves.[28] The Calcutta Commission of Enquiry Report contended that if the shipments of indentured continued, "the waste of human life and misery that will fall on the Coolies exported under the name of free labourers will approach those inflicted on the negro in the middle passage by the slave trade. . . . It seems to us that the permission to renew this traffic would weaken the moral influence of the British government throughout the world, and deaden or utterly destroy the effect of all future remonstrances and negotiations respecting the slave trade; and this effect would ensue, however stringent, minute or restrictive might be the regulations framed to check abuses."[29] In May 1838, the lieutenant-governor of Bengal demanded an embargo on ships carrying indentured Indians. He was concerned that the racism that enabled the commodification of slaves was being replicated with respect to "shiftless, simian-like Indians," who supposedly were ignorant of the ship's destination and running away from familial obligations. In response to an article in the *Asiatic Journal* on July 5 about kidnapping and coercion of Indians by recruiters to Mauritius, a town meeting was called to petition the governor to end the practice. Emboldened by a debate in the House of Lords in March 1838, the petitioners, according to Kale, insisted that they were not interested in "interfering with the free agency and civil rights of the emigrants" but that "the system was radically bad and contained in itself the elements of a new species of slavery."[30]

Opposing the "free choice" and "new form of slavery" interpretations of indenture naturalizes the apparent division between "free" and "unfree" labor and prevents us from recognizing the "collusion between capitalist and colonial interests."[31] As Nitin Varma points out, "Not only was the labour procured under active patronage of the colonial state, using corrupt means and practices, but the labour process was also characterized by the unrestrained powers bestowed on the planters through legislative enactments."[32] The contract signed by the "coolie," which supposedly indicated volition and thus distinguished free choice from slavery, came to signal the key difference between the two models of understanding indenture. For some theorists, the coolie's signature or mark on the contract became the primary signifier of the ability to choose that set the liberal Enlightenment subject apart from the category of chattel slavery. For other theorists, coolies were slaves by another name who signed contracts—if, indeed, they signed anything—under extreme duress. Neither of these interpretative models, however, is adequate in addressing the intricacies of South African labor at that time. With Mumbai bureaucrats insisting that "Indians were exercising free choice in indenturing" and the Anti-Slavery Society (with it pro-free-market capitalistic agenda) trying to prevent the "gullible coolie villager" from landing in the clutches of greedy slaveholding planters, neither complete victimization nor sovereign voluntarism seems an adequate explanation for the experience of indenture.

Whichever model we might prefer, indenture was characterized by what Varma calls "unfreedom," a condition distinct from but related to slavery that is often overlooked or taken as a necessary characteristic of colonial capital-labor relations. As Jonathan Grossman elaborates, "Capital can pose as the champion of the removal of . . . unfreedoms, even while it is using the same ideologised notion of the 'needs of the economy' to actually secure the continuation of unfreedoms."[33] One of the ways that capitalism promoted itself as an opponent of "unfreedom" at this time was through a discourse of humanitarianism.[34] Freedom does not distinguish slavery from indenture. Instead, discourses of freedom or unfreedom, which were context-specific and adaptive, contributed to the racialized and gendered exploitation of labor. Thus, the notion of freedom worked to the advantage of capitalist and colonialist interests. As Kale explains, "The critique of chattel slavery . . . rested on a radical opposition between slave and free labor in which the former was vilified as the threatening absence of liberty, while the latter was celebrated as one of its fundamental guarantors. In this framework, liberty meant the right to sell one's labor to the highest bidder; the formulations conceded little significance (if any) to the relative power of the parties concerned, or to the conditions under which the transactions took place."[35]

It is my contention here that *neither* "free labor" nor "a new slavery" adequately characterizes indenture because both concepts leave intact the notion that workers can choose whether to sell their free labor competitively in the open market. Using Grossman's "The Right to Strike and Worker Freedom" as a template of sorts, I describe various unfreedoms attendant to labor that is supposedly free. Signaled by the voluntaristic contract between worker and employer, the concept of free labor implies that workers alienated from the land have the real capacity to exchange the commodity of their labor as they choose. Detailing the unfreedoms bound up with this exchange, as it took place in the colonies, draws attention to those workers who, paradoxically, are locked into the supposed liberty of capitalism and whose challenges to or acceptance of capitalist social relations remain illegible within official narrations. I will rehearse five of Grossman's points that characterize free labor as unfree, applying them specifically to South African indenture:

1. "Free labour is constituted as such by violence, conquest and compulsion. Its freedom emerges out of imposed necessity, not voluntary choice."[36] Thus, the charges of kidnapping, intimidation, misinformation, and exploitation around those "coolies" who boarded ships bound for South Africa do not necessarily point toward slavery as much as toward the unfreedom of free labor.

2. "In exercising their freedom to sell labour power on the market, workers are involved in an exchange between unequal parties.... The 'playing-field' is never actually 'level.'"[37] It is ludicrous even to suggest that disenfranchised laborers desperately seeking alternatives to the imperial and caste systems of exploitation were equal to wealthy planters with financial investments in Africa, India, and the Caribbean and the backing of imperial governments.

3. "Free labour is exploited ... in a set of social relations which involve a range of different forms of oppression including racial and gender oppression. There is a set of social and political unfreedoms which can and have co-existed with economically free labour."[38] Capital was not a march toward universal humanism and freedom, as professed. Instead, social inequities were refined and further developed to ensure the continuing extraction of labor for profit. The calcification of racial categorization integral to slavery is part and parcel of the development of the free market.

4. "Even where there is free labour in developed capitalist economies, there is unfree labour within those same economies."[39] Systems of indenture, slavery, and free labor have operated simultaneously across regions and time periods in South Africa. For example, those Africans who were "rescued" by the British from slave ships and transported to the Cape were incorporated into a complex system of unfree labor that often was

indistinguishable from slavery. Clare Anderson has argued that the discourses and practices of indenture should be understood "in the context of colonial innovations in incarceration and confinement."[40] The resemblance of the colonial practice of penal transportation to indenture, she argues, shifts historical inquiries from a simplistic question of whether indenture was a "new form of slavery" toward a more nuanced investigation of how imaginative discourses of criminalization permeated the experience and organization of indenture. To illustrate this, Anderson cites the Dickens Committee (1838–40) that compared the march of indentures from one area to another to the "conveyance of convicts from one District to another," concluding that "it would be an abuse of terms to say that the Coolies were treated like slaves . . . but they certainly were treated, in practice, like something between impressed seamen and enlisted recruits."[41] Anderson shows further similarities between indenture and incarceration, such as the marking of indentured servants with a stamp on the forehead that resembles the penal tattooing, or *godna*, enforced in Bengal and Madras between 1789 and 1849. The argument that indenture bears more similarities to penal transportation than slavery obscures how all these systems work together as part of the same regime of transnational labor. Coexisting within the same dynamic and contested imperial webs, chattel slavery and formal freedom serve as the beginning and endpoint of the teleological narrative of modernity; thus, belief in their absoluteness only reiterates this narrative and further obscures the multiple unfreedoms that characterize non-slave labor. Indenture, like slavery, constitutes a site of performance where the empire reproduces itself through repeated acts of surrogation. Achille Mbembe suggests that "specific instances and experiences of unfreedom" link slavery with late modern colonialism. According to Mbembe, to be subjected to either regime "is to experience a permanent condition of 'being in pain': fortified structures . . . buildings that bring back painful memories of humiliation, interrogations, and beatings; curfews that imprison . . . bones broken; shootings and fatalities—a certain kind of madness."[42]

5. The capitalist idea that an individual worker can choose to exchange her labor for wages rests on a "formalist notion of freedom and an individualist notion of the worker—extending that individualism into competition, not simply between the worker and employer over terms, but also between worker and another worker."[43]

The notion of the free market contract assumes that an individual can withhold or perform his or her labor and thereby affect the quotidian functioning of capital. It also assumes that workers are competing for limited resources and that "winning" a scarce job or better working conditions depends on the consenting individual's ability and productivity. Such liberalism saturates the discourse of indenture and slavery, defining them in contradistinction to each other. As Grossman points out, the "freedom of free labour under capitalism is a limited freedom, bound up with unfreedoms. . . . Free labour under capitalism is exploited and alienated. The fact that it is free does not mean that it has jobs or decent living conditions or a living wage or political rights—or the capacity to actually meaningfully enjoy such rights."[44] The continuity of the unfreedoms and injustices of slavery belies the supposed transition from slavery to free labor.

To account for this violence—that is, this impoverishment and denial of rights that characterize capitalism—we must fold histories of race- and gender-based subjugation into traditional Marxism. The problem lies not so much with the concept of an abstract freedom as with capital's perpetuation of the unfreedom, exploitation, alienation, and displacement *of some* as a guarantor of the life of more worthy others. Or, as Mbembe puts it, "*The generalized instrumentalization of human existence and the material destruction of human bodies and populations*" supports the life of other privileged bodies.[45] The right to kill or the right to decide who shall be subjugated and who shall live is based on the state of exception that Mbembe locates within the racialized and gendered geographies of the plantation and the colony. Thus, colonial rule brings together extermination and bureaucratic rationalism through necropolitics in which the symbolic and material death of others produces the life of some. The cruelty and terror of necropolitics, Mbembe goes on to say, creates "death-worlds . . . forms of social existence in which vast populations are subjected to conditions of life conferring upon them the status of the living-dead."[46] As "repressed topographies of cruelty," the plantation and the colony blur the distinctions between death and life, resistance and suicide, free and unfree labor.[47]

In her study of service economies in South Korea, Jin-Kyung Lee deftly links the extraction of certain types of labor to the possibilities of death in necropolitics: "Necropolitical labor means the extraction of labor from those 'condemned' to death, whereby the 'fostering' of life, already premised on their death or the disposability of their lives, is limited to serving the labor demands of the state or empire."[48] Indentured servants (whether Khoi in the

Cape or Indians in Natal some one hundred years later) could be disposed of either during or after the performance of labor. This disposal could take the form of actual death, physical removal, or crippling injury. It is no accident that integral to the "Indian" indenture contract was the stipulation that the laborer had to return to where he or she had come from once the period of indenture was over. Similarly, the Khoi were to disappear into the territory not yet settled (by whites) after their term of indenture or inboekstelsel. Indentured servants were thus effectively eliminated or removed from the domain of the plantation when their contractual obligations were up. The end of labor therefore meant annihilation or banishment.

Lee goes on to argue that all proletarian labor can be broadly defined as necropolitics in that the work itself necessarily incurs physical or mental trauma and injury that operate on a continuum with death. Consider the cane stalks that lacerate the skin, the calloused hands that have lost their lifelines to the machete, the stooped back, the crusted-over sore on the foot from a rat bite. Necropolitical labor, however, includes not just this wear and tear but also the infliction of violence by state and non-state actors. This work is constituted not only by a series of embodied ritualized performative gestures but also as authoritarian inscriptions etched onto the body. The rape of indentured women, for example, or severe punishments such as the withholding of food for supposed derelictions of duty further erode the life of the workers, contributing to the process of slow death that reinforces the expendability of labor and perpetuates the imperial state.[49]

Resting on the Enlightenment conception of the human being as the bearer of juridical freedom and abstract equality, Marx's notion of abstract labor requires necropolitical conditions of subjugation as a supplement or prosthesis. As Lee puts it, "The notion of abstract equality [and freedom] creates a marketplace of labor commodities and, in turn, undergirds the possibility of surrogate and prosthetic labor."[50] This surrogate or prosthetic labor is not only fundamentally racialized but also rendered interchangeable. Necropolitics converts workers into surrogates for one another and into prosthetics for those who are serviced by their deaths. The individual operates as a disposable, interchangeable "coolie Sammy" or "Hottentot" whose body becomes the prosthesis that extends the master's reach.

A brief examination of the politics of suicide might allow us to more fully flesh out the relationship between necropolitics and plantation labor. Beginning with the little we know about suicides among slaves, I focus on what has been seen as an unusual characteristic of indentured servitude in Natal: the high suicide rates in the late 1800s and early 1900s. The rates in Natal were second only to those in Fiji and far exceeded the rates in other British colonies, such as Jamaica and Mauritius. Although the exact number of suicides is difficult to determine, Surendra Bhana and Arvinkumar Bhana estimate that the average number per year increased in the late 1890s, from approximately thirteen to about thirty-four between 1900 and 1910. The years with the most documented suicides were 1906 and 1907, with forty-six and fifty-one, respectively. In 1904, the *Indian Opinion* called for a commission of enquiry to be established to investigate the high suicide rates, especially the thirty-one deaths that had occurred the previous year. While their call was not answered, it set in place a series of racial concerns and associations between South African Indians and suicide that persists today.

Historical records show that Cape slaves (of various backgrounds) also routinely committed suicide. The Landdrost and his representatives investigated each suicide for two reasons: to ensure that slaves did in fact die at their own hands, not from mistreatment or murder; and to dissuade slaves from considering suicide. Thus, we have a fairly reliable record of slaves' deaths from which to theorize the necropolitics of the plantation. The numbers documented by Worden are comparable to the rates almost a century later among "Indian" indentured servants. Some fifteen to twenty suicides were reported each year. Worden notes that rates rose during periods characterized by an escalation of the demands of labor placed on slaves—the 1730s, 1740s, and 1780s. He asserts that suicide was most common among those foreign-born men on whom the heaviest demands were placed and who were not fully acculturated to the particular "topography of cruelty." Bhana and Bhana argue similarly with regard to indentured Indians that if "the conditions were satisfactory, the system operated relatively smoothly. It was when conditions became intolerable that the system generated alienation. . . . Suicides, then, were likely to take place on estates where conditions were bad, and where individuals felt absolutely trapped."[51]

I argue that, for the most part, slaves and indentured servants did not commit suicide in response to abnormal abuse or particularly onerous demands on their labor. Their deaths fulfilled the necropolitical logic of slavery in which slaves and other laborers were always already disposable and all labor was injurious and on a continuum with death. Slaves and indentured servants who killed themselves were indeed responding to the terror of their situation, but this terror was commonplace. Each and every slave had just as much reason to commit suicide in light of the "slow death" that is necropolitical labor. Borrowing the term from Berlant, who defines it as the physical wearing out and deterioration of people that comes to define them, "slow death" is the experience of necropolitical labor in which one's death ensures the lives of others.[52] Reminding us not to dismiss any single suicide, Jasbir Puar asks, "[What if we] 'slow' the act of suicide down—to offer a concomitant yet different temporality of relating to living and dying"?[53] We are thus forced to conclude that suicide does not really constitute a sudden crisis of plantation epistemology. These deaths did not rupture the plantation mode of production; on the contrary, they were a byproduct of the necropolitical system. As Eric Cazdyn argues about capitalism, crises occur not when things go wrong but when things go right: "Crises are built right into many systems themselves; systems are structured so that crises will occur, strengthening and reproducing the systems themselves. . . . [The] breakdown in relations is built back up again by a different set of relations within the same system."[54] While morally and administratively inconvenient, suicide often served the interest of the plantations on a superstructural level. It became the language of the exceptional instead of the everyday. Framed as individual crises that supposedly did not extend beyond a specific moment and place, suicide obscured the quotidian violence of plantation labor. Thus, the taking of one's own life was considered a managed crisis of behavior rather than a vivid articulation of the intolerable conditions, the slow death of necropolitical labor.

Such attempts to reduce suicides to exceptional acts committed in response to exceptional conditions were consolidated by the treatment of the suicide victims' bodies. Photographed, documented, investigated, and legally classified, the suicide victim was folded back into the system of necropolitical labor. The dead body became a marker of the expendability of the slave, a crudely articulated gestural repertoire insisting that the value of the laboring body lay only in its enabling of the (way of) life of others. To discourage other workers from committing suicide, the bodies of the suicide victims were left to decompose in highly visible locations, such as hanging from a tree or strategically placed in the Cape execution grounds. An illustration of this treatment occurred in 1786, Worden tells us, when the Landdrost of Swellendam proposed that the body of a slave woman who had drowned herself be made a spectacular example. The recovered woman's body was laid on a plank to decompose "to frighten the other slaves and hopefully by this spectacle they will change their minds if any thoughts of also taking such actions may lie within them."[55] The postmortem continuation of the violence inflicted on the slave body showed that even in death, the slave was working to ensure the survival of exploitative systems of labor. As we move from life to death, only the type of (necropolitical) labor changes: from the productive labor of the living body to the spectacular labor of the dead body.

The similarities abound between suicide among slaves and later indentured servants. Both groups were forced to survive the cruel conditions of "unfree" contractual and non-contractual labor, and they both committed suicide at similarly high rates. Both groups preferred hanging as a method of suicide, and the rates were higher among foreign-born workers with memories of working outside the plantation. Yet little attention has been paid to these performative reverberations across time and the country. Rather, suicide suddenly appears among Indian indentured workers in the nineteenth century with its only precedent being a cultural and genetic essentialism that supposedly renders the coolie's Oriental mind more liable to break. The supposed lack of emotional and physical sensitivity of the slave, who became cast only as black, erased the high incidence of suicide among slaves from the historical record, and this elision further contributed to the developing racist narrative of exceptionality around indentured Indians' suicide rates.

The Logic of Suicide

In 1956, *Drum Magazine* published an article titled, "Why Do Indians Kill Themselves?" in which the author, G. R. Naidoo, describes various instances of suicide, such as that of nine-year-old Savithree David, who set herself on fire, and those of the five Toplan sisters, who were found hanging from wild fig trees. The story leads with head shots of the five sisters captioned, "The day of gloom Durban's five Toplan sisters hanged themselves from two fig trees started what seemed an endless trail of Indian suicides that shocked people of all races."[56] The photographs of Kamalachie, Lilly, Thavern, Dolly, and Baby Toplan are reduced to the women's heads, which were cropped from various photographs and laid out next to each other, like signposts. Absent is any context for the floating heads in white space, any relationship between them, and, strikingly, any hint of a body. These uncanny, almost surreal images, accompanied by only the women's first names, add to the sensationalism of the article. However, the images are very different from the majority of the photographs that follow. Take, for example, the photo of Appal Naidoo, which depicts a serious man dressed in a shirt and tie gazing into the camera. The caption includes his full name and his method of suicide: "hanged himself from syringa tree." The rest of the images are similar to this one,[57]

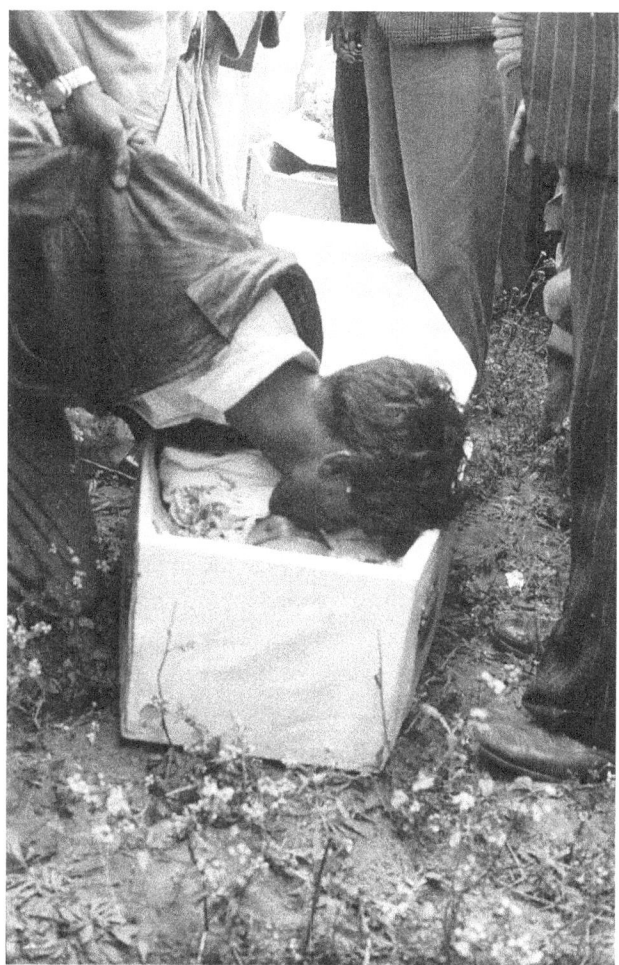

"Kisten Toplan Bids Farewell," 1955. © Bailey's African History Archives.
Photograph by Ranjith Kally.

with the caption always including a full name and method of suicide. As Jon
Soske notes, these images are startling in their familiarity; they resemble the
photographs of indentured Indians taken by the Indian protector that gave
the name of the plantation and the method of death. Soske sees Naidoo's article as "pandering to an almost voyeuristic interest in things 'Indian.' . . . Naidoo's piece illustrates a process characteristic of both colonial social science
and Indian nationalism: the reinterpretation of religious and social practices
in terms of a unitary cultural tradition, which then circulated as a general

matrix through which to interpret Indian behaviour. Experts quoted in the story referenced factors such as poverty and high unemployment. But the article's central explanation for the suicide rate among Indians was a crisis of 'tradition.'"[58]

Soske and others point out that Indianness came to have meaning through ritual enactments of an imaginary culture in need of protection from the erosive forces of modernity. These imaginary reinvestments in Indianness did not reproduce India in various locations across space and time. Instead, they resulted in coerced performances of racialization based on difference from blackness and the loss of cultural authenticity. As Sandhya Shukla argues, "The specificity of an [Indian] subjectivity was based on an idea of ['Indians'] being distinct from 'blacks,' having never been subjected to plantation slavery, and, indeed, as having come . . . as free laborers in response to labor shortages."[59] Forgotten in this dualistic construction of Indianness and blackness were the slaves from Goa and other parts of Asia who worked in Cape Town and on the surrounding plantations. Forgotten were the links among various kinds of labor that enabled capitalist exploitation. Indianness retreated from complex politicized structures of belonging and alliance formed around political and social goals of equity. By writing over the everyday exchanges between (former) indentured servants and indigenous Africans, Indianness came to signify a singular cultural authenticity that needed to be preserved at all costs. This monolithic sign of India as racialized ethnic nationalism and cultural homogeneity violently subsumed deep differences in class, community, caste, and religion.[60]

The development of "Indian" as a monolithic ethnic category was further consolidated by a purported tendency toward suicide. As Arjun Appadurai astutely points out, the mechanism of violence encounters the instability of bodily difference by fixing it in its role as racial/ethnic category for which the body stands in.[61] As one such mechanism, suicide becomes naturalized as culturally "Indian," and a racialized "Indianness" comes to mean, among other things, the proclivity toward suicide. Indians' purported tendencies toward suicide were deemed "cultural," and in turn acts of suicide were evidence of their Asianness. Despite a vast amount of information gathered by district surgeons, resident magistrates, the Office of the Protector, and the planters themselves that suggested other contributing factors, colonial governments resorted to cultural explanations for the large number of suicides. Officials deployed rationales such as cultural tendencies toward alcohol and cannabis use and racialized explanations of pathology and criminality. For instance, the Protector of Immigrants noted:

> The character or temperament of some Indians . . . is such that quite trivial circumstances are sufficient to cause them to threaten to take their lives—a threat too often put into execution. . . . Such men [of the beggar class] will not accept work although they might readily obtain it, and seem to prefer the unsettled life, with its attendant miseries of begging. Eventually apparently, they tire of the existence they have made so little effort to render useful or happy, and put an end to it in some isolated bush or deserted hut.[62]

Something about the innate character of the Indian meant that his or her suicide was a result of difficult-to-separate cultural/racial tendencies, as Julie Parle argues, with "'race' serv[ing] as a self-evident explanation for the behaviour that might otherwise have required closer investigation and intervention by the state."[63] This logic was so much a part of the historiography of Natal indenture that Bhana and Bhana felt compelled almost a century later to address whether the high rate of suicide among indentured Indians was linked to culture and religion. They conclude that, "whereas for the Muslim, Islam took an unequivocal stand [against suicide], for the Hindu there was ambiguity if only because Hinduism condoned suicide under special circumstances."[64] A page later, however, they state that to "the extent that Hinduism determined culturally acceptable behaviour, religion may have influenced suicide. [Given that most suicides were by hanging from a tree,] the choice of a tree may bear some relationship to religiously sanctioned suicide for Hindus . . . , [as] hanging from a tree called 'Vata' (the tree of death) was permissible."[65] Thus, even as Bhana and Bhana attempt to resist the attribution of cultural/racial meaning to suicide, they unwittingly replicate the hegemonic logic that embeds suicide in the language and ideology of race and nation.

The tight coupling of Indianness and suicidal proclivities was further strengthened by the minimal investigation of suicide rates among the rest of South Africa's population groups. As Parle suggests, imperial documentation of suicide was linked to the various governing practices across increasing calcified racial categories. Thus, it was in the state's interest to record suicides among indentured servants for repatriation purposes to India. This contrasts with suicides among white populations, which were largely ignored to protect familial privacy, and suicides among indigenous Africans, whom the colonial government was unable to wholly police or monitor. Parle notes that, due to the relative autonomy of the indigenous African laborers and the limitations of direct colonial management colonial officials relied heavily on chiefs and headmen to inform them of suicides and other untimely deaths. African leaders were actually fined if they failed to report such deaths. "For instance," Parle writes, "when in 1876 in the Magisterial District of Ladysmith, 'Mabala's daughter' killed herself before her wedding ceremony, it was not the matter of her suicide that provoked the ire of the Secretary of Native Affairs, but the failure of the (unnamed) chief, his *induna*, Beje, and the official witness who would have attended the wedding, to report the death. They were fined £25, £10 and £5, respectively."[66]

The "invisibility" of indigenous Africans' suicides helped perpetuate racist stereotypes of a people supposedly incapable of experiencing suffering and therefore not likely to resort to suicide. The few cases that we catch a glimpse of are all the more poignant: the young Banonile, about whom Chief Manqamu kaSomelomo testified in 1909, "She told me that her 'heart' had directed her to cut her throat and accordingly she did so. . . . I asked if she had not quarreled with her husband that she committed such an act and she repeated, 'No, chief, my heart made me do it!'" or Bafilile kaMpepo, who hanged herself after donning her gorgeous beadwork.[67] The absence of suicide from official records became a racialized marker of a black population incapable of deep and subtle grief and pain.

As Parle goes on to develop, imperial record keepers were not sincerely concerned about the victims who were part and parcel of a necropolitical labor force. The apparent concern of these imperial agents instead masked various strategies of governance in which racialized groups were monitored and the findings documented in various sites, such as the offices of Crimes and Statistics Tried by Magistrates and the records of the Indian Protector.[68] Partly because indentured laborers were alleged to be more prone to suicide, they were subject to much more state surveillance than indigenous Africans or whites, which, in turn, contributed to the hypervisibility of Indian suicides. This surveillance began even before workers embarked on their voyage across the Indian Ocean. Specially appointed medical staff analyzed the health of potential indentured laborers, and the transportation ships (some of which had been used during the slave trade) were renovated and restocked to meet carefully calculated specifications regarding ventilation, allocated space, quantity of rations, and amount of water. In the world of speculative finance that was slavery, how a slave died during transportation was crucial in determining whether investors recovered insurance money. For coolie laborers, it was critical that as many reach their destination as possible, as they were not insurable property. What was guaranteed was their labor, and if any of the laborers were found "defective" for any reason (sick, mentally unstable, and so on) when they arrived, they were returned to India on the next ship. Their lives were no more valuable than the lives of slaves. Both groups were disposable, with the injury and trauma of their work operating on a continuum with death. The difference lay in when and where these workers were expendable.

But what led some indentured workers and slaves to kill themselves and others not to? How do we understand where and when agency enters into acts of suicide? The space opened up by rethinking crisis and "slow death" allows for the reconceptualization of normative agency to include what Berlant describes as "activity exercised within spaces of ordinariness that does not always or even usually follow the literalizing logic of visible effectuality, bourgeois dramatics, and the lifelong accumulation or fashioning." Traditionally, suicide gets read as the ultimate form of victimization and sacrifice, where one's inability to exert one's will results in an abandonment of will altogether. In other words, suicide can be conceptualized as the ultimate surrender to forces outside oneself, as one realizes one has no real agency. Suicide can also, paradoxically, be understood as the ultimate instantiation of free will on the part of slaves, indentured and inboekstelsel. Suicide victims can be seen as those determined and brave few who asserted their erased agency in one of the only ways that might have an impact on the colonial capitalist, the deathly cessation of their value as commodity and labor. To a certain extent, this interruption of capital did happen. Suicides, unlike the "natural" death rate of necropolitical labor, resulted in official investigations and documentation of the various conditions that could have led to the deaths. The Reynolds Brothers plantation had to make changes to its labor practices after various investigations of their laborers' suicides.[69] Thus, suicide as agency can be romanticized as tragic, heroic acts of defiance or tragic, heroic instances of defeat. It can be conceptualized as the absolute abandonment or the ultimate instantiation of will.

Yet what happens if we step away from the intentional subject, from the fantasy that life is lived and expressed in what Berlant calls "modes of effective agency that ought justly to be and are ultimately consequential or performatively sovereign"? What happens when we confront the breakdown of traditional notions of agency represented by suicide, as well as the overwhelming knowledge that the historical will of those who committed suicide remains illegible? Whereas Berlant concludes with a bleak vision of life as attrition, motivated only by making a terrible experience less bad or finding momen-tarily relief, such as in drug addiction, I want to turn, as I do throughout this book, toward performances embodied in historical fiction. Through perfor-mance I want to gesture toward a concept of will that does not replicate he-roic notions of agency but nonetheless represents an alternative to the death worlds of capitalism. The multilayered "afterlife" of history thus beckons as I turn to historical fiction and other performative moments to eschew the fic-tion of access implicit in the archive and to critically imagine possibilities of agency that recognize the fictiveness of recovery.

Performing Mati Work: Ruthie, Lindiwe, and the Secret Room

This chapter concludes with the conjuring of a ghostly "afterlife," with a mo-ment in which a community of indentured descendants critically imagine a limited form of agency through ritual, religious faith, and sexual desire. Given my repeated encounters with archival silences around the will of indentured servants and suicide victims, I turn instead to those who survive them, those who go on living with the knowledge of their ancestors' struggles held close. The contemporary writer Agnes Sam is the great-granddaughter of one of those indentured laborers. In a blog post titled "What Does Your Father Do?" Sam tells us that her ancestors "were peasants. They were illiterate. They worked from four in the morning until seven at night. They weren't paid in money, but with rice. They are buried in unmarked graves in South Africa. But their labour has brought each of us to where we are today. That is nothing to be ashamed of."[70] Insisting that "we weren't taught our history in S[outh] A[frica]," Sam mentions her search for records of her family in archives across the country. Finding them largely incomplete, she turns to older people in the family, asking what they can recollect. She writes, "These oral histories may be dimly remembered, but somewhere within those memories may be a nugget of information." Between archival records and nuggets of memory, Sam finds confirmation that her great-grandfather was "shanghaied as a child from Indian to South Africa" and remained in indenture from the date of his arrival in 1860 to his release in 1913, some fifty-three years.[71]

Sam's collection *Jesus Is Indian and Other Short Stories* begins with the absent presence of her great-grandfather. She provides us with the silences necessary to imagine this kidnapped little boy and the unfree man who emerged fifty-three years later, finally able to sell his labor in the so-called free market. While her grandfather is the impetus behind her collection, Sam focuses instead on tracing the lives of indentured women and their descendants and the conversion of some of these women to Christianity to ensure that the state (which refused to recognize Hindu and Muslim marriages) will recognize their children as legal heirs. She thus broadens out the notion of indenture to include not just the experience of the cane fields but also the struggles of these workers' descendants to negotiate the repressive state. "High Heels," the opening story of *Jesus Is Indian*, forces the reader to confront the embodied navigations of power performed by these descendants. In speaking to their particular concerns, the story does not conflate indenture with slavery but also does not gloss over the violent coercion that characterizes daily living. Specifically using the theme of forcible religious conversion, Sam describes a community's struggle to assert some limited form of (queer) agency through ritual practice, belief, and sexuality. Sam links these converted women, born in South Africa, to the biblical character of Ruth, whom she calls the epitome of the "migrant wife." She thus identifies them as displaced even when at home, marginalized even while necessary, forgotten even as they remember. Sam quotes a passage from Ruth 1:16: "Entreat me not to leave thee, or to return from following after thee: for whither thou goest, I will go; and where thou lodgest I will lodge; thy people shall be my people, and thy God my God" (13). The protagonist of "High Heels," a young Indian girl who desperately wants to be included in the boys' game of street cricket, is thus appropriately named Ruthie.

Ruthie is mesmerized by the bright red high-heel shoes with peep toes and shiny buckles that her friend Lindiwe, or Lindi, is wearing to impress the boys. While the boys fail to notice the shoes or Lindi's girlish "sexy" stance, Ruthie pretends to keep her eyes shut while staring at the shoes until she "can't stand to look . . . anymore" (14). "High Heels" is as much a story about a gendered, sexualized, and raced notion of will as it is about indentured Indians' conversion and beliefs. Lindi immediately retracts her offer to let Ruthie try the shoes on, and Ruthie is left angry and screaming in the middle of the cricket game. Now fixated on the shoes and Lindi, Ruthie no longer has any interest in being "the last man" or the "first man" to bat; she goes inside her home only to notice for the first time that there is a locked door behind the now open curtain at the end of the passage, and her mother's sandals are outside the door. Anxious to get back at Lindi for not sharing her shoes, Ruthie excitedly tells Lindi about the door, even as they both realize that Ruthie has no idea what lies behind it. Refusing to be impressed, Lindi replies that she also has a secret door and knows but will not tell what lies behind it.

"Ya have to open it yourself," she tells a frustrated Ruthie (16). After much cajoling, Lindi agrees to give Ruthie the shoes if Ruthie can discover what is behind the door before her birthday in three days.

Ruthie's brother Paul tells her that behind the secret door is a dark, dark room with a dark, dark bed in which an old, old lady lies. The other boys argue that the room is a cupboard, a lavatory, the entrance to a secret tunnel. Ruthie's desire for Lindi's red shoes grows and grows. Her mother's shoes fit only if one does not look at the back; no other birthday present will suffice—Ruthie wants the shiny, red high heels or nothing. On Saturday, after Lindi urges Ruthie to give up, Ruthie destroys her mother's room in search of the key to the secret door. She empties drawers, throws pillows on the ground, dumps out the contents of her mother's trinket box and, in the process, breaks a pearl necklace. The mother, Hama, angrily decides that there will be no birthday party, despite attempts by Ruthie's father, Tata, to mollify both her and Ruthie. Eventually, Tata takes Ruthie's hand, moves aside the curtain, unlocks the door with the key that is above the doorframe, and removes his and Ruthie's shoes.

Sam writes: "I turn the handle and we go through the secret door. I've gone through the door" (22). The same action is described twice using different tenses—"go" and "gone"—and separated by a paragraph break in the original text, suggesting a temporal and epistemic break or chasm. Behind the door is a hidden Hindu prayer room. Ruthie runs out to Lindi to claim her red shoes, and she rushes to show Father O'Malley the room, her actions revealing that although she knows what lies behind the secret door, she does not understand its significance. Lindi refuses to hand over the shoes until Ruthie understands the reason that the prayer room is concealed. "What's a use of gwain through the door," Lindi says, "if ya don't know the secret?" (23). In other words, seeing and understanding are two different things. While Ruthie has seen, she clearly has not yet understood.

Various scholars such as Pallavi Rastogi have suggested that the hidden prayer room puts the past into conversation with the present. For Rastogi, the hidden prayer room "recovers the history of many indentured Indians"—those who were forced to convert to Christianity and those who, via a concealment of their cultural practices, assimilated into mainstream society. For Ronit Frenkel, the prayer room is further evidence of the *geniza* world these women are forced to create as, like the biblical Ruth, they adapt to strange lands and strange customs.[72] Frenkel suggests, "The closed geniza room is reinvented in this context as one in which arcane knowledge systems may be stored or secret heretical selves may be maintained."[73] Ruthie's entrance into the prayer room, according to Rastogi, therefore symbolizes "South Africa's discovery of its subcontinental population as one whose Indianness may be harbored under several layers of assimilation, but which nevertheless refuses to be eradicated."[74] In other words, the prayer room functions as an alternative archive, chronicling not only the presence of indentured Indians in South Africa but also their obscured legacies and forgotten resistance. The discovery of the prayer room becomes a powerfully seductive device that shows the will of a subjugated people who never stopped fighting back. This is undoubtedly a crucial aspect of "High Heels." However, I would take this reading one step further by arguing that, through its foregrounding of performance and desire, "High Heels" queers this literary project of recovery.

My use of the word "queer" does not simply translate into a retrieval of hidden "gay" identity that would result in a simplistic reading of the relationship between Ruthie and Lindi as "proto"-lesbian in some way. While retaining the term's links to non-normative desire, I wish to move away from individual bodies, their choices of sexual objects, and the resulting identitarian categories. As Roderick Ferguson discusses, those communities whose trajectory departs from Western teleological narratives of individuals "coming out" as political subjects are denigrated as backward, homophobic, or not truly liberated.[75] Instead, in the spirit of Audre Lorde, I am using the term "queer" here to mark disruptions to racial, gender, and sexual norms that, as Natasha Tinsley reminds us, enable "connecting in ways that commodified flesh was never supposed to [and] forging interpersonal connections that counteract imperial desires for Africans' living deaths."[76] Queer as embodied, ritual performance of desire—as what Jafari Allen calls "a site of knowledge production and energy, which is alternative to regimes of the state and received culture"[77]—denaturalizes race and gender to expose their cacophonous contradictions.

I am puzzled by why none of the theoretical readings of "High Heels" address the titular shoes and what they represent. As the primary unit of exchange and object of desire between the two girls, the shoes should direct our attention to processes of gendering and other kinds of self-making. Lindi's gendered performance of beauty and sexuality results in Ruthie's desire not only *to be like* Lindi, but also *for* Lindi. This desire is displaced on the shoes, which are accessible only via the secret represented by the locked door.[78] The shoes and, by extension, the secret behind the door are therefore fetishized. The ensuing erotic challenge between the two girls to keep the shoes and to obtain them is paralleled by the struggle to keep the secret of the prayer room and the discovery and revelation of this secret.

In queer theory, the notion of the secret has its theoretical equivalent in the discourse of the closet. Here the Western modern subject marks his individual entrance into the political realm of rights by emerging from the locked door of the closet and claiming a same-sex object choice as a gay identity in the public realm.[79] Such a "liberated" subject supposedly leaves behind more primitive modes of expressing desire where closeted individuals refuse to enter into the public realm for various reasons including shame and fear. As Marlon Ross so astutely points out, "The 'coming out' or closet paradigm . . . fix[es] homosexual identification . . . because it enables this powerful narrative of progress, not only in terms of the psychosexual [and sociopolitical] development of an individual . . . but also more fundamentally as a doorway marking the threshold between up-to-date fashions of sexuality and all the outmoded, anachronistic others."[80]

Ross goes on to argue that "coming out" may not play the essential role that dominant discourses assume because the binary between secrecy and revelation proves inadequate when addressing the complex realities of racialized subjects. Rather than knowing/not knowing or in/out, he suggests a continuum of knowing that varies according to degree, audience, context, and time. For Ruthie, being able to "out" the secret prayer room proves inextricable from obtaining the fetish onto which she displaced her desire—Lindi's shoes. After experiencing Tata's ritual performance inside the prayer-room (to which I will return), she immediately runs out into public space to reveal the secret and claim the shoes. She expects that her "coming out" will guarantee her the queer object of her desire. Instead of a simple exchange of information for shoes, however, Lindi petulantly moves away from binaries toward an understanding of knowledge as operating on a continuum. It is not enough to know that the prayer room exists; one must comprehend why is it a secret, when is it a secret, and to whom is it a secret. Lindi asserts early on in the story that she and most of the community know what lies beyond the door. In other words, the practicing of Hinduism by Christians is an open secret, like the pervasiveness of non-normative desire that permeates all communities.

Gloria Wekker, in her work on Surinamese women, identifies what she terms "mati" work, that is, a system of erotically charged relationships, sexual and non-sexual, between women that does not result in identitarian categories. Mati, a creolization of the Dutch *maatjie* or *maat* meaning "friend" or "mate," is a performance of work that recognizes and nurtures the desire between two women but that does not preclude relationships with other partners, male or female. Ruthie and Lindi's relationship, fueled by an eroticism signaled by the red shoes, constitutes a form of mati work—two girls loving each other, desiring each other and protecting each other. Despite the fact that it might result in the loss of her shoes, Lindi helps Ruthie understand the significance of the prayer room and prevents her from showing the room to Father O'Malley. Lindi never denies Ruthie's desire but instead engages with it in multiple ways that are playful, sometimes tender, and occasionally self-centered. As an everyday form of self-making and community formation, the girls' mati work energizes and influences their various social groups.

Jafari Allen writes that "transcendent erotics and politics insist on the creation of a new space, which may become a political organization or a heretical theoretical paradigm, but also may be a new name that defies, reappropriates or refuses old labels, or a complex of acts beyond what is interpolated within prevailing ideologies."[81] Ruthie and Lindi's desire creates just such a space, disrupting the boundary of in/out, concealment/revelation. Instead of the prayer room being a "dark dark" tomb, it becomes a site of alternate embodied performance where the repertoire of practices constitutes important systems of knowing and transmitting knowledge. Consider Sam's description of Tata praying:

> Tata lifts the red glass chimney from the lamp. He strikes a match. A yellow flame leaps up. He lights the lamp. Then he touches the orange stone. It has two hollows. Tata takes a handful of grey powder from one hollow and places it in the other. Then he strikes another match. Again a yellow flame leaps up. He puts the flame to the powder. Blue smoke curls up into the room. Tata says, "Saamberani" . . . Then Tata sits cross-legged on a red cushion . . . I kneel on the cushion [next to him]. He joins his hands and begins to sing softly. (22)

Ruthie describes a sensual tactile way of knowing that locates agency and desire not only in the individual body but also in the ritualized performance of collective belief. This is a collective belief, not only in other gods, but also in the ability of subjugated peoples to remember the somatic and verbal language of ritual engagement. Sometimes, groups faithfully repeat behaviors and pass them on, even when the memory of their meaning has been forgotten and lives only in ritual acts. Diana Taylor reminds us that "cultural memory is . . . a practice, an act of imagination and interconnection . . . Memory is embodied and sensual, that is conjured through the senses; it links the deep private with social, even official practices."[82]

The presence of an image of Jesus in the corner of the prayer room is therefore significant. As Taylor writes, certain religious performances "seem to be transferred and reproduced within the very symbolic system designed to eliminate them . . . The transfers occurred not just in the uneasy tensions between religious systems but within the religious systems themselves."[83] Thus what appears to be the parents' performance of acquiescence to Christianity represented by Father O'Malley could actually represent a performance of multiple allegiances that cannot be reduced to a binary of true belief/false belief. The prayer room represents a queer desire (for freedom) that does not necessarily rupture imperial rule but that nevertheless acknowledges self and community by foregrounding remembered and re-performed erotic acts of creation. Yvette Christianse's stunning historical novel *Unconfessed* takes up this challenge of remembering and performing queer communities in the next chapter.

BECOMING UNDONE

Performances of Vulnerability

> I am a small boat bobbing just there off Cape Town. . . . I have come
> to pick up Hester and her babies. . . . Kom, Hester. I am your boat. . . .
> Come, Hester.
> —YVETTE CHRISTIANSE, *UNCONFESSED*, 76

The snow was falling, and her month-old son was crying in his crib. Rocking
herself back and forth on the floor near the closet, she resorted to sticking her
fingers in her ears. Nothing she did made any difference. She knows now that
her son was hungry (the carefully measured recommended ounces of breast
milk were woefully inadequate) and that he hates being alone when he sleeps.
But it was January and she knew nothing other than her despair and longing
for home were so deep that they followed her into every room. They were
her only companions as her mother was far away. She missed the scent of salt
in the air, the curling heat of a Durban day that burned the soles of her bare
feet. She was *hertseer* (heart sore) and sick of the cold. Her month-old son
was crying in his crib. All she could focus on was the messiness of the house,
the hurt of her body, and how fragile she felt. The woman began to fantasize
about opening the window and carefully tossing the baby out. He would land
softly on the ground, his eyes startled wide open. The snow would quickly fill
his mouth, muffling him and eventually drowning that incessant crying. She
would not have to fight her tremendous desire to be elsewhere, the urge to
pinch and hit at him and the ache that he widened with every blasted wail.

Across the ocean, in the dance performance *Cargo*, Levern Botha dances vulnerability as she imaginatively embodies Sila van de Kaap's attempts to drown her children and herself. Botha as Sila moves her arms like broken wings, tries to pirouette, runs across mud and water, and falls. When lying on the ground, Botha arches the small of her back and reaches out with both arms, only to bring them back empty. Her arms are full of loss as she enacts a painful and complex genealogy of black performance and loving, joy, and vulnerability. Botha repeats this sequence for the length of her solo.

The snowbound mother and son both survived that time, though far from intact. Now she knows, without a single doubt, that if need be she would kill *for* her son and, perhaps even more difficult, *live* for him and for herself. Her son shines in the light; he is a gorgeous chocolate river. He has many mothers who have helped him learn how to swim and know when to listen. He still does not sleep well, though now he and the mother reach for each other in those morning hours when the ghosts are too thick and good days feel too far away. She is careful to avoid open windows during this time, as the specters bring fresh waves of loss. She hears what they call her, and it catches in her throat: the woman who wanted to drown her child in snow.

But this chapter does not originate only with this mother and son. It starts and ends, pauses and stalls with the archival trace of Sila van de Kaap cutting the throat of her nine-year-old son, Baro, the day before Christmas in 1822. It begins with Sila talking to the dead Baro during her imprisonment on Robben Island. It also springs from the terrifying story of Hester, who came before Sila. On August 16, 1819, Hester jumped into the ocean at Roggeberg with her three children. She had filled their pockets with stones. The day was windy, and her children's eyes were wide open. Men rescued her and one child. Different men then proceeded to try and sentence her with "all possible speed" to death by strangulation. They wrapped a leather strap around her throat, Sila narrates, and pulled at opposite ends to strangle her before they "threw her [back] into the sea."[1] Colonial authorities chose the how, where, and when of Hester's death. Their interruption of her suicide was meant not to reaffirm the value of her life but, rather, to reiterate her lack of value and the meaninglessness of her death. We know nothing of the rescued child.

Sila van de Kaap, gazing on the choppy water of Table Bay on a windy day, narrates this to her dead son, Baro, in Yvette Christianse's novel *Unconfessed*, and we overhear. Sila tells Baro this story perhaps so he can forgive her taking his life. She tells Baro about being hertseer. We listen trembling over the sound of waves, desperate to understand. Between Hester's case in 1819 and Sila's case in 1823, at least three other women were brought to trial in South Africa for the killing of children. These years were not particularly exceptional; mothers killed their children before and after this period, although the circumstances that brought these women to trial were historically specific. Perhaps this chapter, then, is not about mothers wanting to kill or killing their children. Maybe this final chapter is about love in the face of devaluation, commodification, and abuse. This love gracefully traverses the borders of life and death and biological kinship, affiliation, and property. This chapter follows the stories of women who recognize a similar vulnerability in others and learn to painstakingly construct community based on that recognition. After all, as Sila reminds us, "What is there if we who live like this do not cling to each other? What is there if we cannot trust each other? What makes us betray each other?" (279).

Illegibility of Will in the Archive (Reprise)

In his essay "The Colonel and the Slave Girls," James Bradley chronicles his attempt to assemble histories from a lack of adequate source materials. He writes, "Charged . . . with the duty of reclaiming the past for the present, and creating living voices for the deathly voiceless, we run headlong into the effects of power, sometimes totalizing, sometimes fragmentary, but always working to efface any sense we gain of whole subjects with discernable selves."[2] Indeed, "Colonial archives always impose their own logics of legibility," as Christianse suggests in her critical essay "Heartsore."[3] Thus, Sila van den Kaap could not simply be retrieved from within the archive and her absent life thickly described. Relegated to criminal disturbance, her thoughts, her feelings, and her very being appear nowhere. In the plenitude of paper that is the archive, what is documented is less a trace where a black woman might be than the bureaucracy of imperial rule itself. In other words, the colonial archive does a fantastic job of documenting itself and its inability to recognize certain lives as relevant.

Contemporary archivists at the Cape Archives, which are currently under the jurisdiction of the National Archives and Records Service of South Africa (NARS), have a different agenda. Insisting that South Africans have a right to their pasts, current archivists are part of the push to foster a postapartheid nationalism that is complete with proud histories of struggle and triumph. Their work seems persistently to exclaim, "Look at how much we have endured and overcome to become South African citizens." However NARS's agenda is often thwarted. The documents it catalogues point toward global flows of capital that undercut the illusion of discrete national entities. For those subject to the past who seek their "proud histories," the archive is full of significant silences. Stephanie Li writes about her search for something that resembles "their own words" in legal arguments involving property rights and inheritance. Amid pages and pages of documents, all she finds is "a crooked, unsteady 'X'" where the signatures of women of color should have been. Li writes, "Each X stopped me. They broke the surrounding lines of easy, sloping cursive, interrupting pages of text that said so little, and yet these Xs seemed to say still less."[4] Each X deepens the silence, pointing toward an archival plenitude that failed to include certain people as subjects, as well as toward a historical absence that resulted from a failure of attention or deliberate erasure. In "Heartsore," Christianse describes Li's "X" as "a triple discursive imprisonment: black female slave. Each term designates a structure of foreclosure, a mode of categorical exclusion from the full and putatively universal subjecthood of a 'free white male.'"[5] Archival histories with their problems of absence and presence can never reveal the criminalized and supposedly aberrant will of (slave) women of color; they can only gesture to the places where this agency could have and should have been.

How, then, does one approach that place where a woman lingers, the place that Christianse describes as "the place from which . . . speech may emanate but not to be heard, a place in which the muted being is relegated to a position that she must try to make her body signify. . . . How, then, does one approach a story whose referent is constantly circling back and around itself in the archive or, rather, constantly circling the moment in which a slave woman becomes the subject of legal action and punishment, namely that moment in which she killed her son?"[6] The X is not an invitation to fill in the blank. Much in the way that Malcolm deployed his X, it testifies to a historical erasure, to the incommensurability of black experience with traditional historical narratives, to a silence that seethes and bleeds. Sila's will remains inaudible *except*, as I argue throughout this book, through critical imaginative performances such as Christianse's novel or Jazzart Theatre's and Magnet Theatre's collaborative dance piece *Cargo*, discussed in the introduction. These performances do not uncover what "really happened," as these women's wills remain forever illegible. Instead, the performances embody alternative moments in which "will" can surface, in which the afterlife of history conjures nonlinear genealogies of black diasporic performance.

The last page of *Unconfessed* exemplifies this process of critical imaginative performance. In response to the question "*You want to know. What happened to her?*" (341), Christianse gives us an array of possible scenarios for Sila's life, each one poignant, tragic, beautiful, and incomplete. She repeats the refrain "some say," drawing attention to how these possibilities persist as retellings. The characters of the novel, then, reenact these various historical scenarios, like ghostly players, quietly opening a space of performance for Sila's historical narrative. As Bradley says, "It is a live-thing this [performance] space, almost organic, but our actors, shadows or not, must submit to its strictures, its structure and its props. These will present meaning to our audience, who will now understand the sufferings of our captive players, their momentary joys, their daily fears and perhaps, their deepest loves."[7] Stories that have nowhere to go are staged here, and we encounter the possibilities of Sila's life. The performance of "mothering under crisis" demonstrated in Sila's cutting the throat of her son, Baro, reverberates and accrues meaning when experienced with similar performances, such as that of Tryntjie of Madagascar sticking pins into her crying child's body. These instances do not cause each other, but they repeat embodied responses to the violence of subjugation, thus contributing to a black diasporic repertoire. These are performances of survival and vulnerability that expose the jugular and derive immense strength from such precarious openness.

To talk of slave mothers who laughed at, refused to listen to, cut, hacked, sawed, poked, and drowned their children may seem a strange route toward an exegesis of will. However, it is precisely at such moments that the silences around black women's agency are the loudest. As Christianse reminds us, Sila's "failed but effectual attempt to summon the law . . . nonetheless forced some opening through which we can glimpse her, perhaps even hear her, some 150 years later."[8] Throughout *Unconfessed*, the critical "failure" of black bodies and the silences of the archive imaginatively re-create possibilities of will based not just on what has happened in the past but also on what is happening now. The novel rests on the realization, as Darieck Scott suggests, that "if the particular logic of the deed and the world that made it possible has through the passage of time faded like an ancient painting to near invisibility, its frame, capacious and insidiously flexible, still sets the boundaries of our own world. . . . Our freedom is relative and measured by rods other than hers, but we, too, are imprisoned."[9] To speak of killing one's child forces us to confront the thorny issue of will, moving us beyond illusions of choice or self-possession to arrive at a critical fictional landscape that, in Scott's words, can "illuminate the political possibilities [and impossibilities] those devastations enable."[10]

The Politics of Family: My Own Blood

Unconfessed rehearses the racial and sexual dynamics of slavery and its fraught constitution of kinship and property relations. Notions of property were sutured onto patriarchal familial structures by the habitual sexual violence of transatlantic slavery. Various historical moments that operate across time, as C. Riley Snorton writes, construct (and interpret) "black sexuality while simultaneously providing a rationale for contemporaneous technologies for the disciplining and surveill[ance] of black bodies."[11] Consider Christina Sharpe's example of the South Carolina politician and slave owner James Henry Hammond, who carefully documented who was family and who was fungible, despite biological ties to him. In 1839, Hammond purchased eighteen-year-old Sally Johnson and her one-year-old daughter, Louisa. An outspoken white supremacist who wrote virulently against miscegenation, Hammond documented his long-term sexual exploitation not only of Sally, but also of Louisa once she reached twelve. He took care to record which of Sally's and Louisa's children he believed were his offspring or the offspring of his eldest son, Harry. In a letter to Harry quoted by Sharpe, Hammond makes provisions for their fate in the event of his death. Insisting in the language of paternalism that it would be a disservice to free them, he stipulates, "[I] would [not] like that any but *my own blood* should own as Slaves *my own blood* or Louisa. . . . Do not let Louisa or any of my children or possible children be slaves of Strangers. Slavery *in the family* will be their happiest earthly condition."[12] He goes on to write, "Take care of [Louisa] and her children who are both of *your* blood if not of mine. . . . Do not let Louisa or any of my children or possible children be slaves of Strangers."[13]

Hammond insists that both his and his legitimate family's slave offspring be "protected" from strangers by being owned by family. But this should not be mistaken to mean that Hammond and Harry regarded their slave offspring as family. Indeed, as Christopher Peterson writes, "The situation of consanguinity [exists] in the absence of acknowledged paternity."[14] Instead, Hammond's legal argument that his "own blood" should own his "own blood" separates his legal heirs from his children with Sally and Louisa. In a letter to Harry— the son who inherits—Hammond distinguishes between "blood" that can own (genealogy) and "blood" that can be owned (what I will term "pedigree" for clarity). As the basis for a patriarchal legitimacy, the concept of family enables the legal bequest of property, including the inheritance of a privileged social and legal belonging coded as "white." The legal scholar Cheryl Harris identifies this code of social and legal "belonging" as the "possessive invest- ment of whiteness."[15] Harris argues that the legally protected expectations of white privilege become "tantamount to property that could not permis- sibly be intruded upon without consent."[16] Whether or not the slave master's "blood" courses through their veins, slaves' pedigrees mark them as black and thus reproduce their coerced fungible status as property. For the slave, the language of blood indicates kinship while also reinforcing the disinheritance of offspring that, at least legally, are never recognized as kin. Thus, the fol- lowing dichotomies, anchored by the white patriarch's sexuality, are set into play: genealogy versus pedigree, (white) owner versus (black) property, and legitimate family versus enslaved offspring.

In a first scenario, the white patriarch uses his sexuality to ensure his wife's legal and social subjugation, as well as the production of legitimate heirs who will bear the family name. In the second (generally acknowledged but never publicly articulated) scenario, the master's sexuality configures sexual vio- lence as a routine perpetuation of black captivity. The two deployments are constitutive of each other: sexual violence as a form of racialized labor repro- duction is a crucial part of what is passed on legally from father to legitimate son. In a closed circuit of deprivation and abundance, the white son inherits the right to own, which includes the right to rape.

The enslaved child fathered by his or her master is orphaned, kinless with no rights. Hortense Spillers famously postulates that to be kinless is to be de- nied "the vertical transfer of a bloodline, of a patronymic, of titles and entitle- ments, of real estates and the prerogatives of 'cold cash,' from fathers to sons and in the supposedly free exchange of affectional ties between a male and female of his choice."[17] Enslaved black offspring reside in the breach where "'kinship' loses meaning, since it can be invaded at any given and arbitrary moment by . . . property relations."[18] Thus, the slave's status follows the con- dition of the mother; the slave inherits either his or her mother's bondage or her vulnerable and tenuous freedom. One must be careful with Spillers's postulation, however, as it can leave intact a romanticized notion of pure so- cial belonging under attack from property relations. In this model, "kinship" can be seen as analogous to a host cell, and property relations function as the virus that hijacks the cell's workings. I would argue that property relations and kinship acquire meaning only in relation to each other. They *both* are predicated on a similar logic of individual ownership; the jealous lover asserts her ownership of her partner with the claim "mine," just as the slave master claims the slave as his property. Thus, Hammond uses the logic of possessive individualism to articulate both his claims of pedigree on the fungible bodies of his slaves as well as his claims of genealogy on the bonds of family cemented by the transfer of property—"*my* own blood," "*my* children," "*mine.*"

In *Unconfessed*, the crisis that precipitates Sila's killing of Baro also revolves around the distinction between genealogy and pedigree, between ownership and being owned. The killing takes place during the betrothal festivities of Susan Van der Wat, the daughter of the slave master. All of the neighbors are invited, and they gather in front of the house for the various performances of wealth meant to establish the Van der Wat family's social superiority. Everyone's clothes are new or freshly cleaned. Van der Wat's wife asks Sila to fetch her "best jug" for lemonade while Van der Wat shows off his new horse, much to the delight of his youngest son, who also wants to ride. Calling out "Papa," he runs after his father, who lifts him onto the horse. The crowd waves and cheers as the father and son ride to the hill and back in a perfect staging of genealogy (through patrilineal lines) and wealth. The tableau, however, is an illusion. Van der Wat's clothes do not look good on him, no matter how much money he spends on them. His wealth is not just based on slavery but has been stolen from his mother, Oumiesies, not his father: he did not purchase most of his slaves but tricked his mother into giving them to him. He also re-enslaved others whom Oumiesies had freed in her will by destroying the document.

Sila's son, Baro, cuts the only real swath of truth through this tableau of abundance and patriarchy. Sila recounts Baro's actions with disbelief:

> He called out a terrible word that stopped the whole world. *What made him do that?* . . . Everyone, all the neighbors knew that I had come to the farm with three children at my side and one inside me, and Baro was one of the three who came on their own legs. But that day they forgot, I could see and what I saw stopped my heart. They all thought, so, Van der Wat goes to her at night. Why else would their faces have turned the hot summer day to ice? And even when De La Rey tried to laugh it off, the shock remained. And why else would the missus's eyes have gone from her husband to Baro to me to her husband to her guests and back to me? And when she looked at me again, she hated me even more. And when she looked at Baro I saw bad things in her heart. (265)

Baro's terrible word stops the whole world even as it sets in motion a chain of devastating events that lead to Sila's murder of Baro. Sila drops and breaks her mistress's best jug, providing her owners with an excuse to brutally beat her. Baro is then left at the mercy of Van der Wat, who exacts such vicious punishment that the child is seriously injured. Sila repeatedly asks Baro why he uttered what he said: "And you. I see you run after Van der Wat and before you call out I know what is going to come out of your mouth, in front of all those people. *What were you thinking?*" (258). Baro's terrible word could have been somatic, as well as verbal. Perhaps he raised his arms up to Van der Wat to be lifted up as he was overcome by the simple longing of a boy to be publicly acknowledged by a father figure. Perhaps he gave in to the desire for affection instead of violent humiliation, affection for a father on a horse rather than an absent father and a mother treated like a horse. Sila never repeats Baro's terrible word. As readers, we fill in the silence with some version of "papa," some performative utterance that refuses the categories of orphan/social dead/slave. Whatever word we choose, it is merely shorthand for the anguished and "monstrous intimacy" of slavery and the desire for "freedom" and belonging.

In uttering his dreaded word, Baro neither mistakes Van der Wat for his father nor even articulates a desire for a father per se, given the evacuation of the category for the enslaved child. Instead, Baro's terrible word exposes the denial of his legal claims to own himself or anyone else. Baro's word exposes how within the plantation, as Aliyyah Abdur-Rahman writes, slave masters were " 'fathers' to a population for whom legal paternity was not as much mollified as it was vacated."[19] In the face of quotidian violation and limited choice, Baro rearticulates the injury of slavery and the need for redress as a desire for a publicly recognized patrilineal kinship. He attempts to transform the disenfranchising bonds of slavery into the affective ties and legal entitlements of family. Baro might have felt, in Sharpe's words, that he had "no choice but to erase the lack of agency, to turn violation into affection, to be silent about the sadomasochism of everyday black life."[20] Baro's attempts to metamorphose bonds of slavery into familial ties fail, and the events that follow force him to recognize his rejection from the realm of the father and his relegation to the realm of the mother.

Van der Wat is *not* Baro's father, and his role of white master/reproducer of labor banishes Baro's biological father. The possessive individualism at work in both slavery and patriarchal family structure empties out the role of the black father; Baro's father is only briefly mentioned in the novel. In an attempt to give the child a lineage, Sila names Baro after "a box that holds something from my father's people" (118). Although she wishes to provide him with a paternal lineage, she must continually contend with the reality that her children's only legacy is her status as property. Sila writes, "I saw them and their generations chained to each other in a line that went right up into that land, over mountains, through rivers. I felt my body as if it was giving birth to generations already dead" (304). Her children do not inherit freedom. Instead, freedom inherits the logic of slavery. What Saidiya Hartman calls the "stamp of the commodity" haunts Sila's relationship to her children and her children's relationship to their children.[21]

Abdur-Rahman quotes Spillers as saying that slavery was a matrilineal system, with the enslaved black woman functioning as the "principal point of passage between the human and the non-human world."[22] Baro inherits his status as illegitimate, inhuman, and enslaved from Sila, even as she is "ungendered" by the violent labor of slavery that makes her unable to fulfill normative gender requirements of racialized heterosexuality. Matt Richardson argues that this nonconformity to gender expectations is born out of absolute subjugation.[23] It nonetheless can foster some small freedoms from the strictures of gender and family and disabuse blacks of idealized, contractual notions of love, children, and sexuality. Similarly, Darieck Scott writes that the "break that looks to all concerned like *broken* gender and sexuality . . . provides an opportunity for different configurations of gender and sexuality."[24] *Unconfessed* beautifully illustrates this break as an open door that enables Sila to love Lys, another woman imprisoned on Robben Island, and in the numerous stories Sila tells of various slaves in non-normative relationships. For example, she receives word from Philipina, a friend on a former plantation who would "never go with a man" (157). Sila tells Spaasie that Philipina "will care for me and my children as a husband would." Expressing skepticism at this notion of family, Spaasie says, "Philipina will have no one to look after her when she gets old. I said, I will. And my children" (188). In a perfect response to the fictive threat of queer kinlessness, Sila insists on family and inheritance beyond the confines of normative gender formation even as she recognizes the threat of violence that haunts them. She imagines a familial arrangement in which inheritance does not conform to either patriarchy or politics of "blood." In an attempt to sidestep both genealogy and pedigree, Sila gestures toward replacing the discourse of blood with what Peterson calls an ethics of "assuming responsibility." She and her children will be responsible for Philipina even though the hegemonic rationale of "blood" would make them uncaring strangers.

Sila also mentions Isac, the "good man" who "lay with Anthony who would be quieter after but not happier" (157). The source of Anthony's unhappiness lies not in his non-normativity but in his inability to "choose" a sexual partner. It would be inaccurate to call any sexual relations between slaves, whether normative or queer, a "free choice," given that under slavery, as Scott writes, "Agency is criminality and consent is constraint." Scott goes on to say that while "'choice' . . . presupposes a certain (implicitly male) bourgeois subject endowed with certain social status and political rights, the capacity of the slave to 'have' his or her 'own' sexuality . . . is not something that can be assumed."[25] We return once more to the problem of racially determined concepts of agency and consent, which are anything but universal and impossible to read historically but can be imaginatively re-created. Over and over, Christianse depicts sexual "choice" as contingent and constrained by the incompatibility of slavery with individual notions of will and consent. She peoples her critically imaginative landscape of slavery with enslaved and imprisoned men and women whose "will" surfaces when they kill, laugh, (do not) hear, and love. In the rest of the chapter, I focus on reading the novel closely, with an eye to performative modes of killing, laughing, not hearing, and loving, to outline what I see as specific instantiations of "will" as it operates within systems of coercion. Taking a child's life, letting a laugh escape, becoming deaf, making oneself vulnerable to another: the historical revisioning inherent in these instantiations gesture toward the illegibility of black will and the thick vibrancy of its imaginative re-creation.

Legally Free to Mother

According to the historian Pamela Scully's indispensable work, at least three other women were tried for murdering their children between Hester's case in 1819 and Sila's in 1823.[26] While the number of deaths was probably consistent with that of previous years, the number of women brought to trial and the subsequent documentation around these trials were not. If, as Sharon Harris asks, the criminalization of an act and responses to that criminalization "are as much about controlling public discourse, especially by [and about] unruly women, as they are out meting about punishment," then what do we make of these cases of child murder?[27] The interest in identifying these particular crimes results from attempts by abolitionists to chronicle the horrors of slavery. For instance, the prominent abolitionist Wilbur Wilberforce argued before the House of Commons that the moral depravity of slavery corrupted slaver and enslaved alike. Wilberforce based his argument on the notion that enslaved people would rather kill themselves and their children than submit to such a vile regime, citing the testimony of R. B. Fisher, a soldier in the colonial army who recounted infants' corpses frequently washing up on Cape beaches. To defend itself against a litany of abuses that Wilberforce presented in 1817, the Colonial Office asked the Cape's Governor Lord Charles Somerset to investigate. Aided by Chief Justice John Truter, Somerset insisted that slaves were well cared for and relatively content and that all "unwanted" children were given homes. In cases such as Hester's, Cape officials saw an opportunity to spectacularize their vigilance and utter intolerance for such "abnormal" behavior. Reporters such as Samuel Eusebius Hudson could thus assert that "prior to the English first taking the Cape of Good Hope many a poor Unfortunate babe found a Grave in the Sea from inhuman depraved Mothers."[28] According to this reasoning, colonial rule corrected and prevented dead infants' bodies from washing up on shore, and the severity of the court's judgment against inhuman slave women who killed their children provided evidence of this. Cases of mothers killing their children were thus used simultaneously to index the corruption of slavery (dead babies as the tragedy of slavery) and justify the need for colonial law and order to control barbaric slaves (inhuman and depraved mothers that the state needed to discipline through slavery).[29]

It is important to bear in mind the culturally specific meanings and rationales for the killing of infants in various contexts. Scully cites Nancy Scheper-Hughes to argue that "members of the rural poor of the Western Cape participated in a complex and heterogeneous cultural life with links to the African societies of East and Central Africa, as well as to Malaysia and India, the creole slave culture of the Cape, and the indigenous Khoi and San societies. The women involved in these cases possibly brought to the killing of infants a different cultural perspective than that of the British or the Dutch."[30] Rationales such as birth spacing (practiced by the Khoisan) and the prohibition against twins must have influenced enslaved women's behavior, but resorting to notions of authentic, precolonial practices and belief ignores the ways that indigenous cultures adapt to imperial domination. To assume a simple continuation of "authentic" cultural practices underestimates the violence of imperialism while positing culture as a static repository of belief that indigenous peoples merely access, regardless of the context.

In 1823, the year that Sila killed her son, the first amelioration laws were passed at the Cape. British officials readied themselves to direct an emancipated slave population into an economy that exploited wage labor, stressed consumption, and morally prescribed the "civilizing" force of patriarchal nuclear family units. As Scully writes, "The infanticide cases illustrate the centrality of the ideas and practices of sexuality, morality, and autonomy to the fashioning of the colonial order in the postemancipation era. . . . The infanticide proceedings became symbolic trials, serving as platforms from which colonial officials described what was not acceptable, legitimated state legislation in the sphere defined as 'private,' and sought to inculcate practices and values conducive to the reproduction of a self-reproducing rural elite and stable [racialized] working class needing minimal state intervention."[31] Thus, legislation around enslaved and newly freed women killing their children had as much to do with imperial notions of morality as it did with these women's unequal entry into wage labor and capitalist consumerism. Enslaved and freed women and their children became the center of struggles over the procurement of the "rights" to their labor. To the colonial regime, a mother killing her child was a usurpation of state sovereignty over the child's labor. The trials publicly performed a ritualistic battle for ownership over future generations in the closed circuit of deprivation and abundance that is slavery and its afterlife.

Dana Rabin documents infanticide's reputation in eighteenth-century England, in its reinscription of gender roles, as a crime thought to be specifically feminine.[32] Infanticide was assumed to be a crime committed solely by (white) unwed mothers as a last-ditch effort to avert the social ostracization that resulted from illegitimate children. As such, it was associated with secrecy and concealment, with the child's corpse considered privileged evidence. Defense arguments against charges of infanticide focused on how prepared and welcoming the expectant mother was. Thus, a baby hat or blanket procured before the baby's birth worked against the charge of infanticide. A married mother killing her child was seen as an unfathomable rejection of the gendered trajectory of white women. This began to change as the eighteenth century progressed. Courts increasingly were faced with mothers who pleaded that they could not claim responsibility for their actions due to their emotional and mental distress. Rabin argues that the term "sensibility" came to refer to physical sensory capabilities: "By the mid-eighteenth century 'sensibility' [came to denote] a special and admirable susceptibility to one's own feelings and the feelings of others."[33] Women brought to trial thus claimed diminished responsibility for their actions based on the emotional sensitivities that came from being members of the "weaker," more easily distressed gender.

The crime of infanticide was configured around the illegitimate births of unmarried white mothers and their supposedly delicate emotional constitution. Since enslaved black women were "ungendered" and excluded from marriage and the politics of legitimate patrilineage, I hesitate to label Sila's murder of Baro "infanticide." In a structure that depended on the sexual and labor exploitation of black women and their children, slave children were always already illegitimate; social and cultural orphans. Moreover, stereotypical notions of slave women's imperviousness to physical and emotional pain complicated their relationship to the gendered legal narratives of infanticide, which relied on notions of the fragile constitutions of white women. The "ungendered" black woman was expected to give birth in the fields and go back to work, to be unaffected as she watched her child brutally beaten by the master, to shrug off rape after rape with the callous disregard and lack of sensitivity that characterized her race.

Given that Sila's crime does not easily fit into traditional notions of infanticide, how do we understand her actions? While the will of the historical Sila remains inaccessible, the novel *Unconfessed* uses the murder to anchor its critical exploration of issues of will, choice, and resistance. Sila's "choice" to kill a child she loves raises all sorts of questions about the slave mother's ability and inability to choose to act in conditions of domination. Could murdering one's child be a form of resistance, and if so, what are the consequences of such theorizations of resistance? Stephanie Li's *Something akin to Freedom* focuses on "a legacy of seemingly anti-intuitive modes of resistance in which self-violation becomes agency and freedom represents a complex negotiation for power and the protection of loved ones."[34] Like Hartman, Li thinks through forms of contestation that are difficult to recognize, since they rarely resemble conventional notions of autonomy and agency exercised by self-possessed individuals. Heroic actions such as running away get configured as resistance while accommodation and contingency are often read as types of compliance.[35] Li however wants to move away from such conceptualizations of liberty based on "rugged individualism and self reliance" toward "radical assertation[s] of care and desire."[36]

The story of a fellow prisoner on the island named Jacob, who cuts off his finger in *Unconfessed*, though brief, is an important opening through which to consider Li's rethinking of liberty. Sila tells Baro of the struggles between Jacob and Pedder, the head guard on the island. She begins with Pedder's body language; he keeps his hands behind his back in a gesture that suggests his superiority: "I am the one and you better know it" (48). His insistence on performing his mastery means that although he is fond of whipping the enslaved prisoners with the cat-o'-nine-tails, he never wields the whip himself, as he is above manual labor. Instead, in a scenario familiar on slave plantations with overseers, Pedder manages the prisoners by creating and exploiting differences among them. He allows some prisoners greater privileges and control over others. As a way to show favor, Pedder allows Jacob to whip, jeer, and shout at other slaves. An unnamed event fractures the men's relationship. While the novel never reveals what happened, one assumes an unexpected willfulness on Jacob's part as he balances between acting and being acted upon. A short time later, Pedder puts Jacob in the Black Hole for eight days, ostensibly because Jacob has failed to make Pedder three shirts in a short amount of time. The heat, the meager diet of bread and water, and the humiliation mean that Jacob emerges from the Black Hole a different man. Pedder then has Jacob beat so badly by his "new favorite" prisoner that Jacob has to be sent to the hospital. "When Jacob came back, he was quiet. He spoke to no one. But Pedder was not finished with him" (49), Christianse writes. Pedder attempts to further break Jacob's spirit by setting the slave the impossible task of making two shirts in two days. When Pedder sends another man around on the deadline, it is not to get the shirts but to take Jacob back to the Black Hole. At this point, Jacob takes a knife from the carpenter's shed and "cut his finger off. Just like that!" (50). Jacob thus puts himself in the role of victimizer. In his acts of self-harm, he preempts and outperforms Pedder's brutality. The consequences of Jacob's actions include Pedder's being reprimanded by the superintendent of police. In this way, Jacob also refuses the labor of making shirts. However, Jacob's performance has a price: he remains the victim. Wendy Brown writes that this self-injury constitutes a form of freedom that is "neither a philosophical absolute nor a tangible entity but a relational and contextual practice that takes shape in opposition to whatever is locally and ideologically conceived as unfreedom."[37] Rather than measuring practices of resistance against imaginary ideals of autonomous heroic agency, we should include those acts that emerge in the relational spaces between people and that is not simply the property of self-possessed individual persons. *Unconfessed* illustrates a world in which neither men nor women are able to define themselves as autonomous individuals as their identity is entangled in affective ties. Theirs is a relational ontology in which the meaning of objects and people is forged from an ensemble of their relations.[38] Given the legal strictures binding mother and child together, the notion of freedom for slave mothers in particular cannot revolve around a determined, independent individualism. Sila's ability to care for, protect, and ensure her children's survival (or the safety that only death can bring) qualifies freedom for her, defining it so that its meaning shifts and congeals at various points and contexts. Sila's "decision" to "summon death and draw a space for it in the world through the living throat of her boy" (15) represents a dilemma about the meaning of freedom for a subject constituted not through individual autonomy but through affective ties. Does one have to be legally free to mother? Can mothering exist within the economy of slavery, in which a mother's ability to care for her child means less than what she has bequeathed to him—that is, his status as property?

In her summoning of Baro's death, Sila feels "*her* life going out of the body that had been *her* very own burden in this world" (15). While it might seem counterintuitive that *her* life ebbs out of Baro, the reiteration of the possessive pronoun "her" is key to understanding the scene. Sila is not so much killing Baro as releasing him from the possessive logics of slavery and traditional understandings of mothering, both of which bear the "stamp of commodity" (where the child "belongs" to the parent). Using the work of the legal scholar Barbara Bennett Woodhouse, Christopher Peterson points out the striking similarities between parental rights (even though parents cannot enjoy, sell, or transfer their children per se) and property rights: "Indeed, parental 'rights' have historically been upheld under the rubric of the Fourteenth Amendment's guarantee of liberty. This ironic appeal to the constitutional protection of freedom to assert a property claim in one's children recalls the ideology of slavery whereby Southerners insisted on their 'right' to own slaves."[39] Sila's relinquishing of her claim on Baro by killing him might be the *very condition of their relationship's possibility*. She does not claim possession of Baro by murdering him. She is not saying that he is hers and she can do what she wills with his life. Rather, she attempts another kind of mothering not saturated with the logic of ownership. At the moment Sila kills Baro, she remembers details that she is unable to articulate: "I could not say that the hand that stole the knife shook, or that I had lifted my dear boy into my lap and held him, and stroked him and known that he was already beyond all of them, even me" (232). Sila's love is premised not on Baro's "belonging" to her. Rather, her recognition that Baro is "beyond" them all lends an unfathomable depth to her love for him.

Abdur-Rahman quotes Spillers as saying that the enslaved black woman is the "principal point of passage between the human and the non-human world."[40] Sila sees death as another place and another time, with different possibilities in accordance with African cosmologies where the dead live on as ancestors. The barriers between life and death are not vigilantly maintained, nor are the dead carefully sequestered. In *Unconfessed*, the dead are instead a promiscuous and uncontainable lot with different agendas. They pop in, terrify, lure, guide, and haunt the living, appearing unexpectedly on the dirt path or as voices on the wind. Baro appears (always incompletely) to Sila and this relationship, which traverses the boundaries of mortality, drives the narrative, and enables the complex claims and disavowals of mother and son. The actual horror of Sila killing Baro recedes in light of the relationality that death ushers in, what Peterson calls a "spectral form of kinship—an alternative idiom" of belonging.[41] Baro's murder ends his relationship with his master, but not with his mother. Sila and Baro's "spectral form of kinship" relationship does not revolve around corporeal possession or the assimilation of the Other into the volitional subject. Instead, it insists that the Other can never be fully claimed or possessed or even known and that self-presence cannot and should not be achieved through the assimilation of the Other. The Other is always absent, always lost, residing someplace that is not here. Sila thus acknowledges that Baro has traveled from someplace else to see her, as he does not have "the look of anyone from this island, or from that town over the water" (39). When Sila's daughter Meisie is kidnapped, Sila thinks, "*I knew. I knew. I knew-knew-knew.* . . . They took her in a boat in this weather and with that cough. I will kill them all. Get me a gun. Get me an axe. I will chop this world up into tiny pieces. . . . *Ag. Farewell. Farewell. What else can I do?*" (191–92). In bidding Meisie farewell, Sila confronts, once again, the necessity of a language of kinship articulated around absence and dispossession, around loss and grief.[42] She begs Baro to watch out for Meisie and to watch out for Mina's daughter, Flora. Sila is undone by her caring and her pain, not only for the children she bore, but also for Flora. She refuses to stop grieving, as loss helps constitute the spectral form of kinship necessary to depart from models of individual will and possession.[43]

Most of the characters in the novel view Sila's act as a barbaric, racialized departure from normative mothering or as a form of maternal love so strong as to be unintelligible. These competing explanations are clearly outlined in the opening pages of the novel. Only toward the end of the novel do we get a description of the scene from Sila's perspective. Crucially, she does not justify her killing of Baro. Rather, the scene refuses reductive explanations and focuses instead on the illegibility of Sila's will, on colonial law's inability to understand her actions. I quote at length the scene in which she points out this illegibility even as she insists on the incommensurability of her experience as a slave mother and the religious, moral, and legal imperatives of colonialism:

> And therefore I could not say as they wanted me to say. That I had taken my boy. *Cruelly?* Or even that I had loved him and held him in my lap when he at last cried himself to sleep. I could not say ... that there was no hope, already, long before I stroked my boy's throat, that he would not sleep in the ground for three days and rise again to tell me that I had made him greater than all of them. No. I could say nothing of the way that love had required that I crush all horror even as I faced it. I looked at them. They looked at me and looked away. *Speak,* they said. To say what? What is it you have in your minds when you ask me to make the picture? ... They wanted to know about that last moment my boy was of this earth. But not if he suffered. (232–33)

Sila's refusal to translate her actions into a form legible to colonial authorities constitutes one of the most striking aspects of this passage. Conjuring forth the heartbreaking moment when she watches her beaten son cry himself to sleep, she insists that nothing she could say would explain her actions. The moment will remain ultimately indescribable for two reasons. First, the colonial officials' preconceived notions about her actions, those "pictures they have in their minds," result in their asking the wrong question. The specific moment of death for Sila pales in comparison with the life of a slave that Baro endured. His murder can begin to make sense only if one understands that Baro suffered for Sila's "sin" of being a slave mother. Second, it ritualistically performs vulnerability and intimacy between Baro and Sila, and them alone, in what Sarah Cervenak describes as "strategic information withholdings."[44] Although Cervenak is talking specifically about Harriet Jacobs, the ability to maneuver epistemologies and histories by refusing forces that interrogate, explain, and understand is a crucial strategy practiced by slave women. Sila, like Harriet Jacobs, attempts to "untether justice from its entrapment in understanding ... at precisely those moments when it bends away from the forces that attempt to translate or read" (14–15). In other words, Sila refuses to share her wondering, even if it might mitigate her sentencing.

The Christian notion of death as an impermeable barrier, as well that of God sacrificing his son to save humanity, lie at the heart of Sila's rejection of Christianity. Sila repeatedly compares the veneration with which God's sacrifice of Jesus is met with the criminalization and ostracization she faces after she has "saved" Baro from this world. Furthermore, in its insistence that resurrection is only possible for Jesus, Christianity would deny Sila her children even after their death. Why should only her children remain dead in the ground? As Meg Samuelson writes, "Freedom from the 'social death' of slavery . . . can only be attained by sundering from the world of the living those who have passed on; by killing off once more a past that the enslaving Cape has already trampled under foot."[45] By insisting that "death is all there is to death," Christianity would deny Sila her children for the second time (275). And interacting with her children after they are gone enables Sila to continue living. Remembering a son who died in the town prison before she could name him, Sila describes being able to name him after death: "He came to me, laughing. I said, your name is Laughter. I held him to me and that was between us, what we felt" (277).

Laughter, or What My Mother Named Me

Christianse introduces the idea of laughter as a very specific form of "will" for the enslaved peoples in the novel and for those living with the "afterlife" of slavery. Black laughter, or what Stephen Best and Saidiya Hartman call "black noise," spills over into non-speech, into moans, shouts, and cries that mark a terrain where conventional articulation is not enough. Such unstable and indeterminate sonic frequencies index "the kinds of political aspirations that are inaudible and illegible within the prevailing formulas of political rationality. . . . These yearnings are illegible because they are so wildly utopian and derelict to capitalism."[46] Black noise, then, in its refusal of certain structures of coherence, informs and deforms power even while it attests to other ways of living. Cape slavery regulated the sounds of slaves, making it difficult to hear black noise in any substantive public way. Slavery's soundscape was thus characterized by enforced silence and carefully dictated noise, by agonized screams of pain rather than joyful laughter. Mike Chasar writes that, for the slave, "the ability to control sound and silence could mean freedom . . . for survival and escape were contingent on an acute appreciation of the . . . plantation soundscape."[47]

The master's laugh exercised like a whip to enforce his superiority characterized the plantation soundscape, and accompanying this laugh were the slaves' fake grins or coerced performances of joviality which supported illusions of slavery's paternalistic benevolence. The white laugh signaled the alleged sophistication of the master while black laughter supposedly marked the primitivism of slaves. Chasar describes the work of scholars who theorized well into the twentieth century "either that black laughter was different from white laughter by virtue of its childishness and innocence or that laughter itself had behavioral or physiological roots in Africa and was thus a primitive, immature, or uncivilized element in the Western world."[48] Thus, slaves' performances of humor were deemed immature and simplistic due to the primitivism of their "African" roots.

It is therefore no accident that, especially for black humorists, performances of black laughter became crucial to redefining the soundscape of slavery and its aftermath. Signifying on the "limited scope of the possible in the face of the impossible," black humorists, according to Glenda Carpio, "enact symbolic rituals of redress with respect to the breach of slavery."[49] The ritual of black laughter marks a possible eruption of will, the emergence of acoustic revolt that pragmatically turns to the law even while gesturing beyond it to another, as yet unrealized way of being beyond the regimes of unfree labor. Black laughter, Carpio goes on to document, "outlines . . . a communal life whose redemption and transformation present a still to be realized alternative to capitalist colonialism."[50] Black laughter changes and adapts; it is always a product of a specific time and context. Rather than an essentialized expression of individual agency, it constitutes complex, interdependent interactions with a deeply racist and sexist soundscape.

Laughter, especially the laughter of Lys, Sila's lover and friend, pays a crucial role in *Unconfessed*. The novel returns to the formulation of the laugh repeatedly, insisting that it is key to understanding possible redress even as it gestures toward a still deferred justice. Christianse suggests that Lys's laugh ritualistically embodies black noise that echoes across time into the present:

> I did not hear her called Lys when I first met her. . . . The guard was calling a small woman lazy yellow bitch. I heard laughter and there she was, laughing at the guard. . . . She looked at me and laughed again but with good laughter. Here, you know, laughter is a way of crying or of adding salt to a beating, but her laughter is not like that. I took my spare dress and gave it to her. What did that make her look like, the smallest one in the tallest one's dress? . . . She laughed about that. Right there and then, she laughed. Lys is the one who taught me how to live here. . . . We laugh. Listen. (52)

This passage outlines at least two different ways that laughter functions: as threat or humiliation and as a catalyst for the creation of alternative structures of kinship. Laughing in the face of power requires the ability to operate in multiple acoustic registers at once. Lys's laughter at being called a "lazy yellow bitch" by the prison guard draws our attention to the limits of liberal conceptions of law and property. Her black noise intervenes in the public soundscape of the prison island, unsettling the guard who does not know what to make of her skillful deflection. His insult appears to have backfired, as it is not Lys but he who is humiliated by Lys's ill-fitting dress. The valence of the laugh shifts, however, when Lys looks at Sila. This "good" laughter at recognizing an ally mitigates the implied threat of her laughter when aimed at the guard. With nothing dry to wear except the ill-fitting dress, Lys laughs not only at her own humiliating predicament but also at the similarly desperate plight of all of the women. The dress, like the laughter, metaphorically conceals Lys's shame. It hides her potential "nakedness" just as her "good" laughter masks her threat to the guards who mistreat her.

The shortest woman (Lys) wearing the dress of the tallest woman (Sila) exemplifies humor resulting from incongruity. The humor of incongruity is not just the arrival of the unexpected but also the suspension of normativity through a consideration of alternative possibilities. As Carpio argues, "At its best, the humor of incongruity allows us to see the world inverted, to consider transpositions of time and place and to get us . . . to question the habits of mind that we may fall into as we critique race."[51] Through this humor, which turns things upside down and inside out, the women of the novel temporarily distance themselves from unbearable and dangerous situations, thus becoming onlookers who gaze in at themselves while looking out. Lys's laughter suggests what could be possible in face of the impossible. On an island where women are faceless bodies raped in the dark every night, Lys's laugh insists on their resilience despite their incredible vulnerability. Her humor results in what Victor Turner calls "communitas," the bond created by the humorist and the people with whom she shares the joke. One need only consider the estrangement caused by "not getting the joke" to realize the communitas generated by the ability to participate in the social rituals of humor. Although the women are not bound together by racial, social, or philosophical sameness, their laughter generates temporary and shifting alliances:

> Lys says to me, look at that guard, he stinks like the meat he has hanging in his room. Now, why that should make us laugh I do not know, but laugh we do. Even when Mina says the guards keep us hanging in our huts at night as if we too are meat, we laugh. Ja, we laugh together. Sometimes one of us will start—me, or Lys, or Mina, or Rachel. Or Deel, who is not strong enough to break or lift stones and will die if the warden does not take her out of the quarry. Even Deel can find some laughter. (207)

There is nothing inherently funny about the parallels drawn between meat and the way the women are consumed/raped. Yet the contagiousness of black laughter allows the women to look from the outside in at the ridiculous parallel between meat on hooks and their bodies. Their laughter is subversive both in its generation of a communitas across difference and in the implicit threat of that laughter to power. The women wield laughter like a collective battle ax or a knife with which to quietly cut throats.

In his novel *Watt* (1953), Carpio tells us, Samuel Beckett writes about laughter that is not strictly laughter but, rather, a mode of ululation: "The bitter laugh laughs at that which is not good, it is the ethical laugh. The hollow laugh laughs at that which is not true, it is the intellectual laugh. . . . But the mirthless laugh is the dianoetic laugh, down the snout—Haw!—so. It is the laugh of laughs, the *risus purus*, the laugh laughing at the laugh, the beholding, saluting of the highest joke, in a word the laugh that laughs—silence, please!—at that which is unhappy."[52] Laughter as ululation is key to *Unconfessed*. Ululation is a high-pitched vocal trilling typically practiced by women in Africa, the Middle East, and Central and South Asia. Used either to express mourning (similar to the Irish practice of keening at a wake) or to celebrate events such as weddings and homecomings, ululation marks significant communal events. The sound resonates throughout my body as I recollect outdoor Sunday Christian/Zulu prayer sessions when women dressed in white raised their heads and laughed. They laughed both out of sheer joy at the presence of God in one another and in grief at the misery of apartheid South Africa. Their exultations, as Carpio might put it, were "loud, mournful, protracted, and rhythmical expressions of grief [that] testif[ied] to a history of dispossession.[53] Ululation as a simultaneous expression of celebration and grief, a laughing in sorrow accompanied by weeping in joy, ritualistically redistributes the burden of the person laughing as well as of the person listening. It functions as a communal ritualistic release and containment that includes and exceeds the individual participants. Sila describes the day that Van der Wat took away her children Carolina and Camies as the day she had stones in her throat and stomach. Signifying on the coerced quarrying of limestone by prisoners on Robben Island, Sila is sick of swallowing stones year after year. Addressing Baro, she says, "Ag, when you laugh . . . I hear you laugh. Do not forget that laughter, real laughter, keeps the stones from breaking into tears and drowning the world" (67). Laughter reconfigures Sila's affective relationship to labor—both the backbreaking quarrying of stone and the work of creating a communitas.

Black noise or laughter is not only heard by the dead but also helps to conjure them up, thereby revealing black bodies as breathing, pulsating membranes of memory that can traverse the world of the living and the world of the dead. In this collective mode of storytelling, the practitioner weaves the narrative spell of laughter in the spaces that connect people. Conjuring laughter resides in-between, where it cannot be contained, mastered, or possessed by an individual consciousness and bounded body; it enables one to leave one's body, to travel, to move away from notions of ownership over bodies, and to desire and touch without the need to possess. To laugh is to conjure is to laugh.

The secret of Lys's laughter is her ability to travel without her body, as well as her ability to trust someone with her body when she is absent. Sila claims, "That is the secret of her laughter. Here is not where she belongs and here is not what keeps her in place. There is no prison for Lys. But when she comes back from this kind of sleeping, on days like this, she does not answer to Lys and I alone whisper her name to her, her name that her mother called her, the name that her father called her. *Kammean*" (134–35). For Lys to be called by the name her parents gave her gestures toward a time that she was not imprisoned or enslaved. That time was not prior to slavery and imprisonment, or even after. Rather, Lys's laughter suggests a time outside slavery, what Best and Hartman call "a loophole between hope and resignation . . . between the no longer and not yet."[54] This is the gap between formal emancipation and freedom, between the injustice of the present and the justice yet to come. Lys's laughter refuses her imprisonment and, in the face of the enduring dispossession and fungibility of black people, conjures a moment in which an inhabitable death world becomes a place where one can dwell again, fully embracing the poignancy of loss.

The Sweetness of (Not) Hearing: Alternative Listening Practices

> Can you see how the light is already tightening with a sweetness in that direction? It is a tightening of light and air, of the thin layer that I have learned how to see, the one between light and air. It is like the thin membrane that holds a yolk together. That is how I hear the world. The world drums, like little feathers against that membrane
> —YVETTE CHRISTIANSE, *UNCONFESSED: A NOVEL*, 320

Sila is deaf in one ear as a result of a vicious beating from Van der Wat. Instead of equating this deafness with a lack of hearing, however, Sila incorporates the "big silence" (320) into a listening practice that allows her to hear around corners. This alternative listening practice remembers vividly the pain that accompanied her loss of hearing; it enables her to hear and see differently and constitutes a strategic deployment of "will" that is both visible and invisible at the same time. For the most part, scholars of sound have focused on the sounds of slavery (those of work, punishment, and play). Little attention has been paid to black listening practices and deafness; to the compelling questions of how and what slaves hear. This lack of critical attention is in all probability due to the illegibility of black will within the archive; black listening practices index an interiority that is largely missing in the historical record. Actual black listening practices are something we can only guess at, such as the constant scream of the sea and a child crying quietly by the door at night while the master rapes his mother.

Recent years has seen an increase in scholarship on sound that emphasizes the aural as a critical practice and as an important, but often overlooked, aspect of historical life. The sound historians Mark M. Smith and Richard Rath argue that the visual emphasis with which historians traditionally have imagined early American life consolidated racial and ethnic otherness. They claim that whites were "strategically hard of hearing" when it came to registering slaves' grievances or black speech but extremely attentive when it came to listening for sounds of revolt.[55] A racial hierarchy thus permeates and shapes the aural, rendering black "noise" the antithesis of the law. When black hearing was discussed, it was in terms that reinforced the racial ideology of white supremacy. The notorious Samuel A. Cartwright of New Orleans wrote that sound bypassed the Negro's brain, directly pleasing the ear in visceral, intuitive, and non-cerebral ways.[56] The Negro, Cartwright went on to argue, has better hearing than his white peers and therefore greater powers of imitation—in fact, it is the simple repetition or mimicry of what he hears that allows the Negro to appear more intelligent than he actually is.

Roland Barthes suggests that listening organizes time and space through intimate connections between people. For Barthes, "The appropriation of space is also a matter of sound: domestic space . . . is a space of familiar, recognized noises whose ensemble forms a kind of household symphony."[57] This imagining of domestic space obviously fails to take into account the nightmare of transatlantic slavery and how tenuous any formulation of domestic space for slaves would be. In the context of chattel slavery, listening operates on multiple registers based on the power dynamics within any single domestic space; the slave listens to the familiar voice of the master or mistress that excludes her from domestic space even as it demands her labor. But listening can also provide us with a space within which to imagine the slave's illegible will. Even though Barthes did not take into account the complexities of slave aurality, what I find useful is his notion that "what is plumbed by listening is intimacy."[58] Listening brings one subject into relation with another as sound pulls the listener into the speaker's intimate orbit. Aural forms of knowledge are crucial in the generation of empathic understanding across difference. During the course of his public performances and in writings such as "My Bondage and My Freedom," Frederick Douglass grew to believe that the aural circumvented some of the political problems of abolitionist spectacles of injured blackness. Struggling with the politically regressive voyeuristic sympathy and sexual titillation many white viewers felt when confronted with sentimental images of the suffering black body, Douglass gradually began to de-emphasize the visual in favor of the aural. In "The Heroic Slave" he writes that the voice and not the suffering black body is the "index of the soul."[59] Describing the act of listening as "sound[ing] the mysterious depths of the thoughts and feelings of a slave," he suggests that more politically transformative and generous relations can only emerge when one becomes vulnerable to the interpersonal differences that emerge through interactions.[60] Genuine listening performs a vulnerability that erodes blind conviction and rigid self-righteousness. Listening not only to what but to *how* people speak develops interpersonal connections that exceed the spectacularization of the black body.

Sila uses alternate sound ways to remap Robben Island and various sites of memory. The familiar, recognized sounds that remap her landscape are the stuff of nightmares, not symphony. She tells us about the sound of the lock being forced at night when the guards come to rape the female prisoners, the drone of waves against the hull of the slave ship, the gulls that sound like babies crying. Her directions to Baro around Robben Island are largely aural: follow the sound of the ocean until you hear this or block your ears when you see this.

For Sila, to listen is to remember the terrible beating by Van der Wat that took her hearing in one ear and changed the way she hears forever. On the day she screamed that Van der Wat could not sell her children because Carolina and Camies were the free children of a free woman, he "took care of this ear for good," she says. "He hit me all around my head with open hands and with a knobkerrie. He hit and hit and shouted and my hearing was bursting and spraying away" (316). The pain of Sila's perforated eardrum temporarily drives her mad, and she imagines her children as ghostly specters. After a couple days, the pain recedes enough for her to realize her children are alive, but her view of her own existence is fundamentally altered by an awareness that she could, at any moment, fall into a "great hole in the world." Located at Sila's threshold for pain and violence, this hole represents a non-porous, Western type of death that would sever her from her children. It is a silence that is all-encompassing; a sonic void from which there is no return.

Sila has to learn how to "hear the world all over again" (319) and does this by incorporating her knowledge of the "great hole"—her deafness in one ear and her hearing in the other—to create an alternative listening practice. This practice does not privilege normative hearing. Sila sees her inability to hear certain sounds as an advantage: "I can say how happy I am not to hear certain things. . . . Waves breaking can make me sick to the stomach when I hear them. A gull crying makes me think of babies" (320). For every sound Sila is unable to hear, there are others that only she can access. Her listening then becomes embodied; a conjuring of memory, movement, and second sight; "a way of tricks and guesses" (319). Consider the following pivotal passage:

> I can hear sounds that others do not. I used to hear *Oumeisies* come look-ing through the *fynbos* for me and my children. I can still hear the way the world shifts when King *Poff-Adder* comes into the compound. I used to hear the way the guards scratched themselves. These other sounds do not bother me because they are a trick that I have named sound. You see, Johannes, the world is full of shifting and other kinds of movement. . . . There. You see. I knew that guard was coming by. Tshhh. Wait. It is not that he always goes running down there at this time of day—he visits one of the men prisoners behind that hut. I have come to know how things move here and I have put this together with my memories of sounds, but also together with things that I see. And I do hear what he gets up to with that prisoner. (320)

Sila hears the dead—those demons that want to torture the living; those who, like Oumeisies, want to suck the living into their loneliness; and those, like Hes-ter's children, whose voices will break your heart. Sila repeatedly asks the dead Baro to block his ears even as he must listen for "the difference. . . . Close your ears. Quick. Listen" (177). The juxtaposing of blocking one's ears with an injunction to listen suggests that for Sila, listening is more than auditory and requires voluntary and involuntary acts of deafness. This sort of hearing happens not only through vibrating eardrums but also via the entire body. It is with her entire body (deaf ear included) that Sila hears those sounds that are supposedly inaudible: the puff adder slithering into the compound; the guards scratching themselves; and a guard secretly raping a male prisoner behind the hut. She detects these resonances by tracking the orbits of the dead, light and shadow, and weighing them against her memories of time and sound. On a day when Sila is overwhelmed by despair and unable to move, she is tossed out of her cot by Lys: "The floor speaks to the bones in my body. Hardness to hardness. The floor makes me feel what lies beneath all the flesh. A truth we all carry and fear when life is good. . . . My bad ear is the ear that hears what the floor says to the bones in my body. My bad ear was born for this" (99). Sila uses her entire body to listen: muffled voice in one ear, the voice of the floor in the other, sonic memory housed in the flesh and buried in the bone.

Sila deploys this complex of listening and deafness to contest her subjugation. "I pretended I could not hear. I pointed to my ears and shook my head. They were cross. They wanted to put out my lights but I was cheating them again" (149). If listening is the stage on which the two deities of power and desire confront each other, as Barthes remarks,[61] then Sila, with her power not to hear, manipulates the guards' desire that she obey. Over and over she chooses not to hear by pointing to her ears and thereby staging an act of disability that masks her disobedience. In this way, Sila rejects certain listeners by insisting on a hostile deafness that refuses any mode of intimacy. Through this aggressive deafness, she pushes her abusers away even as she attacks. Combining deafness, body memory, resistance, aggression, and intimacy, Sila's alternative listening practice instantiates a counterintuitive will that is almost impossible to detect within the archive. For the historian searching through written documents for examples of such politicized listening, the difficulty of distinguishing between intentionally not hearing and not being able to hear is compounded by accessing what could be heard only by slaves and not by slave owners and archivists. The aural landscapes of slaves, slave owners, and colonial archivists overlapped but were not identical. These landscapes were shaped by sonic experiences specific to non-Western cultures and the system of enslavement. Christianse's skillful imagining of Sila's listening practice unfolds a space for slaves' will to emerge. The fictive possibilities suggested by Sila's will—for example, her listening and deafness and whom and how she chooses to love—engage the silences of the archive, critically conjuring alternative modes of being.

Brenna Munro writes that queer characters often render visible disavowed histories. The queer figure in South African history writing is particularly noteworthy, given the specific role gay rights have played in postapartheid liberalism. South Africa's groundbreaking incorporation of gay rights into its constitution departed from the well-rehearsed heteronormative familial scripts and iconography of nationhood. For some, the mythic young gay person supplemented the straight family as the symbol of the democratic nation to come—a "rainbow nationalism," if you will. Yet given the growing antigay sentiment that characterizes a more and more disillusioned postapartheid population, one has to wonder whether this queering of the standard family romance of nation is all that progressive. As Munro asks, could queerness as a rights-based recognition of diversity simply enable a neoliberal nationalism "that places people's hopes in a utopian future that may never arrive?"[62] Ignoring the mutual imbrication of identity politics and the "free" market, this queered family romance reinforces the legitimacy of the state without questioning the power dynamics inherent in its workings. Being acknowledged and legitimized by the state becomes more important than any structural critique of the state itself. Herein lies one of the major factors behind the current government's failure to move toward socioeconomic racial equity.

Christianse's queering of intimacy intercedes in current South African struggles around gay rights, wealth redistribution, and capital. Her turn toward queer families and *not* queer individual rights offers us crucial lessons about the creation of ethical and equitable political community. The queer families of *Unconfessed* critique Western and "traditional" African ideals of romantic love, both of which subordinate women to patriarchal demands of labor. The reality of racialized women's labor does not match these fantasies of the heterosexual family unit; instead, as Sila reflects, "Mothers and children, and mothers of children not theirs. That is how we are in this country" (127). Rewriting the overused maxim that it takes a village to raise a child, Sila states, "If I counted everyone I call family, we would fill a village" (164). In one of the most moving scenes in the novel, Sila steals two pieces of orange from the warden's kitchen where she works. One piece goes to her daughter and the other to Flora, Mina's daughter. Sila intends to provide the girls with some reprieve, some sweet nourishment and pleasure, not just from the oranges but also from the shared act of two black girls eating oranges. Sila's radical and consistent care and desire for Flora constructs a family of multiple mothers and multiple (non)biological offspring.

Sila's generosity toward Flora is all the more striking when one remembers the animosity between Sila and Mina. Their mutual hostility arises from their differing strategies of surviving the horrors of Robben Island. Sila sees Mina's fearful, seemingly acquiescent responses to life on the island as a way of "hid[ing] in the darkness, where they want us to be" (313). Mina attempts to placate her abusers, to do as they say in the hope of staving off future cruelty and abuse. In the context of slavery, however, such apparent acts of submission can be read as willful strategies of survival. As Abdul-Rahman notes, "Through technologies of terror and torture, slaves learned to adopt postures of passivity, and even complicity, in rituals designed to showcase the master's dominance.[63] Performing her part in the strained ritualized performance of master-slave/ guard-prisoner, Mina drinks alcohol the guards give her before they rape her: "They like her better now because she does not fight [after she drinks] and they are not afraid of the look in her eyes" (321). Her acts of submission include attempts to protect her daughter by insisting, for example, that Flora not eat the orange piece smuggled to her by Sila in case the warden discovers the "transgression." Sila, by contrast, makes nothing easier for those who would abuse her. "I have been despised and I have opened my mouth and spoken the language that this has taught me. I have wanted to send fleas into their sores and the soft folds of their bodies. I have wanted to send locusts and flies that would carry their cattle away with diseased blood" (259). She wills her body to speak to Van der Wat, not before and not as but *after* he rapes her: "And he trembles always. After. And was confused. And grew angrier by the day" (30). Sila, according to Mina, thinks that she is better than her. Mina's feet, Sila notes bitterly, are locked into the dance of a good girl.[64] Being alive for Sila takes a back seat to living a life worth living. Both characters precariously balance sex and mothering in the absence of the possibility of choice and consent.

Much like listening and not listening, this vulnerability establishes a kind of queer relationality that goes beyond questions of individual willful acts. For all of their disagreements and ill feelings, Sila knows that she and Mina "are of a kind. We are women. It does not matter that they took [Mina] when she was old enough to cry for a life that already had full memories, and that she had to work, like Lys, on a farm for a man who had no wife, and it does not matter that she knows what it is to be ridden like a horse or milked like a cow. That is another kind that we are. We are women who are horses. We are *poese* up to our chins" (312). Their different responses to subjugation do not result in different outcomes. Sila might kick and scream and conjure up retribution while Mina might lie in a drunken stupor, but both women ultimately face the morning violated and heart sore. The shared vulnerability of all of the women, despite their differences, underpins their creation of queer family. As Darieck Scott notes, enslaved people can perform the "deleterious effects [of slavery and imprisonment] not only for the purpose of demonstrating their injurious outcomes but to see how the effects, indeed the injuries themselves, may . . . be tools that can be used either to model or to serve as a means of political transformation."[65] Instead of kinship being defined through various racialized refractions of possession, property, and consumption,[66] *Unconfessed* insists on the political efficacy of a shared physical and social vulnerability that gestures toward freedom.

This vulnerability is not limited to women. Sila writes poignantly about Matroos, Soldaat, Keizer, and Vigiland, four prisoners who are slowly disappearing into madness. All four men are utterly dependent on those who feed them, talk to them, and take care of them. They are made and unmade by others. They reside at the limits of sanity and pain, warning Sila that their fate could easily be hers. Matroos walks leaning too far to one side as if the world has lost its balance. Soldaat, a former soldier, cries when he sees a rifle and holds his right arm like a broken wing. Then there is the beautiful Keizer, who is raped so often that he becomes incontinent, and the youngest, Vigiland, who was arrested for vagrancy and became lost in his dreams. Sila avoids these prisoners because they remind her of Baro and Baro's possible trajectory at the hands of Van der Wat. Thus, they also force her to confront her own vulnerability and psychological fragility.

Negotiating vulnerability is a difficult mode of being, entailing various strategies, one of which, as Judith Butler suggests, is to repudiate weakness through reenactments of violence.[67] Thus, Jephta's brutal attempt to rape Sila, a repetition of Van der Wat's actions, is a way he attempts to contest his weakness. Another strategy is the performance of a lack of affect. Sila manages her vulnerability by desiring and pretending at an affective death to soften the next blow. In the hope that she will no longer hurt, Sila commands her heart to go away: "Heart, I am speaking to you, you who live in me like another. Listen. Go away. . . . We are at war, my heart and I . . . I forget you. . . . Go. *Go!* I dismiss thee. I dismiss thee. I dismiss thee. *Enemy!*" (193–94). In this way, Sila enacts a fantasy of mastery over an ultimately insurmountable vulnerability.

Her heart, however, answers: "My heart speaks back. . . . It is my job to love and to long for love" (194). Despite Sila's best efforts, she cannot will away vulnerability.

Vulnerability demands an acknowledgment that we are constituted by the dispossession ushered in by our relationships. The vulnerable subject is not so much formed by relationality as unraveled into a loose, temporary, and always changing constellation. In our public exposure to others, caresses and violations create us only to undo us. As Judith Halberstam has asserted, to be undone is to fail, and failure can constitute "modes of unbeing and unbecoming [that] propose a different relation to knowledge."[68] Embracing one's fragility, knowing that we can lose one another and ourselves at any moment, can be devastating. When Lys dies, Sila announces that she is *"friend and lover to Lys, mother to children who carry the weight of the world on their faces"* (330). All she has left of Lys is the space in the bed beside her and the absence of that "good, quiet day" created by loving and being loved by Lys.[69] Eventually Sila surrenders that loss to the wind; only the wind can carry such gifts. She makes no attempts to recuperate her loss, because she understands black queer relations as marked by being "undone," a possibility that haunts all social bonds. Sila does not claim Lys before or after death. Rather, she names herself as friend and lover to Lys (alive or not), no matter how difficult this is: "Let me live up to this, what has been demanded of me. It does not matter who has demanded it. All that matters is that I am the one who knows that something has been demanded of her and I am the one who understands that there is no escape in refusing to answer" (339). This is a queer intimacy premised on the knowledge that one is made and broken by our relations, beautifully articulated by Butler, who writes: "One is hit by waves. [One] finds oneself foiled. One finds oneself fallen. . . . Something is larger than one's own deliberate plan, one's own project, one's own knowing and choosing. Something takes hold of you: where does it come from? What sense does it make? What claims us at such moments, such that we are not the masters of ourselves? To what are we tied? And by what are we seized?" (21).

This model of relationality suggested by the intimacy of shared vulnerability offers us a unique way to think through questions of will and the discernment of "will." By working through relations of vulnerability, *Unconfessed* reveals the sovereign subject to be a myth that obscures dependence, affiliation, and ethical responsibility: "All we have is each other and that too is our downfall" (279). Christianse's poignant depictions of Sila's acts of love provide us with politically generative modes with which to imagine the "will" of slave women that is rarely individually discernible. By accessing narratives of shared vulnerability, one can begin to flesh out new modes of being within coercive regimes. These modes do not function despite our debilities. Sila's deafness and the sores of her lips work together with Lys's leprotic decay, for example, to create a relational ontology in which the idea of the human is remade. We, like Sila and Lys, have to learn how to see and "hear the world all over again" (319) with the understanding that physical deterioration and illness are part of living, with an awareness that one person's will exists only in relation to another's and that it is when we are at our most fragile that we are the most "beautiful" (321). Moving away from notions of individual, masculinized purposive agency allows us to gesture instead toward those illegible moments of will within the archive that are never empty.

Epilogue

This volume ends with theft—not the theft of human beings, which has been the focus of the book, but with the theft of artistic production. On April 20, 2012, unknown people broke into the home of the South African photographer Zanele Muholi. Leaving behind numerous other items of value, the thieves stole twenty external hard drives and backup systems; a laptop with digital files of her work; and interviews, images, and notes for a new series called *Queercide*. The series documents violence against queers of color, not only through non-stereotypical representations but also by photographing the trials of perpetrators and the funerals of those who did not survive. Muholi says that this theft of "the most valuable content [she had] ever produced" left her feeling "like a breathing zombie."[70] In an interview with the *New York Times*, she laments, "It's about our lives, as a community, trying to make sense and negotiate a space in homophobic spaces. It's not about me, it's a project produced by me, but of other people, who are very important to me, whose lives are so dear to me."[71]

Muholi's work, like many contemporary postapartheid commemorative projects, seeks to give voice to those who historically have been muted and whose absence has long gone unnoticed. In some ways, her project resonates with the agendas of various institutional cultural sites, such as the Robben Island Museum, which suture together restorative histories into teleological narratives. Even as these sites seek to commemorate a history that should not be forgotten, they nonetheless obscure the messiness of the move from apartheid into democratic capitalism. As Rosalind Morris argues, the "experiences that are narrated in these spaces—of . . . lost children and missing parents, of prohibited and punished love—are inserted into an expanded and expanding image of the past, one that seeks to displace the ideological occlusions of the apartheid era."[72] A politics that begins and ends with the state's recognition and granting of rights overwrites the continuation of capital's exploitation of labor under various guises. I would argue that Muholi's stolen series exists in the chasm between South Africa's "rainbow" nationalism where gay rights are constitutionally guaranteed and the reality of racialized homophobia and exploitation. Despite de jure constitutional protection, one out of two black lesbians will be raped at least once during her lifetime in what has become known as "corrective rape."[73] Many queer women suffer from AIDS-related illnesses, and opportunities for paid work are scarce. Rather than basing equality on the public recognition of erased identities—neoliberal multiculturalism's main concern—Muholi's work insists that issues around capital and material inequality are integral to queer rights. In many ways, this volume is haunted by her stolen series, those images that document the undocumented, those moments that give flesh to the name and the wound. As stand-ins for the illegible will of black women in the archive, these pilfered images do not incite us to recover what is lost as much as they insist on acknowledging what has been stolen and what is illegible. Feeling their absence renders us alive and vulnerable in the face of state-imposed death, in the face of the diasporic theft of ourselves and all of our "stuff."

Just as we have to critically imagine will where none is legible, the best way to see Muholi's lost photographs is look askance, to turn to her other images that speak to a queer relationality. I thus cast my eye toward some of Muholi's photographs from the *Being* series, in which she stresses the role that material exchanges perform in models of intimacy. These images of women who love, live, and laugh together through vicissitudes of poverty and fear of violence demonstrate a queer familial interdependence that is always already bound up in issues such as deprivation, accessibility, dependence, and freedom. As Muholi explains on her website:

> The *Being* series continues to explore the love and intimacy within our relationships regardless of the on-going pain and struggles that we face. My projects are about our histories, struggles and lives. Lovers and friends consented to participate in the project, willing to bare and express their love for each other. Each photograph features a couple in their different settings of their daily lives, and within their daily routine. . . . And it is

through seeing ourselves as we find love, laughter, joy that we can sustain our strength and regain our sanity as we move into a future that is sadly still filled with the threat of insecurities—HIV/AIDS, hate crimes, violence against women, poverty and unemployment.

Particularly important to me is a set of gorgeous photographs of Katlego Mashiloane and Nosipho Lavuta, Ext. 2, Lakeside, Johannesburg 2007. The pictures were taken in one small room where, it seems, the women perform most of their living. Muholi understandably denied me permission to reproduce the images, as she felt that all of her images were being overused. So let us imagine them instead. One photograph shows the women sitting on the floor against a brick wall, legs intertwined as they laugh at something or someone off-camera. Another has them squeezed at the edge of the frame next to an old-fashioned yellow-and-green stove that is the focal point. While their cramped position shows the smallness of the room, this smallness becomes intimacy as one woman sits on the other's lap. They quickly kiss each other in the midst of smiling. Yet another picture shows them standing naked side by side in a small, startlingly blue tub. They are both bent over toward the camera, scooping up soapy water as they bathe. In the background stands a crowded table on which are set a couple of white candles. The candles speak less to romance than to the obvious lack of electricity in their sparse surroundings. There are two other images of them naked, one in which they separately lotion their feet and faces and another in which, seated on the bed, one cradles the other from behind. Their faces are turned to each other, and they appear to be in mid-sentence. A final photograph depicts one of the women clad in a chaste white lace bra and full panties, sitting on the edge of the bed with a book of photographs on her lap. She studies what appears to be a reclining nude. The other woman, clad in brightly colored boxers and what Americans call a "wife beater" bends over to tie her braids into a ponytail. The image implies affinity even though the women do not touch or even look at each other. The brick wall behind them, the flowered sheet, the sunlight, and the closeness of the scene all suggest the indescribable performance of intimacy predicated on their vulnerability to each other.

The book of photographs on the lap of one of the women reminds us that traditional artistic representations of black (queer) women reduce them to sexualized commodities that can be bought, sold, and consumed. The nakedness or near-nakedness of the woman reading the magazine, however, resists this type of gross sexualization even as it reminds us of Mashiloane and Lavuta's material presence. As Pumla Gqola writes, "Through Muholi's lens, these Black lesbians exist and relate to each other in the midst of regimes that attempt to violate and co-opt their lives; they are not wholly defined by the terms of such definition. The shifting physical positions in the images, during which they are ... only briefly and fleetingly concerned with the world represented by a/the camera—point to the fluidity of intimacy [and] the impossibility of packaging it."[74] Through their performances of vulnerability embodied in the rituals of the everyday, the two women come into being by being undone by each other. It is such performances of vulnerability that point toward the illegible will in the archive and make me wonder out loud at their beauty as I am slowly and meaningfully undone.

NOTES

INTRODUCTION

1. C. Riley Snorton, *Nobody Is Supposed to Know: Black Sexuality on the Down Low* (Minneapolis: University of Minnesota Press, 2014), 39.

2. Dwight Conquergood, "Performance Studies: Interventions and Radical Research," *TDR* 46, no. 2 (Summer 2002): 148.

3. Joseph Roach, *Cities of the Dead: Circum-Atlantic Performance* (New York: Columbia University Press, 1996), 1079, 1081.

4. Robin Bernstein, *Performing American Childhood from Slavery to Civil Rights* (New York: New York University Press, 2011), 12–13.

5. Diana Taylor, "Performance and/as History," *TDR* 50, no. 1 (Spring 2006): 83.

6. The modern archive is often invoked as a technical cipher for what Sven Spieker calls the "modern dream of total control and all-encompassing administrative discipline, a giant filing cabinet at the center of a reality founded on ordered rationality": Sven Spieker, *The Big Archive: Art from Bureaucracy* (Cambridge, MA: MIT Press, 2008), 1. This archive's evidentiary power is thought to derive from its ability to simply register specific moments in time, ignoring the fact that the archive produces its own meaning.

7. Anjali Arondekar, *For the Record: On Sexuality and the Colonial Archive in India* (Durham, NC: Duke University Press, 2009), 2.

8. Arondekar, *For the Record*, 1.

9. Arondekar, *For the Record*, 3.

10. Jennifer Wenzel defines "afterlife" as the "denot[ation of] relationships of people to time that produce multilayered dynamics of presence and absence, anticipation and retrospection": Jennifer Wenzel, *Bulletproof: Afterlives of Anticolonial Prophecy in South Africa and Beyond* (Chicago: University of Chicago Press, 2009), 5.

11. Alexander G. Weheliye, *Habeas Viscus: Racializing Assemblages, Biopolitics, and Black Feminist theories of the Human* (Durham, NC: Duke University Press, 2014), 18–19.

12. Weheliye, *Habeas Viscus*, 29–30.

13. Oyeronke Oyewumi, *The Invention of Women: Making an African Sense of Western Gender Discourses* (Minneapolis: University of Minneapolis Press, 1997). Chandra Mohanty, *Feminism without Borders: Decolonizing Theory, Practicing Solidarity* (Durham, NC: Duke University Press, 2003).

14. Weheliye would insist here on the concept of racializing assemblages that "articulate relational intensities between human physiology and flesh, producing racial categories, which are subsequently coded as natural substances": Weheliye, *Habeas Viscus*, 50.

15. Ann Laura Stoler, *Race and the Education of Desire: Foucault's History of Sexuality and the Colonial Order of Things* (Durham, NC: Duke University Press, 1995), 72.

16. Stoler, *Race and the Education of Desire*, 90.

17. Zine Magubane, *Bringing the Empire Home: Race, Class, and Gender in Britain and Colonial South Africa* (Chicago: University of Chicago Press, 2004), 185–86.

18. Stoler, *Race and the Education of Desire*, 92.

19. John Edwin Mason, *Social Death and Resurrection: Slavery and Emancipation in South Africa* (Charlottesville: University of Virginia Press, 2003), 32–33.

20. "By the end of the VOC period, the development of a heightened colour consciousness was spreading; as Giliomee stated, 'by 1820 a racial order was firmly established' ": Nigel Worden, *Slavery in Dutch South Africa* (Cambridge: Cambridge University Press, 1985), 151.

21. Linda E. Merians, *Envisioning the Worst: Representations of "Hottentots" in Early-Modern England* (Newark: University of Delaware Press, 2001), 26; emphasis added. Magubane makes a similar point, referring us to original travelers' accounts by John Barrow (1801), William Burchell (1827), Henry Lichtenstein (1812), Thomas Pringle (1834), and George Thompson (1827): Zine Magubane, "Which Bodies Matter? Feminism, Poststructuralism, Race, and the Curious Theoretical Odyssey of the 'Hottentot Venus,'" *Gender and Society* 15, no. 6 [2001]: 822.

22. Magubane, "Which Bodies Matter?," 823.

23. Diana Taylor, *The Archive and the Repertoire: Performing Cultural Memory in the Americas* (Durham, NC: Duke University Press, 2003), 4.

24. Jean Comaroff and John Comaroff, *Ethnography and the Historical Imagination* (Boulder, CO: Westview, 1992), 79.

25. Magubane, *Bringing the Empire Home*, 4.

26. Timothy Burke, " 'Sunlight Soap Has Changed My Life': Hygiene, Commodification, and the Body in Colonial Zimbabwe," in *Clothing and Difference: Embodied Identities in Colonial and Post-Colonial Africa*, ed. Hildi Hendrickson (Durham, NC: Duke University Press, 1996), 190–91.

27. Weheliye, *Habeas Viscus*, 6.

28. Neville Hoad, "Miss HIV and Us: Beauty Queens against the HIV/AIDS Pandemic" CR: *The New Centennial Review*: 18. Hoad is talking not about Miss Landmine Angola but about the Miss HIV Stigma Free pageant, first held in Botswana in 2003. Its goals include the humanization and "normalization" of the person living with HIV, education about the pandemic, prevention, and treatment.

29. Hoad, "Miss HIV and Us," 26.

30. Elizabeth A. Povinelli, *The Empire of Love: Toward a Theory of Intimacy, Genealogy, and Carnality.* (Durham, NC: Duke University Press, 2006), 7.

31. Povinelli, *The Empire of Love*, 8.

32. Hortense Spillers talks about how African American women are so burdened by an excess of historical meanings that it is almost impossible for the "agents" buried under them to surface, except by inventing a new grammar: Hortense J. Spillers, "Mama's Baby, Papa's Maybe: An American Grammar Book," *Diacritics* 17, no. 2 (Summer 1987): 64–81. This formulation forms the backbone of Weheliye, *Habeas Viscus*.

33. Spillers, "Mama's Baby, Papa's Maybe," 67.

34. Elizabeth A. Povinelli and Kim Turcot DiFruscia, "A Conversation with Elizabeth A. Povinelli," *Trans-Scripts* 2 (2012): 78.

35. Povinelli and DiFruscia, "A Conversation with Elizabeth A. Povinelli," 79.

36. Achille Mbembe, "Necropolitics," trans. Libby Meintjes, *Public Culture* 15, no. 1 (Winter 2003): 12.

37. Achille Mbembe, "On Politics as a Form of Expenditure," in *Law and Disorder in the Postcolony*, eds. Jean Comaroff and John Comaroff (Chicago: University of Chicago Press, 2006), 324.

38. Orlando Patterson, *Slavery and Social Death: A Comparative Study* (Cambridge, MA: Harvard University Press, 1982), 35–76.

39. Carrie Noland, "Introduction," in *Migrations of Gesture*, eds. Carrie Noland and Sally Ann Ness (Minneapolis: University of Minnesota, 2008), xiii.

40. Juana Maria Rodriguez, *Sexual Futures, Queer Gestures and Other Latina Longings* (New York: New York University Press, 2014), 4.

41. Rodriguez, *Sexual Futures, Queer Gestures and Other Latina Longings*, 6.

42. Susan E. Phillips, "Physical Graffiti West: African American Gang Walks and Semiotic Practice," in *Migration of Gestures*, eds. Carrie Noland and Sally A. Ness (Minneapolis: University of Minnesota Press, 2008), 38.

43. Rodriguez, *Sexual Futures, Queer Gestures and Other Latina Longings*, 101.

44. Noland, "Introduction," xv.

45. Jonathan Crush and Clarence Tshitereke, "Contesting Migrancy: The Foreign Labor Debate in Post-1994 South Africa," *Africa Today* 48, no. 3 (Fall 2001): 49–70.

46. Phaswane Mpe, *Welcome to Our Hillbrow: A Novel of Postapartheid South Africa* (Athens: Ohio University Press, 2001).

47. See Paul Gilroy, *The Black Atlantic: Modernity and Double Consciousness* (Cambridge, MA: Harvard University Press, 1993).

48. Loren Kruger, "Black Atlantics, White Indians, and Jews: Locations, Locutions, and Syncretic Identities in the Fiction of Achmat Dangor and Others," *South Atlantic Quarterly* 100, no. 1 (2001): 113.

49. Pier M. Larson, *History and Memory in the Age of Enslavement: Becoming Merina in Highland Madagascar, 1770–1822* (Portsmouth, NH: Heinemann, 2000), xvi.

50. Larson, *History and Memory in the Age of Enslavement*, 272.

51. Larson, *History and Memory in the Age of Enslavement*, xix.

52. Tony Ballantyne and Antoinette Burton, eds., "Introduction: Bodies, Empires, and World Histories," in *Bodies in Contact: Rethinking Colonial Encounters in World History*, eds. Tony Ballantyne and Antoinette Burton (Durham, NC: Duke University Press, 2005), 3.

53. The Dutch West India Company not only supplied Surinam with slaves during the eighteenth century but also played a key intermediary role in the transatlantic trade: Nigel Worden and Gerald Groenewald, eds., *Trials of Slavery: Selected Documents Concerning Slaves from the Criminal Records of the Council of Justice at the Cape of Good Hope, 1705–1794* (Cape Town: Van Riebeeck Society for the Publication of South African Historical Documents, 2005), ix.

54. Worden and Groenewald note a few exceptions, such as the "chance capture of a Portuguese slaver with Angolan slaves aiming for Brazil in 1658": Worden and Groenewald, *Trials of Slavery*, xi.

55. Robert Shell, cited in Worden and Groenewald, *Trials of Slavery*, xii.

56. Worden and Groenewald, *Trials of Slavery*, 57.

57. Worden and Groenewald, *Trials of Slavery*, 4.

58. In 1754, Rachel Van de Caab was found guilty of collaborating with Joseph to poison their mistress with mercury. To make Joseph talk, their master spans his body into the *poolsche bok*, which leads to Joseph's suicide. In the *poolsche bok*, the slave's hands are tied together and placed over the drawn-up knees. A stick or some equivalent is placed under the knees and across the arms so the slave is unable to defend herself in any way. Slaves were usually undressed and whipped while in this position. This practice was widespread in the Cape from the seventeenth century on: see Worden and Groenewald, *Trials of Slavery*, 267n4.

59. Quoted in Mason, *Social Death and Resurrection*, 74

60. See Nigel Worden, *Slavery in Dutch South Africa* (Cambridge: Cambridge University Press, 1985), 53, table 5.1. In 1687, there were 230 male slaves, 44 female slaves, and 36 children. By 1793, there were 9,046 male slaves, 3,590 female slaves, and 2,111 children.

61. See "1749 Jon Lategaan" and "1740 Michiel Lourich," in Worden and Groenewald, *Trials of Slavery*, 276–81 and 176–87.

62. Suzette Spencer, "Historical Memory, Romantic Narrative, and Sally Hemings," *African American Review* 40, no. 3 (Fall 2006): 509.

63. Nell Irvin Painter, "Representing Truth: Sojourner Truth's Knowing and Becoming Known," *Journal of American History* 8, no. 2 (1994): 462–63.

64. William Wright, *Slavery at the Cape of Good Hope* (1831) (New York: Negro Universities Press, 1969), 15.

65. Mason, *Social Death and Resurrection*, 95.

66. Quoted in Anders Sparrman, *A Voyage to the Cape of Good Hope: Towards the Antarctic Polar Circle, and Round the World: but Chiefly into the Country of the Hottentots and Caffres, from the Year 1772–1776*, trans. Georg Forster (London: G. G. J. and J. Robinson, 1785), 72.

67. Sharon Holland, *The Erotic Life of Racism* (Durham, NC: Duke University Press, 2012), 46.

68. Worden, *Slavery in Dutch South Africa*, 59.

69. O.F. Mentzel, *A Description of the African Cape of Good Hope, 1787*, Vol. II (Cape Town: The van Riebeeck Society, 1944), 125.

70. George M. Frederickson, *White Supremacy: A Comparative Study of American and South African History* (New York: Oxford University Press, 1982), 81.

71. Wright, *Slavery at the Cape of Good Hope*, 19.

72. Magubane, *Bringing the Empire Home*, 15.

73. Donald Donham, *Violence in a Time of Liberation: Murder and Ethnicity at a South African Gold Mine* (Durham, NC: Duke University Press, 1994), 110.

74. Sara Ahmed, *Willful Subjects* (Durham, NC: Duke University Press, 2014), 42.

75. Looking specifically at the gold mines in South Africa, Donham writes that the "stated purpose of racial separation was not just to maintain white purity and privilege, but also to protect black workers from the corrosive effects of market exchange, particularly in a world in which, as jural minors, they were seen as incapable of protecting themselves": Donham, *Violence in a Time of Liberation*, 111. The resulting paternalist bond undercut the idea of black South Africans as individual citizens with the rights of free labor to control the economic life of mine workers and to discourage unions that aimed to protect workers' rights.

76. Donham, *Violence in a Time of Liberation*, 111.

77. Rosemary Wiss, "Lipreading: Remembering Saartjie Baartman," *Australian Journal of Anthropology* 5, nos. 1–2 (1994): 19.

78. Carole Pateman, *The Disorder of Women: Democracy, Feminism, and Political Theory* (Stanford, CA: Stanford University Press, 1989), 152; emphasis added.

79. Pateman writes, "The implications of the convention that a wife must bow to the authority of and be economically dependent upon her husband, who is 'head of the household,' are obscured more thoroughly in the late twentieth century than in earlier times, because it is now firmly held that marriage can properly be based only on the consent of two individuals. But this appearance of equality between two individuals cloaks the unequal status of husband and wife created through the marriage contract. . . . The contemporary significance of the contract theorists' reconciliation with patriarchalism has been hidden behind the liberal conviction that marriage is a matter of 'individual' choice": Pateman, *The Disorder of Women*, 153. According to Pateman, behind the language of individual choice lie structures of inequity that mask the meaninglessness of choice for certain participants caught up in its structures. Despite well-meaning feminist reinventions, the marriage contract itself is haunted by fundamental inequities that structure gender inequity. One need only think of the difficulties in extending the protections of rape law to married women raped by their husbands to be reminded that the consequence of entering into a marriage contract is the legal and social presupposition of a woman's "consent" to her husband's authority.

80. Carl F. Stychin, "De-Meaning of Contract," in *Sexuality and the Law: Feminist Engagements*, eds. Vanessa E. Munro and Carl F. Stychin (London: Routledge Cavendish, 2007), 79.

81. Stychin, "De-Meaning of Contract," 79.

82. Spillers, "Mama's Baby, Papa's Maybe," 67.

83. Elizabeth B. Clark, "'The Sacred Rights of the Weak': Pain, Sympathy, and the Culture of Individual Rights in Antebellum America," *Journal of American History* 82, no. 2 (1995): 465.

84. Terence Ball, "Two Concepts of Coercion," *Theory and Society* 5, no. 1 (1978): 98.

85. Saidiya Hartman, *Scenes of Subjection: Terror, Slavery and Self-Making in Nineteenth-Century America* (New York: Oxford University Press, 1997), 20.

86. Roach, *Cities of the Dead*, 3.

87. Ball, "Two Concepts of Coercion," 107.

88. Ball, "Two Concepts of Coercion," 98.

89. Ball, "Two Concepts of Coercion," 107.

90. Daniel Markovits, "Contract and Collaboration," *Yale Law Journal* 113, no. 7 (May 2004): 1450.

91. Sara Ahmed's "queer ethics of clumsiness" suggests something similar. She suggests an ethics of those who are not attuned to one another—those with various capacities and incapacities who clumsily bump into one another. "Corporeal diversity, how we come to inhabit different kinds of bodies . . . , would be understood as a call to open up a world that has assumed a certain kind of body as a norm. Rather than equality being about smoothing a relation perhaps equality [and I would add collaboration] is a bumpy ride": Ahmed, *Willful Subjects*, 51.

92. Here Stychin directly engages with Wendy Brown's famous argument that "'the constitutive terms of liberal political discourse depend upon their implicit opposition to a subject and a set of activities marked "feminine"' . . . a sexual division of labor, and a gendered antinomy between individual and family as well as in the terms expressing the respective ethos of civil society and the family; 'self-interest' on the one hand and 'selflessness' on the other": Wendy Brown, *States of Injury: Power and Freedom in Late Modernity* (Princeton, NJ: Princeton University Press, 1995), 81. Thus, Brown suggests that the usefulness of a language of rights is questionable.

93. Ahmed, *Willful Subjects*, 9.

94. Nigel Penn, *Rogues, Rebels and Runaways: Eighteenth-Century Cape Characters* (Cape Town: David Philip, 1999).

95. Andre Brink, *The Rights of Desire* (New York: Harcourt, 2000).

96. Agnes Sam, *Jesus and Other Short Stories* (Portsmouth, NH: Heinemann, 1994).

97. Gloria Wekker, *Politics of Passion: Women's Sexual Culture in the Afro-Surinamese Diaspora* (New York: Columbia University Press, 2006).

98. Yvette Christianse, *Unconfessed: A Novel* (New York: Other Press, 2007).

99. Christianse, "'Heartsore': The Melancholy Archive of Cape Colony Slavery," *Scholar and Feminist Online* 7, no. 2 (Spring 2009). http://www.barnard.edu/sfonline.

100. Christianse, *Unconfessed*, 279.

CHAPTER 1. RETURNING TO HANKEY

1. Joseph Roach, *Cities of the Dead: Circum-Atlantic Performance* (New York: Columbia University Press, 1996), 28.

2. Jin-Kyung Lee, *Service Economies: Militarism, Sex Work, and Migrant Labor in South Africa*. Minneapolis: University of Minnesota Press, 2010), 227.

3. Clifton Crais and Pamela Scully, *Sara Baartman and the Hottentot Venus: A Ghost Story and a Biography* (Princeton, NJ: Princeton University Press, 2009).

4. As mentioned in Fezile Jacobs's testimony in Ciraj Rassool, Leslie Witz and Gary Minkley. "Burying and Memorialising the Body of Truth: The TRC and National Heritage." In *After the TRC: Reflections on Truth and Reconciliation in South Africa*, eds. Wilmot James and Linda van de Vijver (Cape Town: David Philip, 2000), 115–27.

5. See the South African Truth and Reconciliation Commission Videotape Collection, Yale Law School Lillian Goldman Law Library, New Haven, CT, http://trc.law .yale.edu. Joyce Mthimkulu's story is referenced in Rassool, Witz, and Minkley 125. This incident resonates strangely with Stamp Paid in Toni Morrison's novel *Beloved*, who carries with him "a red ribbon knotted around a curl of wet woolly hair, clinging still to its bit of scalp." While the scalp and ribbon invoke in him a desperate desire to dwell on "what in the world was harmless," Stamp Paid also insists on carrying it in his pocket until such a time that the horror that resulted in that scrap of hair, scalp, and ribbon is redressed or at least addressed: Toni Morrison, *Beloved* (New York: Plume, 1988), 180–81.

6. Rassool, Witz and Minkley, "Burying and Memorializing the Body of Truth: The TRC and National Heritage," 125.

7. Ciraj Rassool, "Human Remains, the Disciplines of the Dead, & the South African Memorial Complex." In *The Politics of Heritage in Africa: Economies, Histories, and Infrastructures*, ed, Derek Peterson, Kodzo Gavua, and Ciraj Rassool (Cambridge: Cambridge University Press, 2015), 133–56. http://ebooks.cambridge.org/chapter.jsf ?bid=CBO9781316151181&cid=CBO9781316151181A014.

8. This comes from the title of Zakes Mda's novel, *Ways of Dying* published by Picador in 2002.

9. Rebekah Lee, "Death 'On the Move': Funerals, Entrepreneurs and the Rural-Urban Nexus in South Africa." *Africa: The Journal of the International African Institute* 81, no. 2 (May 2011): 227.

10. David B. Coplan, *In the Time of Cannibals: The World Music of South Africa's Basotho Migrants* (Chicago: University of Chicago Press, 1994), 33, 124.

11. Eddy Tshidiso Maloka, *Basotho and the Mines: A Social History of Labour Migrancy in Lesotho and South Africa, c. 1890–1940* (Dakar, Senegal: Codesria, 2004), chap. 6. Another important source is Eddy Tshidiso Maloka, "Basotho and the Experience of Death, Dying, and Mourning in the South African Mine Compounds, 1890–1940 in *Cahiers d'Études Africaines* 38, no. 149 (1998): 17–40.

12. Maloka, "Basotho and the Experience of Death, Dying, and Mourning in the South African Mine Compounds," 20.

13. Diana Taylor, *The Archive and the Repertoire: Performing Cultural Memory in the Americas* (Durham, NC: Duke University Press, 2003), 28.

14. Joseph Roach, *Cities of the Dead: Circum-Atlantic Performance* (New York: Columbia University Press, 1996), 2.

15. Connie Rapoo, "Just Give us the Bones! Theatres of African Diasporic Returns," *Critical Arts* 25, no. 2 (June 2011): 132.

16. We could even consider the African National Congress's exhumation and reburial of Thembu Paramount Chief Sabata Dalindyebo, who was dumped in the women's section of a pauper's grave in 1989: Rebekah Lee, "Death 'On the Move,'" 239.

17. Rapoo, "Just Give us the Bones!," 132.

18. There are numerous linguistic, physical, and cultural differences among the various clans of Khoisan, all called "Hottentots" by Europeans: see Linda E. Merians, *Envisioning the Worst: Representations of "Hottentots" in Early-Modern England* (Newark: University of Delaware Press, 2001). Baartman belongs to the Khoikhoi people, a group that was recently officially recognized by the United Nations as an indigenous "First Nation." For more in-depth discussions of issues of nomenclature, indigenous status, and politics of Khoisan identity, see Andrew Bank, Hans Heese, and Chris Loff, eds., *The Proceedings of the Khoisan Identities and Cultural Heritage Conference* (Cape Town: Institute for Historical Research Infosource, 1997).

19. Around 1991, the World Bank began an initiative to aid indigenous peoples of the area, eventually funding the Griqua National Conference's establishment of sacred sites on a farm named Ratelgat in the Western Cape: Crais and Scully, *Sara Baartman and the Hottentot Venus*, 157.

20. Lee, "Death 'On the Move,'" 241.

21. Lydie Moudileno, "Returning Remains: Saartjie Baartman, or the 'Hottentot Venus' as Transnational Postcolonial Icon," *Forum for Modern Language Studies* 45, no. 2 (2009): 208–9.

22. Rapoo, "Just Give us the Bones!," 132.

23. Crais and Scully, *Sara Baartman and the Hottentot Venus*, 155.

24. Crais and Scully, *Sara Baartman and the Hottentot Venus*, 109.

25. Choosing to bury Baartman on International Indigenous People's day and South Africa's Women's Day gestured toward these concerns.

26. His speech can be found on http://www.dfa.gov.za/docs/speeches/2002/mbeko809.htm. All further references to his speech are from this site.

27. Mbeki's shortsighted accusations that Western science had invented HIV/AIDS for its own racist purposes severely hampered prevention and management of the virus and disease, causing South Africa's infection rates to soar.

28. Ann M Kakaliouras, "An anthropology of Repatriation: Contemporary Physical Anthropological and Native American Ontologies of Practice," *Current Anthropology* 53.S5 (2012), S212.

29. Martin Legassick and Ciraj Rassool, *Skeletons in the Cupboard: South African Museums and the Trade in Human Remains, 1907–1917* (Cape Town: Iziko Museum, 2015), 102.

30. See Ann Kakaliouras, "An Anthropology of Repatriation."

31. Katherine McKittrick, "Science Quarrels Sculpture: The Politics of Reading Sarah Baartman." *Mosaic* [Winnipeg] 43, no. 2 (2010): 113–30, 123.

32. Philip in McKittrick, "Science Quarrels Sculpture," 123.

33. Thomas DeFrantz defines "corporeal orature" as the "align[ment of] movement with speech . . . to incite action": Thomas DeFrantz, "The Black Beat Made Visible: Hip Hop Dance and Body Power," in *Of the Presence of the Body: Essays on Dance and Performance Theory*, ed. Andre Lepecki (Middletown, CT: Wesleyan University Press, 2004), 64–81, 4.

34. Crais and Scully, *Sara Baartman and the Hottentot Venus*, 151–52.

35. Moudileno, "Returning Remains," 210.

36. "Charou" is a slang term, often derogatory, used to refer to a Hindu of Indian descent. Hindus practice cremation and not burial of the dead and thus would not use coffins in their death rituals. The reference to "thinking on one's feet" alludes to stereotypes about the cunning and conniving "Asiatic" often used to describe indentured laborers and their descendants. I include this joke to point to the ubiquity of issues concerning the relocation of the dead in popular culture and because it brings together discussions of Baartman with discourses about Indian Africans developed later in the book.

37. Adam Ashforth, *Witchcraft, Violence, and Democracy in South Africa* (Chicago: University of Chicago Press, 2005), 165.

38. Crais and Scully, *Sara Baartman and the Hottentot Venus*, 167.

39. Candice Bailey, "Muti Killing Is a Way of Life in Rural Areas," *IOL News*, January 16, 2010.

40. See also Mary Braid, "Witchcraft Returns to Haunt New South Africa: Children Murdered and Their Bodies Used in Rituals." *The Independent*, January 21, 1998.

41. Ashforth, *Witchcraft, Violence, and Democracy in South Africa*, 136.

42. See Braid, "Witchcraft Returns to Haunt New South Africa"; Gareth Van Onselen, "Pervasive Problem of Witchcraft Needs a More Urgent Response," *Business Day Live*, July 2, 2013. Braid writes that, as "South Africa struggles to be seen as a progressive player on the world stage, much of its culture remains rooted in the past. Perhaps the most horrific evidence of this is the continuing kidnapping and murder of children so that their body parts can be used in traditional medicine."

43. Ashforth, *Witchcraft, Violence, and Democracy in South Africa*, 311.

44. Ashforth, *Witchcraft, Violence, and Democracy in South Africa*, 259–60.

45. Crais and Scully, *Sara Baartman and the Hottentot Venus*, 25.

46. Yvette Abrahams, "Disempowered to Consent: Sara Bartman and Khoisan Slavery in the Nineteenth-Century Cape Colony and Britain," *South African Historical Journal* 35 (1996): 99–101.

47. Quoted in Z. S. Strother, "Display of the Body Hottentot," in *Africans on Stage: Studies in Ethnological Show Business*, ed. Bernth Lindfors (Bloomington: Indiana University Press, 1999), 43.

48. Rosemary Wiss, "Lipreading: Remembering Saartjie Baartman," *Australian Journal of Anthropology* 5, nos. 1–2 (1994): 16.

49. Crais and Scully, *Sara Baartman and the Hottentot Venus*, 90. Crais and Scully cite this letter, which in all likelihood was written for Cesars by Dunlop, as Cesars

could neither read nor write. Most free blacks in the Cape did not have access to an education that would allow them to acquire these skills.

50. Quoted in Crais and Scully, *Sara Baartman and the Hottentot Venus*, 89. Though this letter's author chose to remain anonymous, there is little doubt that the author was Macauley, especially since the letter appeared directly after his visit.

51. Crais and Scully, *Sara Baartman and the Hottentot Venus*, 91–92.

52. Edlie Wong, *Neither Fugitive nor Free: Atlantic Slavery, Freedom Suits, and the Legal Culture of Travel (America and the Long Nineteenth Century)* (New York: New York University Press, 2009), 11.

53. See Zine Magubane, "Which Bodies Matter? Feminism, Poststructuralism, Race, and the Curious Theoretical Odyssey of the 'Hottentot Venus,'" *Gender and Society* 15, no. 6 (2001): 822–24; Linda E. Merians, *Envisioning the Worst: Representations of "Hottentots" in Early-Modern England* (Newark: University of Delaware Press, 2001).

54. Sadiah Qureshi, "Displaying Sara Baartman, the 'Hottentot Venus,'" *History of Science* 42, 2 (2004): 241.

55. Magubane, "Which Bodies Matter?," 829.

56. Magubane, "Which Bodies Matter?," 828.

57. Wiss, "Lipreading," 19.

58. Crais and Scully, *Sara Baartman and the Hottentot Venus*, 88.

59. The less than successful tour in Ireland occurred in April 1812.

60. Crais and Scully, *Sara Baartman and the Hottentot Venus*, 98.

61. Quoted in Strother, "Display of the Body Hottentot," 45.

62. I develop this idea using Lauren Berlant's concept of "slow death" later in the book.

63. Wiss, "Lipreading," 34.

64. Wilfred Carsel, "The Slaveholders' Indictment of Northern Wage Slavery," *Journal of Southern History* 6, no. 4 (1940): 504. See also George Fitzhugh, *Sociology for the South; Or, the Failure of Free Society* (Richmond, VA: A. Morris, 1854) and *Cannibals All! Or, Slaves without Masters* (Cambridge, MA: Belknap Press of Harvard University Press, 1857). In a review of *Cannibals All!* Theodore D. Harris asserts that Fitzhugh's depictions of the abuses of laissez-faire capitalism and the benevolence of slavery were so vivid that William Lloyd Garrison devoted more time to refuting his argument in the *Liberator* than to that of any other pro-slavery advocate.

65. Carsel, "The Slaveholders' Indictment of Northern Wage Slavery," 508–10.

66. Quoted in Strother, "Display of the Body Hottentot," 43–44.

67. Quoted in Strother, "Display of the Body Hottentot," 44.

68. Saidiya Hartman, *Scenes of Subjection: Terror, Slavery and Self-Making in Nineteenth-Century America* (New York: Oxford University Press, 1997), 54.

69. Crais and Scully, *Sara Baartman and the Hottentot Venus*, 90.

70. Hartman, *Scenes of Subjection*, 36.

71. *Small Island* is Levy's fourth novel and won the Orange Prize for Fiction, the Whitbread Novel Award and the Commonwealth Writer's Prize.

72. Andrea Levy, *Small Island* (New York: Picador Press, 2004), 4. Hereafter, page numbers are cited in parentheses in the text.

73. Veit Erlmann, " 'Spectatorial Lust': The African Choir in England, 1891–1893," in *Africans on Stage: Studies in Ethnological Show Business*, ed. Bernth Lindfors (Bloomington: Indiana University Press, 1999), 110.

74. Zine Magubane, *Bringing the Empire Home: Race, Class, and Gender in Britain and Colonial South Africa* (Chicago: University of Chicago Press, 2004), 44.

75. Crais and Scully, *Sara Baartman and the Hottentot Venus*, 69.

76. Crais and Scully, *Sara Baartman and the Hottentot Venus*, 71.

77. Wiss, "Lipreading," 14. The first broadsheet was published on September 18, 1810, and later circulated throughout Europe. Of particular interest is that both aquatints list Baartman as the publisher. Thus, she held the copyright to what would become iconic images of her in the present.

78. The short pipe became part of a standard iconography for the Khoikhoi. The smoking of tobacco was actively promoted through the use of tobacco as part of payment for wage labor. Tobacco replaced the traditional Khoikhoi use of dagga, or *cannabis sativa*. Smoking the pipe became symbolic of the supposed indolence of the Khoikhoi that justified Europeans' theft of their land and their relegation to the legal status of minors. The walking stick became emblematic of the nomadism of the Khoikhoi that supposedly made them unfit cultivators—hence, the "necessity" for taking their land: see Strother, "Display of the Body Hottentot," 4–16.

79. Crais and Scully, *Sara Baartman and the Hottentot Venus*, 12. She was given the tortoise shell necklace after her first menstruation as an initiation into the Khoekhoe world of gendered obligations. It was also one of the very few objects she had with her when she died.

80. Strother, "Display of the Body Hottentot," 33.

81. Magubane, *Bringing the Empire Home*, 45.

82. Apropos here would be the description in the *Times* on May 18, 1853, of the "Caffres at Hyde-Park-Corner" performance: "They seem utterly to lose all sense of their present position, and, inspired by the situations in which they are placed, appear to take Mr. Marshall's scenes for their actual abode in the vicinity of Port Nation": Bernth Lindfors, "Charles Dickens and the Zulus," in *Africans on Stage: Studies in Ethnological Show Business*, ed. Bernth Lindfors (Bloomington: Indiana University Press, 1999), 66.

83. T. Denean Sharpley-Whiting, *Black Venus: Sexualized Savages, Primal Fears, and Primitive Narratives in French* (Durham, NC: Duke University Press, 1999), 18–19.

84. Strother, "Display of the Body Hottentot," 31.

85. Coco Fusco, *English Is Broken Here: Notes on Cultural Fusion in the Americas* (New York: New Press, 1995), 49.

86. Matthews, quoted in Wiss, "Lipreading," 15. Qureshi likens this poking and prodding to audiences' responses to animals at a local menagerie that were "teased and agitated," further arguing that such behavior demonstrated the blurring of the boundaries between human and animal displays: Qureshi, "Displaying Sara Baartman, the 'Hottentot Venus,' " 238.

87. Barbara Chase-Riboud, *Hottentot Venus* (New York: Doubleday, 2003); Anne Fausto-Sterling, "Gender, Race, and Nation: The Comparative Anatomy of 'Hottentot' Women in Europe, 1815–1817," in *Deviant Bodies: Critical Perspectives on Difference in Science and Popular Culture*, eds. Jacqueline Urla and Jennifer Terry (Bloomington: Indiana University Press, 1995), 19–48; Sharpley-Whiting, *Black Venus*.

88. Sarah Jane Cervenak, *Wandering: Philosophical Performances of Racial and Sexual Freedom* (Durham, NC: Duke University Press, 2014), 5–6.

89. Cervenak, *Wandering*, 3.

90. Cervenak, *Wandering*, 14–15.

91. Significant work has been done on freak shows: see, e.g., Rachel Adams, *Sideshow U.S.A.: Freaks and the American Cultural Imagination* (Chicago: University of Chicago Press, 2001); Robert Bogdan, *Pornography or Entertainment? The Rise and Fall of the Freak Show* (Chicago: University of Chicago Press, 1988); Rosemarie Garland-Thomson, ed., *Freakery: Cultural Spectacle of the Extraordinary Body* (New York: New York University Press, 1996). Bodgan emphasizes the business aspects of the freak show. He suggests that freaks, for the most part, were independent entertainers who were playing a role on-stage and lived complete and ordinary lives otherwise. He downplays the aspects of coercion in the interests of recovering the agency of the freak.

92. Jacqueline Urla and Jennifer Terry, "Introduction: Mapping Embodied Deviance," in *Deviant Bodies: Critical Perspectives on Difference in Science and Popular Culture*, eds. Jacqueline Urla and Jennifer Terry (Bloomington: Indiana University Press, 1995), 2.

93. Wiss, "Lipreading," 13.

94. Strother, "Display of the Body Hottentot," 29.

95. Magubane, "Which Bodies Matter?," 826.

96. Crais and Scully, *Sara Baartman and the Hottentot Venus*, 67.

97. Qureshi, "Displaying Sara Baartman, the 'Hottentot Venus,'" 240.

98. Qureshi, "Displaying Sara Baartman, the 'Hottentot Venus,'" 240–41.

99. Adams, *Sideshow U.S.A.*, 40.

100. Adams, *Sideshow U.S.A.*, 40.

101. Adams, *Sideshow U.S.A.*, 43.

102. Crais and Scully, *Sara Baartman and the Hottentot Venus*, 36.

103. Crais and Scully estimate a community of almost four hundred Khoekhoe in the Eastern Papendorp area, most of them survivors for the great Hottentot Rebellion of 1799–1802 where they rebelled against their masters: Crais and Scully, *Sara Baartman and the Hottentot Venus*, 44.

104. Crais and Scully, *Sara Baartman and the Hottentot Venus*, 42.

105. Crais and Scully, *Sara Baartman and the Hottentot Venus*, 50.

106. John Robert Robinson, *"Old Q"; a Memoir of William Douglas, Fourth Duke of Queensberry, K.T., One of 'the Fathers of the Turf,' with a Full Account of His Celebrated Matches and Wagers, Etc.* (London: Sampson Low, Marston, 1895), 245.

107. Charles Kessler, ed., *Berlin in Lights: The Diaries of Count Harry Kessler, 1918–1937* (New York: Grove, 2002), 283.

108. Kessler, *Berlin in Lights*, 283.

109. Kessler, *Berlin in Lights*, 284.

110. Kessler, *Berlin in Lights*, 284.

111. Kessler, *Berlin in Lights*, 284.

112. Ann E. Nymann, "Sally's Rape: Robbie Mccauley's Survival Art," *African American Review* 33, no. 4 (1999): 583.

113. Okwui Enwezor, "Reframing the Black Subject: Ideology and Fantasy in Contemporary South African Representation," in *Race-ing Art History: Critical Readings in Race and Art History*, ed. Kymberly N. Pinder (New York: Routledge University Press, 2002), 372.

114. Hartman, *Scenes of Subjection*, 22.

115. Enwezor, "Reframing the Black Subject," 372.

116. See http://africanhistory.about.com/od/slaveryimages/ig/Slavery-Images -Gallery/TestingForSickness.htm.

117. Roach, *Cities of the Dead*, 215.

118. Urla and Terry, "Introduction," 2.

119. Walter Johnson, *Soul by Soul: Life inside the Antebellum Slave Market* (Cambridge, MA: Harvard University Press, 1999), 171.

120. Hartman, *Scenes of Subjection*, 61.

121. I am aware that to European audiences, all musical performances by Others were heard as rude, unmusical, and primitive. However, here I am reading descriptions of Baartman's against the author's intentions.

122. Judith Halberstam, *The Queer Art of Failure* (Durham, NC: Duke University Press, 2011), 12.

123. Hartman, *Scenes of Subjection*, 38.

124. Johnson, *Soul by Soul*, 129.

125. Quoted in Johnson, *Soul by Soul*, 180.

126. Quoted in Johnson, *Soul by Soul*, 179.

127. Johnson, *Soul by Soul*, 34.

128. Johnson, *Soul by Soul*, 21.

CHAPTER 2. "FORCE REFIGURED AS CONSENT"

1. Cape women retained their maiden names after marriage. The Partible Inheritance rule was in force at the Cape, where half of the estate went to the surviving spouse and the other half was divided among children of the deceased. While this changed slightly in the nineteenth century, it meant that a woman could become the head of a household either as a surviving spouse or as an offspring. Elizabeth Lingelbach thus inherited and owned the slaves as head of her household: see Robert C. H. Shell, "A Family Matter: The Sale and Transfer of Human Beings at the Cape, 1658 to 1830," *International Journal of African Historical Studies* 25, no. 2 (1992): 335.

2. Consider our four convicted slaves: one was from Madagascar; one, from Bengal; one, from Tutucorijn; and one, from Masulipatam. Their diverse origins point to the Dutch East India Company's repeated importation of slaves from its Eastern colonies

such as Bengal via Batavia and places along the Coromandel and Malabar coasts. According to Parbavati Rama, the Cape's first two slave imports came from West Africa when a Dutch ship intercepted a Portuguese slaver. Due to later prohibitions from procuring slaves from the West Coast, the Dutch East India Company resorted to Mozambique, Madagascar, India, Sri Lanka, and the Indonesian Archipelago as a source for its slaves (Rama 21–22). Robert Shell in *Children of Bondage* states that of the approximately 63,000 slaves who came to the Cape between 1652 and 1808, nearly 26 percent were from India (30–40). Rama's research builds on Shell's work to state that in the years between 1658 and 1819, 42 percent of foreign slaves brought to the Cape were Indian with 3,660 males and 645 females (Rama 50).

3. Shell, *Children of Bondage,* 288.

4. This decree appears originally in George McCall Theal's 39 volume compilation, *Records of the Cape Colony, 1793–1831, copied for the Cape Government, from the Manuscript Documents,* vol. 9 (Charleston, SC: BiblioLIFE, 2009), 153.

5. John Edwin Mason, *Social Death and Resurrection: Slavery and Emancipation in South Africa* (Charlottesville: University of Virginia Press, 2003), 33.

6. See Peter Kolb, *The Present State of the Cape of Good Hope,* trans. G. Medley (London: W. Innys, 1731), 360–63. http://repository.up.ac.za/dspace/handle/2263/8675.

7. For an analysis of the execution, see Mary Louise Pratt, *Imperial Eyes: Travel Writing and Transculturation* (New York: Routledge, 1992), 48.

8. Victor Turner, *Dramas, Fields, and Metaphors: Symbolic Action in Human Society* (Ithaca, NY: Cornell University Press, 1974).

9. Diana Taylor, *The Archive and the Repertoire: Performing Cultural Memory in the Americas* (Durham, NC: Duke University Press, 2003), 4.

10. Taylor, *The Archive and the Repertoire,* 28.

11. Tony Ballantyne and Antoinette Burton, eds., "Introduction: Bodies, Empires, and World Histories," in *Bodies in Contact: Rethinking Colonial Encounters in World History,* eds. Tony Ballantyne and Antoinette Burton (Durham, NC: Duke University Press, 2005), 3.

12. Suzette Spencer, "Historical Memory, Romantic Narrative, and Sally Hemings," *African American Review* 40, no. 3 (Fall 2006): 509.

13. Quoted in Anders Sparrman, *A Voyage to the Cape of Good Hope: Towards the Antarctic Polar Circle, and Round the World: but Chiefly into the Country of the Hottentots and Caffres, from the Year 1772–1776,* trans. Georg Forster (London: G. G. J. and J. Robinson, 1785), 72.

14. Nigel Penn, *Rogues, Rebels and Runaways: Eighteenth-Century Cape Characters* (Cape Town, South Africa: David Phillip, 1999), 18.

15. Mason, *Social Death and Resurrection,* 99.

16. Lady Ann Barnard. *South Africa a Century Ago: Letters Written from the Cape of Good Hope (1797–1801),* ed. W. H. Wilkins (London: Smith, Elder, & CO., 1910). http://digital.library.upenn.edu/women/barnard/letters/letters.html.

17. Hortense Spillers, "Mama's Baby, Papa's Maybe: An American Grammar Book," *Diacritics* 17, no. 2 (Summer 1987): 64–81.

18. Sharon Holland, *The Erotic Life of Racism* (Durham, NC: Duke University Press, 2012), 42.

19. Patricia Williams, *The Alchemy of Race and Rights: Diary of a Law Professor* (Cambridge, MA: Harvard University Press, 1991), 17, 19.

20. Hans F. Heese, *Reg en Onreg: Kaapse Regspraak in die Agtiende Eeu* (Belville: Universiteit van Wes-Kaapland, 1994); Penn, *Rogues, Rebels and Runaways: Eighteenth-Century Cape Characters* (Cape Town: David Philip, 1999), 71. Hans F. Heese was extremely kind in providing me with a copy of the sentencing and assisting me with other sources, as was Nigel Penn.

21. Christina Sharpe, *Monstrous Intimacies: Making Post-Slavery Subjects* (Durham, NC: Duke University Press, 2010), 4.

22. Spillers, "Mama's Baby, Papa's Maybe," 76.

23. Sharpe, *Monstrous Intimacies*, xxv.

24. I use the term "enjoyment" in its legal sense throughout this book to suggest not only the use of an object or person for satisfaction or pleasure but also the exercise of rights and privileges.

25. Penn, *Rogues, Rebels and Runaways*, 35. Hereafter, page numbers are cited in parentheses in the text.

26. Sharon Block, *Rape and Sexual Power in Early America* (Chapel Hill: University of North Carolina Press, 2006), 4.

27. Heese, *Reg en Onreg*, appendix. Hereafter, page numbers are cited in parentheses in the text.

28. The discussion in chapter 1 of muti and the power of Sarah Baartman's bodily remains is also relevant here.

29. Clifton Crais, *The Politics of Evil: Magic, State Power, and the Political Imagination in South Africa* (Cambridge: Cambridge University Press, 2009), 5.

30. Crais, *The Politics of Evil*, 12.

31. I thank my colleague Scott Stevens for telling me about "touching for the King's Evil," the belief that the king or pregnant queen could cure scrofula by virtue of touch.

32. We also see evidence of the power of the king's hand to heal in British folklore. Mabel Peacock recounts a story that appeared in the *Stamford Mercury* on March 26, 1830, in which "two women came forward [during the execution of three men in Lincoln] to rub the dead men's hands over some wens or diseased parts of their bodies, [one of them bringing] a child with her for the same purpose": Mabel Peacock, "Executed Criminals and Folk-Medicine," *Folklore* 7, no. 3 (September 1896): 268.

33. I examine this vexed topic of infanticide in my chapter on *Unconfessed* that revolves around a slave's life imprisonment on Robben Island for the murder of her children.

34. Jenny Sharpe, *Ghosts of Slavery: A Literary Archeology of Black Women's Lives* (Minneapolis: University of Minneapolis Press, 2003), 62.

35. Spencer, "Historical Memory, Romantic Narrative, and Sally Hemings," 511.

36. Saidiya Hartman, *Scenes of Subjection: Terror, Slavery and Self-Making in Nineteenth-Century America* (New York: Oxford University Press, 1997), 92.

37. Hartman, *Scenes of Subjection*, 88.

38. Hartman, *Scenes of Subjection*, 89.

39. Hartman deals extensively with the meaning of this phrase as does Jenny Sharpe, who states, "Unlike Hartman . . . who reads the phrase for its greater proximity to 'nonconsent' and hence evidence of a sexual practice that is practically indistinguishable from rape, I am interested in the opening the phrase provides for considering slave women's manipulation of their sexual exploitation to their own advantage": Sharpe, *Ghosts of Slavery*, xx.

40. Lingelback's attempts to free herself of her marriage contract that slaves were denied access to illustrate the structural inequities built into the contract form.

41. Spencer, "Historical Memory, Romantic Narrative, and Sally Hemings," 508.

42. Hartman, *Scenes of Subjection*, 111.

43. Block, *Rape and Sexual Power in Early America*, 16.

44. J. A. Scutt, "The Standard of Consent in Rape," *New Zealand Law Journal* (January 1976): 466.

45. Block, *Rape and Sexual Power in Early America*, 21.

46. Quoted in Block, *Rape and Sexual Power in Early America*, 21.

47. Block, *Rape and Sexual Power in Early America*, 54.

48. Marli F. Weiner, *Mistresses and Slaves: Plantation Women in South Carolina, 1830–80* (Urbana: University of Illinois Press, 1998), 2.

49. Mason, *Social Death and Resurrection*, 73.

50. Sharon Block, "Lines of Color, Sex, and Service: Comparative Sexual Coercion in Early America," in *Sex, Love, Race: Crossing Boundaries in North American History*, ed. Martha Hodes (New York: New York University Press, 1999), 152.

51. While white women's direct sexual enjoyment of slaves was rare, there is evidence to suggest that it did occur. A year after Tryntjie's trial, court records mention Maria Mouton of Middelburg and her slave "lover," Titus of Bengal, on trial for the murder of Maria's husband. Maria's sentence was extraordinary harsh: she was half-strangled, scorched, and then strangled to death after being found guilty. Her gruesome punishment—as opposed to that of Menssink, who did not even have to appear before the court—speaks volumes about the exceptional and therefore shocking status of a white woman who not only murdered her husband but also "voluntarily" had sexual dealings with a slave.

52. Pamela Scully, "Rape, Race and Colonial Culture: The Sexual Politics of Identity in the Nineteenth-Century Cape Colony, South Africa," *American Historical Review* 100, no. 2 (April 1995): 356.

53. Andre Brink, *The Rights of Desire* (New York: Harcourt, 2000). Hereafter, page numbers are cited in parentheses in the text.

54. Andre Brink, "Interrogating Silence: New Possibilities faced by South African Literature," in *Writing South Africa: Literature, Apartheid, and Democracy, 1970–1995*, eds. Derek Attridge and Rosemary Jolly (Cambridge: Cambridge University Press, 1998), 22.

55. Brink, "Interrogating Silence," 25.

56. Sharpe, *Ghosts of Slavery*, xi.

57. H. L. Malchow, *Gothic Images of Race in Nineteenth-Century Britain* (Stanford, CA: Stanford University Press, 1996), 2–3.

58. Patrick Brantlinger, *Rule of Darkness: British Literature and Imperialism, 1830–1914* (Ithaca, NY: Cornell University Press, 1990), 227–28.

59. The entire poem appears in Wallace Stevens, "The Motive for Metaphor," in *The Collected Poems-The Corrected Edition*, eds. Chris Beyers and John N. Serio (New York: Vintage Books, 2015), 304.

60. J. M. Coetzee, *Disgrace: A Novel* (New York: Viking Adult, 1999), 89.

61. Coetzee, *Disgrace*, 25.

62. Coetzee, *Disgrace*, 90.

63. Alan Hyde, *Bodies of Law* (Princeton NJ: Princeton University Press, 1997), 82.

64. Alan Hyde, *Bodied of Law*, 83.

65. Quoted in Hyde, *Bodies in Law*, 86.

66. See Patricia Williams, *The Rooster's Egg: On the Persistence of Prejudice* (Cambridge, MA: Harvard University Press, 1997), 16–17.

67. Hyde, *Bodies of Law*, 87.

68. Hyde, *Bodies of Law*, 95.

69. Carl F. Stychin, "De-Meaning of Contract," in *Sexuality and the Law: Feminist Engagements*, eds. Vanessa E. Munro and Carl F. Stychin (London: Routledge Cavendish, 2007), 83.

70. Stychin, "De-Meaning of Contract," 82.

CHAPTER 3. PERFORMING DEBILITY

1. Morten Traavik's career took off after the Miss Landmine pageants. After being made the first artist-in-residence for the Norwegian Armed Forces, he continues to provoke controversy with his collaborations with North Korea, most specifically an album of A-Ha covers with North Korean musicians. He is also responsible for the performance piece "Pimp My Aid Worker" (Lusaka, Zambia, 2011), which draws attention to the problems of liberal humanitarian aid to Africa.

2. Traavik, as told to Robyn Stubbs, Norway. "Redefining Beauty: Crowning Miss Landmine," blog post dated November 28, 2007, http://www.orato.com/current-events/2007/11/28/redefining-beauty-crowning-miss-landmine.

3. Quoted Stan Feingold, dir., *Miss Landmine*, documentary (Cineflix Productions, 2010).

4. Quoted in Feingold, *Miss Landmine*.

5. Benjamin Reiss, *The Showman and the Slave: Race, Death, and Memory in Barnum's America* (Cambridge, MA: Harvard University Press, 2001), 19.

6. Joseph Roach, *Cities of the Dead: Circum-Atlantic Performance* (New York: Columbia University Press, 1996), 25, 30.

7. McMillan makes an excellent connection between Heth's performative embodiment of history and the way that President Barack Obama discussed the 106-year-old Ann Nixon Cooper during his acceptance speech in Chicago: Uri McMillan, *Embodied*

Avatars: Genealogies of Black Feminist Art and Performance (New York: NYU Press, 2015), 242n115. Cooper became the backdrop against which historical "progress" was mapped, beginning with the abolition of slavery and culminating in the election of America's black president.

8. McMillan, *Embodied Avatars*, 13–14.

9. Reiss, *The Showman and the Slave*, 4.

10. Barnum was a great admirer of Maezel. According to James Cook, while on tour with Heth in Boston, he wrote, "I had frequent interviews and long conversations with Mr. Maelzel. I looked upon him as the great father of caterers for public amusement, and was pleased with his assurances that I would certainly make a successful showman": quoted in James W. Cook Jr., "From the Age of Reason to the Age of Barnum: The Great Automaton Chess-Player and the Emergence of Victorian Cultural Illusionism," *Winterthur Portfolio* 30, no. 4 (Winter 1995), 253. They both understood the role of the press in manufacturing an audience for their curiosities and recognized each other's virtuosity in manipulating the "types and inks." The Turk was proved a hoax, yet it still occupied a central place in the public imaginary.

11. Cook, "From the Age of Reason," 251.

12. Michel Foucault, *Discipline and Punish: The Birth of the Prison*. Trans. Alan Sheridan (New York: Vintage Books, 1995), 180.

13. Foucault, *Discipline and Punish,* 138.

14. Reiss, *The Showman and the Slave*, 4.

15. Reiss, *The Showman and the Slave*, 191.

16. In 1854, Barnum described himself as "the proprietor of the negress." In 1869, as Reiss points out, he revised his description to read "the proprietor of this novel exhibition": Reiss, *The Showman and the Slave*, 24.

17. Edward H. Dixon, M.D., ed., "Barnum and Joice Heth," *The Scalpel: A Journal of Health, Adapted to Popular and Professional Reading, and the Exposure of Quackery* 3, no. 1 (November 1850): 58. I would like to thank Uri McMillan for alerting me to this in an unpublished draft of his manuscript that would become *Embodied Avatars*.

18. Throughout the manuscript, I deploy the term "enjoyment" in a legal sense, to suggest both the use of an object or person for pleasure and the exercise of rights and privileges.

19. Quoted in Reiss, *The Showman and the Slave*, 87.

20. Mark Smith. *How Race is Made: Slavery, Segregation, and the Senses* (Chapel Hill: University of North Carolina Press, 2008), 13–14.

21. Saidiya Hartman, *Lose My Mother: A Journey along the Atlantic Slave Route* (New York: Farrar, Straus and Giroux, 2007), 153.

22. Walter Johnson, "On Agency," *Journal of Social History* 37, no. 1 (Autumn 2003): 115.

23. Hartman, *Lose My Mother*, 137.

24. In some ways, as my colleague Patrick Walter suggests, we can think about this as two different models of truth. The "historical" model grounds truth in empirically verifiable archival facts. While it aspires to apolitical objectivity, it actually reifies the

political system it pretends to recount. A more political methodology grounds truth in events, insisting that fidelity to the event creates political subjects.

25. Hartman uses Mieke Bal's *Narratology: Introduction to the Theory of Narrative* to define fabula as a "series of logically and chronologically related events that are caused and experienced by actors": Saidiya Hartman, "Venus in Two Acts," *Small Axe* Number 26, Vol. 12, no. 2 (June 2008): 7. Bal emphasizes the performative in that actors both are moved by as well as move the action along. Thus narration includes not just the textual and oral, but also the gestural and embodied.

26. Hartman, "Venus in Two Acts," 11.

27. Colleen Ballerino Cohen, Richard Wilk, and Beverly Stoeltje, eds., *Beauty Queens on the Global Stage: Gender, Contests, and Power* (New York: Routledge, 1996), 3–4.

28. Robert Lavenda, "Minnesota Queen Pageants: Play, Fun, and Dead Seriousness in a Festive Mode," *Journal of American Folklore* 101, no. 400 (April–June 1988): 172.

29. The controversy over Carrie Prejean, first runner up in Miss USA 2009 pageant, provides an interesting case about women's respectability. Erotic pictures of a scantily clad Prejean, whose statements against gay marriage during the pageant and subsequent involvement in the National Organization for Marriage's campaign against gay marriage were posted on the web after she won. Prejean insisted that the photos had been leaked to discredit her "protection of opposite marriage"—namely, marriage between a man and a woman. Despite precedent, the pageant's owner, Donald Trump, initially overrode pageant rules when he decided that Prejean could retain her crown. We see here a distinct reverberation of Barnum's struggle with the putative morality and respectability of the participants. The crown was later stripped because Prejean supposedly failed to fulfill "other" pageant obligations.

30. Mary H. Moran, "Carrying the Queen: Identity and Nationalism in a Liberian Queen Rally," in *Beauty Queens on the Global Stage: Gender, Contests, and Power*, eds. Colleen Ballerino Cohen, Richard Wilk, and Beverly Stoeltje (New York: Routledge, 1996), 149–50.

31. Traavik, as told to Robyn Stubbs, Norway. "Redefining Beauty: Crowning Miss Landmine," blog post dated November 28, 2007, http://www.orato.com/current-events/2007/11/28/redefining-beauty-crowning-miss-landmine <no longer active>.

32. Moran, "Carrying the Queen," 150.

33. Angela Robson, "Miss Landmine: The Beauty Pageant with a Difference," *Marie Claire*, May 28, 2008, http://www.marieclaire.co.uk/news/lifestyle/257750/miss-landmine-the-beauty-pageant-with-a-difference.html.

34. Sarah Banet-Weiser, *The Most Beautiful Girl in the World: Beauty Pageants and National Identity* (Berkeley: University of California Press, 1999), 2–3.

35. Lavenda, "Minnesota Queen Pageants," 173.

36. Quoted in Saeed Ahmed, "Landmine Victims Star in Angola Pageant," CNN.com, April 1, 2008, http://www.cnn.com/2008/WORLD/africa/04/01/angola.landmine/index.html.

37. Baartman's appellation of the Hottentot Venus provided the rationale for this game. As the goddess of love, she was supposed to be the ultimate object of men's

desires and love. As the Hottentot, she was putatively repellant. The cruel game, where the men's obviously parodic and "comic" declarations of love, was at the expense of Baartman. Whether or not Baartman got the "joke," we will never know.

38. Banet-Weiser, *The Most Beautiful Girl in the World*, 7.

39. Vanessa Williams resigned in 1984 due to the publication of erotic photographs that involved some homosexual content.

40. Richard Iton, *In Search of the Black Fantastic: Politics and Popular Culture in the Post–Civil Rights Era* (New York: Oxford University Press, 2010), 12–13.

41. The Miss America swimsuit competition recently changed its name to the "physical fitness competition."

42. Meg McLagan, "Principles, Publicity, and Politics: Notes on Human Rights Media," *American Anthropologist* 105, no. 3 (September 2003): 609.

43. Teri Silvio, "Animation: The New Performance," *Journal of Linguistic Anthropology* 20, no. 2 (December 2010): 427.

44. Natalie Underberg, "Virtual and Reciprocal Ethnography on the Internet: The East Mims Oral History Project Website," *Journal of American Folklore* 119, no. 473 (Summer 2006): 304.

45. Krista Thompson, *Shine: The Visual Economy of Light in African Diasporic Aesthetic Practice* (Durham, NC: Duke University Press, 2015), 6.

46. Quoted in Feingold, *Miss Landmine*.

47. Roach, *Cities of the Dead*, 31. Roach refers to Addison's description in the June 1, 1711, issue of *The Spectator* of two rivals, one of whom uses her slave girl to upstage the other. The story derives its meaning in a social world where the possibility of racial surrogation constitutes a dramatic threat.

48. Banet-Weiser, *The Most Beautiful Girl in the World*, 173.

49. Rosemarie Garland-Thomson, "Integrating Disability, Transforming Feminist Theory," *NWSA Journal* 14, no. 3 (Autumn 2002): 24.

50. See http://www.orato.com/home-family/miss-landmine.

51. Garland-Thomson, "Integrating Disability," 24.

52. Sarah Baartman's "disease" of steatophygia in indigenous contexts was a sign of her fitness, where fat demonstrated good nutrition and increased reproductive ability. However, to the Western eye, Baartman's "display invoked disability by presenting as deformities or abnormalities the characteristics that marked her as raced and gendered": Garland-Thomson, "Integrating Disability," 7. Thus, disability was explicitly racialized and gendered as nonwhite.

53. Julie Livingston, *Debility and the Moral Imagination in Botswana* (Bloomington: Indiana University Press, 2005), 203.

54. David Serlin shows how prosthetic design made significant advances not only because of its social and sexual implications but also due to its material links with and appropriation by a militarized industry: David Serlin, "The Other Arms Race," in *The Disability Studies Reader*, ed. Lennard J. Davis (New York: Routledge, 2006). For example, Norbert Weiner's design for a cybernetic controlled prosthesis, the "Liberty Limb" or "Boston Arm," was sent first not to so-called rehabilitation centers for amputees but

to big business in the 1960s that developed the industrial robot that replaced manual workers instead of enabled them.

55. Robert McRuer, *Crip Theory: Cultural Signs of Queerness and Disability* (New York: New York University Press, 2006), 111.

56. Livingston, *Debility and the Moral Imagination in Botswana*, 203.

57. Kevin Gaines, *Uplifting the Race: Black Leadership, Politics, and Culture in the Twentieth Century* (Chapel Hill: University of North Carolina Press, 1996), 21.

58. McRuer, *Crip Theory*, 115.

59. Garland-Thomson, "Integrating Disability," 25.

60. Petra Kuppers, *Disability and Contemporary Performance: Bodies on the Edge* (New York: Routledge Press, 2013), 3.

61. Garland-Thomson, "Integrating Disability," 23–24.

62. I have argued throughout this chapter that rather than these images moving from one sphere to the other, they are haunted by and unintelligible without the "private" sensationalized images. However, one should not deny the real work that is done by a strategic deployment of "positive" public images to shift society's common sense toward accepting differential embodiment.

63. Garland-Thomson, "Integrating Disability," 24.

64. Moran, "Carrying the Queen," 150.

65. Tobin Siebers, "Disability in Theory: From Social Constructivism to the New Realism of the Body," in *The Disability Studies Reader*, ed. Lennard J. Davis (New York: Routledge, 2006), 173.

66. Terri Kapsalis, *Public Privates: Performing Gynecology from Both Ends of the Spectrum* (Durham, NC: Duke University Press, 1997), 4–5.

67. Quoted in McRuer, *Crip Theory*, 126.

68. McRuer, *Crip Theory*, 128.

69. Marquard Smith, "The Vulnerable Articulate: James Gillingham, Aimee Mullins, and Matthew Barney," in *The Disability Studies Reader*, ed. Lennard J. Davis (New York: Routledge, 2006), 48.

70. Quoted in Ann McClintock, *Imperial Leather: Race, Gender and Sexuality in the Colonial Contest* (New York: Routledge Press, 1995), 189.

71. Kapsalis, *Public Privates*, 88.

72. Quoted in Kapsalis, *Public Privates*, 33.

73. Kapsalis, *Public Privates*, 39.

74. Michael Davidson quotes Ato Quayson as saying, " 'To have full disclosure about the social and political grounds of an impairment is perforce to go beyond the impairment and to engage the social, political, and cultural forces that produce disability' ": Michael Davidson, "Universal Design: The Work of Disability in an Age of Globalization," in *The Disability Studies Reader*, ed. Lennard J. Davis (New York: Routledge, 2006), 120.

75. The notion of passing arises out of an African American context and is commonly used to describe person who 'passes' as a less disadvantaged race in order to acquire social privilege. While this term has traditionally posited notions of a prior

authentic identity being replaced by a fake identity built around subterfuge, both the prior identity and the identity one is "passing" as are produced through performative reiterations shaped by history, violence, and agency. Sander Gilman applies this term to aesthetic surgery in thought-provoking ways: Sander L. Gilman, *Difference and Pathology: Stereotypes of Sexuality, Race and Madness* (Ithaca, NY: Cornell University Press, 1985), 21–31.

76. Smith, "The Vulnerable Articulate," 50.

77. Smith, "The Vulnerable Articulate," 55.

78. The uneven color of her prosthesis does not exactly match her skin color. As early as 1944, the Naval Graduate Center's samples included a "Negro" ear and a "Caucasian" cheek. Serlin notes that a single mold was used to cast every ear, for example, which may have had the effect of "neutralizing or even erasing, the perceived phenotypic differences between white and black": Serlin, "The Other Arms Race," 56. It also constitutes a homogenizing strategy that insists on a norm in different shades.

79. Johnson, "On Agency," 115.

80. José Esteban Muñoz, *Disidentifications: Queers of Color and the Performance of Politics* (Minneapolis: University of Minnesota Press, 1999), 4.

81. Alexander G. Weheliye, *Habeas Viscus: Racializing Assemblages, Biopolitics, and Black Feminist theories of the Human* (Durham, NC: Duke University Press, 2014), 2.

82. Weheliye, *Habeas Viscus*, 2.

83. Johnson, "On Agency," 119.

4. SLOW DEATH

1. Aziz Hassim, *Revenge of Kali* (Johannesburg: STE, 2009), 168. Hereafter, page numbers are cited in parentheses in the texts.

2. Samuelson, "(Un)settled States," 285.

3. Ashraf Rushdy, *Remembering Generations: Race and Family in Contemporary African American Fiction* (Chapel Hill: University of North Carolina Press, 2001), 10.

4. Antoinette Burton, "'Every Secret Thing?' Racial Politics in Ansuyah R. Singh's *Behold the Earth Mourns*," *Journal of Commonwealth Literature* 46, no. 1 (2011): 4.

5. Isabel Hofmeyr, "Africa as a Fault Line in the Indian Ocean," in *Eyes across the Water: Navigating the Indian Ocean*, eds. Pamela Gupta, Isabel Hofmeyr, and Michael Pearson (Pretoria, South Africa: Unisa Press, 2010), 104.

6. Richard B. Allen, "The Mascarene Slave-Trade and Labour Migration in the Indian Ocean during the Eighteenth and Nineteenth Centuries," *Slavery and Abolition* 24, no. 2 (2003): 45.

7. Afterlife here denotes "relationships of people to time that produce multilayered dynamics of presence and absence, anticipation and retrospection": Jennifer Wenzel, *Bulletproof: Afterlives of Anticolonial Prophecy in South Africa and Beyond* (Chicago: University of Chicago Press, 2010), 5.

8. Nigel Worden, *Slavery in Dutch South Africa* (Cambridge: Cambridge University Press, 1985), 9.

9. Worden, *Slavery in Dutch South Africa*, 48; emphasis added.

10. Mauritius, for example, imported Indian slaves until the 1820s, before it turned to indenture.

11. Robert Semple, *Walks and Sketches at the Cape of Good Hope*, facsimile ed. (Charleston, SC: BiblioLIFE, 2009).

12. Semple, *Walks and Sketches at the Cape of Good Hope*, 47–48.

13. The murder of a VOC official by Buginese and Sumatran slaves led to banning the import of Asian slaves in 1767. Asian slaves were seen as dangerously insubordinate, and the Cape turned to vessels not owned by the VOC, predominantly French ships bound for Saint-Domingue and then Portuguese ships carrying slaves from Mozambique: Pedro Machado, "A Forgotten Corner of the Indian Ocean: Gujarati Merchants, Portuguese India and the Mozambique Slave-Trade, c. 1730–1830," *Slavery and Abolition* 24, no. 2 (2003): 23. While many Asian slaves certainly were mentioned in the legal records of escapes and attacks on slave owners, resistance has more to do with the slave's degree of creolization and her treatment by planters than with her racial origin.

14. This process was not as acute in urban and frontier environments before the end of the eighteenth century, and in the very cosmopolitan Cape Town, social categories remained a little more distinct.

15. Nigel Worden, "Coercion and Freedom in the Cape Colony, 1652–1836," in *The Face of Freedom: The Manumission and Emancipation of Slaves in Old World and New World Slavery*, ed. Marc Kleijwegt (Leiden: E. J. Brill, 2006), 209.

16. By the early nineteenth century, after its legalization, Islam was the predominant religion among working-class Capetonians.

17. Worden, *Slavery in Dutch South Africa*, 4. Worden takes great pains to insist that plantation slavery was not the same as the institutionalized racism that slowly calcified throughout the country after industrialization. Instead, he argues that the newer racial systems exploited their similarities with the racialized hierarchies of Cape slave society to further propagate themselves. Robert Shell also brilliantly demonstrates this: *Children of Bondage: A Social History of the Slave Society at the Cape of Good Hope, 1652–1838* (Hanover, NH: Wesleyan University Press, 1994).

18. Nigel Penn, *Rogues, Rebels and Runaways: Eighteenth-Century Cape Characters* (Cape Town, South Africa: David Philip, 1999), 6.

19. Worden, *Slavery in Dutch South Africa*, 141–42.

20. Worden, "Coercion and Freedom in the Cape Colony," 198.

21. Arnold Itwaru, in Marina Carter and Khal Torabully, *Coolitude: An Anthology of the Indian Labour Diaspora* (London: Anthem, 2002), 38.

22. Indeed, the continuing legacy of plantation labor regimes can be clearly seen in varied labor struggles around mining today. A case in point involves the Marikana platinum mine owned by Lonmin, located close to Rustenberg. Miners went on strike in 2012 due to their low pay, inadequate living standards, and abysmal working conditions that included falling rocks and exposure to dust, noise, intense heat, and fumes. In attempts to gain control over the angry workers, a special unit of the South African

Police opened fire of a group of strikers on August 16, killing thirty-four people and wounding at least seventy-eight people.

23. Véronique Bragard, *Transoceanic Dialogues: Coolitude in Caribbean and Indian Ocean Literatures* (Berlin: Peter Lang, 2008), 27–28.

24. Indentured servants were not filling the need for workers as much as being used to discipline black/indigenous workers in South Africa and the Caribbean. What planters wanted was not more labor but, rather, more coerced labor that was vulnerable socially, economically, physically, and culturally to the technologies of the plantation.

25. Madhavi Kale, *Fragments of Empire: Capital, Slavery, and Indian Indentured Labor Migration in the British Caribbean* (Philadelphia: University of Pennsylvania Press, 1998), 6.

26. Carter and Torabully, *Coolitude*, 47.

27. See Hugh Tinker, *A New System of Slavery: The Export of Indian Labour Overseas, 1830–1920* (Oxford: Oxford University Press, 1974).

28. Carter and Torabully, *Coolitude*, 47.

29. Quoted in Carter and Torabully, *Coolitude*, 48.

30. Kale, *Fragments of Empire*, 30.

31. Nitin Varma, "Coolie Acts and the Acting Coolies: Coolie, Planter and State in the Late Nineteenth and Early Twentieth Century Colonial Tea Plantations of Assam," *Social Scientist* 33, nos. 5–6 (May–June 2005): 49.

32. Varma, "Coolie Acts and the Acting Coolies," 49.

33. Jonathan Grossman, "The Right to Strike and Worker Freedom in and beyond Apartheid," in *Free and Unfree Labour: The Debate Continues*, eds. Tom Brass and Marcel van der Linden (New York: Peter Lang, 1997), 162.

34. For example, Dick Kooiman's archival research on the London Missionary Society (LMS) led him to state that "for the LMS missionaries there was nothing more humanitarian than to enable the people . . . to share the blessings of a capitalist development": Dick Kooiman, "Conversion from Slavery to Plantation Labour; Christian Mission in South India, 19th Century." *Social Scientist* 19, no. 8 & 9 (August/September 1991), 63.

35. Kale, *Fragments of Empire*, 30.

36. Grossman, "The Right to Strike and Worker Freedom in and beyond Apartheid," 147.

37. Grossman, "The Right to Strike and Worker Freedom in and beyond Apartheid," 147.

38. Grossman, "The Right to Strike and Worker Freedom in and beyond Apartheid," 147–48.

39. Grossman, "The Right to Strike and Worker Freedom in and beyond Apartheid," 148.

40. Clare Anderson, "Convicts and Coolies: Rethinking Indentured Labour in the Nineteenth Century," *Slavery and Abolition* 30, no. 1 (2009): 93.

41. Anderson, "Convicts and Coolies," 95.

42. Achille Mbembe, "Necropolitics," trans. Libby Meintjes, *Public Culture* 15, no. 1 (Winter 2003): 39.

43. Grossman, "The Right to Strike and Worker Freedom in and beyond Apartheid," 147–49.

44. Grossman, "The Right to Strike and Worker Freedom in and beyond Apartheid," 169.

45. Mbembe, "Necropolitics," 14 (italics per the original source).

46. Mbembe, "Necropolitics," 40.

47. Mbembe, "Necropolitics," 40.

48. Jin-Kyung Lee, *Service Economies: Militarism, Sex Work, and Migrant Labor in South Korea* (Minneapolis: University of Minnesota Press, 2010), 6.

49. Necropolitical work becomes a tradeoff between the injury incurred and the rewards of work such as food and shelter that enable the worker to live.

50. Lee, *Service Economies*, 14.

51. Surendra Bhana and Arvinkumar Bhana, "An Exploration of the Psycho-Historical Circumstances Surrounding Suicide among Indentured Indians, 1875–1911," in *Essays on Indentured Indians in Natal*, ed. Surendra Bhana (Leeds: Peepal Tree, 1991), 140.

52. See Lauren Berlant, "Slow Death (Sovereignty, Obesity, Lateral Agency)," *Critical Inquiry* 33, no. 4 (Summer 2010): 754–80.

53. Jasbir Puar, keynote lecture at Affective Tendencies Conference, Rutgers University, New Brunswick, NJ, October 8, 2010, excerpted in "In the Wake of It Gets Better," *The Guardian*, November 16, 2010.

54. Eric Cazdyn, "Disaster, Crisis, Revolution," *South Atlantic Quarterly* 106, no. 4 (Fall 2007): 649.

55. Worden, *Slavery in Dutch South Africa*, 135–36.

56. G. R. Naidoo, "Why Do Indians Kill Themselves?" *Drum* (August 1956): 27–31.

57. The one exception is a striking image of Mrs. Pillay and her daughter, who were the survivors of three sons/brothers who committed suicide. This poignant photograph shows a gaunt-faced Mrs. Pillay with downcast eyes being supported by her wide-eyed daughter, whose fearful gaze to the right belies the strength suggested by her arm around her mother.

58. Jon Soske, "Navigating Difference: Gender, Miscegenation and Indian Domestic Space in Twentieth-Century Durban," in *Eyes across the Water: Navigating the Indian Ocean*, eds. Pamela Gupta, Isabel Hofmeyr, and Michael Pearson (Pretoria, South Africa: Unisa Press, 2010), 197–219, 209.

59. Sandhya Shukla, *India Abroad: Diasporic Cultures of Postwar America and England* (Princeton NJ: Princeton University Press, 2003), 35.

60. As early as the 1890s, Gujarati traders attempted to distance themselves from the category of Asiatics/Indians that was used mainly to classify indentured servants and their descendants. They appealed to the colonial state that they should be classified as "Arabs," a category that would enable them to escape the stigma and colonial regulations around indentured servitude, as a coolie heritage was somehow shameful. On how petitions of reclassification reflected deep divisions and animosities that the colonial state ignored and erased in their wish to reinforce pseudo-scientific racial

categories, see Thomas Blom Hansen, "The Unwieldy Fetish: Desire and Disavowal of Indianness in South Africa," in *Eyes across the Water: Navigating the Indian Ocean*, eds. Pamela Gupta, Isabel Hofmeyr, and Michael Pearson (Pretoria, South Africa: Unisa Press, 2010), 109–21.

61. Arjun Appadurai, "Dead Certainty: Ethnic Violence in the Era of Globalization," *Public Culture* 10, no. 2 (Winter 1998): 225–47.

62. "Report for the Protector of Immigrants for the Year 1891," PAR Natal Colonial Publications (NCP) 8/1/10/5/4, 16.

63. Julie Parle, *States of Mind: Searching for Mental Health in Natal and Zululand, 1868–1918* (Pietermaritzburg: University of KwaZulu-Natal Press, 2007), 229.

64. Bhana and Bhana, "An Exploration of the Psycho-Historical Circumstances Surrounding Suicide among Indentured Indians," 156.

65. Bhana and Bhana, "An Exploration of the Psycho-Historical Circumstances Surrounding Suicide among Indentured Indians," 157.

66. Parle, *States of Mind*, 231.

67. Parle, *States of Mind*, 203.

68. Bhana and Bhana's study of indentured suicides made extensive use of the records of the Indian Protector: see Bhana and Bhana, "An Exploration of the Psycho-Historical Circumstances Surrounding Suicide among Indentured Indians." They do not, however, mention the prosecution of Indians for attempted suicide. This information was housed with the colony's other criminal statistics that included all races: the Crimes and Statistics Tried by Magistrates. Thus, suicides and attempted suicides by Indians were two different bureaucratic concerns, housed in different sites.

69. Official Inquiries at Reynolds Bros: Natal Archives Repository (NAR): II 292/1904; 969/1904; CSO 4187/1905: 94 pages; NAR: CSO 2854/1906: 31 pages.

70. See http://www.agnessam.com/blog/what-does-your-father-do, April 14, 2015.

71. Agnes Sam, "High Heels," in *Jesus Is Indian and Other Short Stories* (Portsmouth, NH: Heinemann, 1994), 1. Hereafter, page numbers are cited in parentheses in the text.

72. The term "geniza," derived from the Hebrew root *g-n-z*, originally meant "to hide" or "put away." Later it came to mean a room in a synagogue where texts awaited proper religious disposal. These texts were damaged, heretical, or unimportant documents that contained the name of God; all needed ceremonial burial, as it was forbidden to throw them away. I am unclear about why Frenkel chose this Jewish term to describe a Hindu altar: see Ronit Frenkel, *Reconsiderations: South African Indian Fiction and the Making of Race in Postcolonial Culture* (Pretoria: Unisa Press, 2010).

73. Frenkel, *Reconsiderations*, 136.

74. Pallavi Rastogi, "From South Asia to South Africa: Locating Other Postcolonial Diasporas," *Modern Fiction Studies* 51, no. 3 (2005): 547.

75. Roderick Ferguson, "Race-ing Homonormativity: Citizenship, Sociology and Gay Identity," in *Black Queer Studies: A Critical Anthology*, eds. E. Patrick Johnson and Mae G. Henderson (Durham, NC: Duke University Press, 2005), 52–67.

76. Omise'eke Natasha Tinsley, "Black Atlantic, Queer Atlantic: Imagining the Middle Passage as Queer Borderwaters," *GLQ* 14, nos. 2–3 (April 2008): 199.

77. Jafari Allen, *!Venceremos? The Erotics of Black Self-Making in Cuba* (Durham, NC: Duke University Press, 2011), 96.

78. Ruthie's desire is not just for any high-heeled shoes; it is specifically for Lindi's shoes. She does not ask her parents for a pair of shoes, which might have been simpler than asking them to reveal what is behind the door. Nor are her mother's high heels an adequate substitute. Freud's notion of the fetish is obviously apropos.

79. Eve Kosofsky Sedgwick's *Epistemology of the Closet* (Berkeley: University of California Press, 1990) brilliantly historicizes not only the movement from notions of sexual inversion to notions of homosexuality as the choice of a same-gender object but also the epistemology of the closet at the turn of the nineteenth century. This epistemology is crucial to modern identity, but, as scholars such as Marlon Ross argue, rests on racist ideologies predicated on the uneven development of races with blacks being premodern or primitive: Marlon B. Ross, "Beyond the Closet as Raceless Paradigm," in *Black Queer Studies: A Critical Anthology*, eds. E. Patrick Johnson and Mae Henderson (Durham, NC: Duke University Press, 2005), 161–89.

80. Ross, "Beyond the Closet as Raceless Paradigm," 163.

81. Allen, *!Venceremos?* 95.

82. Diana Taylor, *The Archive and the Repertoire: Performing Cultural Memory in the Americas.* (Durham, NC: Duke University Press, 2003), 82.

83. Taylor, *The Archive and the Repertoire*, 44.

5. BECOMING UNDONE

1. Yvette Christianse, *Unconfessed: A Novel* (New York: Other Press, 2007), 33. Hereafter, page numbers are cited in parentheses in the text.

2. James Bradley, "The Colonel and the Slave Girls: Life Writing and the Logic of History in 1830s Sydney," *Journal of Social History* 45, no. 2 (Winter 2011): 417.

3. Yvette Christianse, " 'Heartsore': The Melancholy Archive of Cape Colony Slavery," *Scholar and Feminist Online* 7, no. 2 (Spring 2009).

4. Stephanie Li, *Something Akin to Freedom: The Choice of Bondage in Narratives by African American Women* (New York: State University of New York, 2010), 86.

5. Christianse, "Heartsore."

6. Christianse, "Heartsore."

7. Bradley, "The Colonel and the Slave Girls," 421.

8. Christianse, "Heartsore."

9. Darieck Scott, *Extravagant Abjection: Blackness, Power, and Sexuality in the African American Literary Imagination* (New York: New York University Press, 2010), 2–3. Scott's discussion of Margaret Garner, another famous slave mother who killed her children, provides a political matrix with which to understand Sila's actions. He writes that the slave woman's "decision to murder her [son]—a decision we should be careful not to name as a choice, at least not without troubling assumptions about individual

agency that are commonplace in a liberal democratic society—is of such a final and extreme nature that it begs readers to differ": Scott, *Extravagant Abjection*, 1.

10. Scott, *Extravagant Abjection*, 16.

11. C. Riley Snorton, *Nobody Is Supposed to Know: Black Sexuality on the Down Low* (Minneapolis: University of Minnesota Press, 2014), 39.

12. Christina Sharpe, *Monstrous Intimacies: Making Post-Slavery Subjects* (Durham, NC: Duke University Press, 2010), 33.

13. Quoted in Sharpe, *Monstrous Intimacies*, 35.

14. Christopher Peterson, *Kindred Specters: Death, Mourning, and American Affinity* (Minnesota: University of Minnesota Press, 2007), 221.

15. Cheryl Harris writes that in "protecting the property interest in whiteness, property is assumed to be no more than the right to prohibit infringement on settled expectations, ignoring countervailing equitable claims predicated on a right to inclusion": Cheryl I. Harris, "Whiteness as Property," *Harvard Law Review* 106, no. 8 (June 1993): 1707–91, 1791.

16. Harris, "Whiteness as Property," 1731.

17. Hortense Spillers, "Mama's Baby, Papa's Maybe: An American Grammar Book." *Diacritics* 17, no. 2 (Summer 1987): 74.

18. Spillers, "Mama's Baby, Papa's Maybe," 74.

19. Aliyyah I. Abdur-Rahman, *The Erotics of Race: Identity, Political Longing, and Black Figuration* (Durham, NC: Duke University Press, 2012), 222 [pagination from book ms.].

20. Sharpe, *Monstrous Intimacies*, 23.

21. Saidiya Hartman. *Lose Your Mother: A Journey along the Atlantic Slave Route* (New York: Farrar, Straus and Giroux, 2007), 80.

22. Abdur-Rahman, *The Erotics of Race*, 81.

23. Matt Richardson, " 'My Father Didn't Have a Dick': Social Death and Jackie Kay's *Trumpet*," GLQ 18, nos. 2–3 (2012): 361–79.

24. Scott, *Extravagant Abjection*, 129.

25. Scott, *Extravagant Abjection*, 156.

26. Pamela Scully's brilliant work on infanticide focuses on the post-emancipation period and the role of Christian missions and mission courts. She shows how women's sexual behavior and reproduction was central to the struggle for power between the missions and colonial authorities. Pamela Scully, "Narratives of Infanticide in the Aftermath of Slave Emancipation in the Nineteenth-Century Cape Colony, South Africa," *Canadian Journal of African Studies* 30, no. 1 (1996): 88–105.

27. Sharon M. Harris, *Executing Race: Early American Women's Narratives of Race, Society, and the Law* (Columbus: Ohio State University Press, 2005), 67. Child murder has acquired a particularly negative stigma, as it works counter to stereotypes about mothering, gender, and sexuality. This continues into the present. At the "Sybil Brand Institute in Fort Worth, TX., [only] two groups of women are required to wear red: informants and those convicted of infanticide": Alexander Cockburn in Sharon M.

Harris, "Feminist Theories and Early American Studies," *Early American Literature* 34, no. 1 (1999): 91.

28. Quoted in V. C. Malherbe, "In *Onegt Verwekt*: Law, Custom and Illegitimacy in Cape Town, 1800–1840," *Journal of Southern African Studies* 31, no. 1 (Mar 2005): 176.

29. Nonlinear genealogies of enslaved women's propensity to murder their children appear in colonial records across the diaspora. For example, in eighteenth-century Saint-Domingue, a "rabid pro-slavery pamphleteer . . . claimed that slave women purposely murdered newborns so that they might be free to engage in lascivious behavior with enslaved males and with slaveholders. . . . 'They destroy their own fruit, or they practice infanticide in order to live without moderation' ": Karol K. Weaver, " 'She Crushed the Child's Fragile Skull': Disease, Infanticide, and Enslaved Women in Eighteenth-Century Saint-Domingue," in *Killing Infants: Studies in the Worldwide Practice of Infanticide*, eds. Brigitte H. Bechtold and Donna Cooper Graves (New York: Edwin Mellen, 2006), 41.

30. Pamela Scully, "Narratives of Infanticide in the Aftermath of Slave Emancipation in the Nineteenth-Century Cape Colony, South Africa," *Canadian Journal of African Studies* 30, no. 1 (1996): 94.

31. Scully, "Narratives of Infanticide in the Aftermath of Slave Emancipation in the Nineteenth-Century Cape Colony," 89, 100.

32. Dana Rabin, "Bodies of Evidence, States of Mind: Infanticide, Emotion and Sensibility in Eighteenth-Century England," in *Infanticide: Historical Perspectives on Child Murder and Concealment, 1550–2000*, ed. Mark Jackson (Hants, UK: Ashgate, 2002), 73.

33. Rabin, "Bodies of Evidence, States of Mind," 81, 89.

34. Li, *Something akin to Freedom*, 2.

35. Eugene Genovese, for example, writes that running away and fighting for freedom are the ultimate forms of resistance: Eugene Genovese, *Roll, Jordan, Roll: The World the Slaves Made* (New York: Vintage Books, 2011).

36. Li, *Something akin to Freedom*, 14.

37. Wendy Brown, *States of Injury: Power and Freedom in Late Modernity* (Princeton, NJ: Princeton University Press, 1995), 6.

38. See the introduction in this book.

39. Peterson, *Kindred Specters*, 70. The relationship between parent and child in the eighteenth century was also used in the United States to describe the rise of a new nation that needed to separate from a "bad parent." John Adams wrote, "But admitting we are children, have not children a right to complain when their parents are attempting to break their limbs, administer poison, or sell them to the enemies for slaves?": quoted in, John Adams, *The Portable John Adams*, ed. John Patrick Diggins (New York: Penguin Books, 2004), 223. In Adams's postulation, children have a right to resist when their parents try to kill them. Thus, American "patriots" had the right to their own nation, since England was a parent attempting infanticide.

40. Abdur-Rahman, *The Erotics of Race*, 81.

41. Peterson, *Kindred Specters*, 34.

42. Peterson, *Kindred Specters*, 77.

43. In an article on the murder of nine people at a church in Charleston, SC, in 2015 and the Black Lives Matter movement, another mother echoed the same sentiment hundreds of years later when asked what it was like being the mother of a black son in America. "The condition of black life is one of mourning," she said; of knowing that at any moment her son might be killed: quoted in Claudia Rankine, "The Condition of Black Life Is One of Mourning," *New York Times Magazine*, June 22, 2015, http://www.nytimes.com/2015/06/22/magazine/the-condition-of-black-life-is-one-of-mourning.html?_r=0.

44. Sarah Jane Cervenak, *Wandering: Philosophical Performances of Racial and Sexual Freedom* (Durham, NC: Duke University Press, 2014), 14.

45. Meg Samuelson, "'Lose Your Mother, Kill Your Child': The Passage of Slavery and Its Afterlife in Narratives by Yvette Christianse and Saidiya Hartman," *English Studies in Africa* 51, no. 2 (2008): 44.

46. Stephen Best and Saidiya Hartman, "Fugitive Justice," *Representations* 92, no. 1 (Fall 2005): 6.

47. Mike Chasar, "The Sounds of Black Laughter and the Harlem Renaissance: Claude McKay, Sterling Brown, Langston Hughes," *American Literature* 80, no. 1 (2008): 61.

48. Chasar, "The Sounds of Black Laughter and the Harlem Renaissance," 63.

49. Best and Hartman, "Fugitive Justice," 1; Glenda Carpio, *Laughing Fit to Kill: Black Humor in the Fictions of Slavery* (New York: Oxford University Press, 2008), 11.

50. Carpio, *Laughing Fit to Kill*, 6.

51. Carpio, *Laughing Fit to Kill*, 6.

52. Beckett, quoted in Carpio, *Laughing Fit to Kill*, 197.

53. Carpio, *Laughing Fit to Kill*, 197.

54. Best and Hartman, "Fugitive Justice," 3.

55. There is no direct quote. See Mark M. Smith, *How Race is Made: Slavery, Segregation, and the Senses* (Chapel Hill: University of North Carolina Press, 2008) and Richard Cullen Rath, *How Early America Sounded* (Ithaca, NY: Cornell University Press, 2005).

56. Samuel A. Cartwright in Mark M. Smith, *How Race is Made*, 43–46.

57. Roland Barthes, *The Responsibility of Forms: Critical Essays on Music, Art, and Representation* (New York: Hill and Wang, 1985), 24.

58. Barthes, *The Responsibility of Forms*, 250.

59. Frederick Douglass, "The Heroic Slave" (1853), in *Frederick Douglass: Selected Speeches and Writings*, ed. Philip S. Foner (Chicago: Lawrence Hill, 1999), 221.

60. Douglass, "The Heroic Slave," 222. For further discussion of this, see Marianne Noble, "Sympathetic Listening in Frederick Douglass's 'The Heroic Slave' and *My Bondage and My Freedom*," *Studies in American Fiction* 34, no. 1 (Spring 2006): 53–68.

61. Barthes, *The Responsibility of Forms*, 260.

62. Brenna M. Munro, *South Africa and the Dream of Love to Come: Queer Sexuality and the Struggle for Freedom* (Minneapolis: University of Minnesota Press, 2010), xxiv.

63. Abdur-Rahman, *The Erotics of Race*, 97.

64. This is the phrase that Sila uses to describe Jeptha, the slave who tried to rape her when she first got to Van der Wat's farm and who later testified against her at the trial. "His feet were locked into the dance of a good boy. I hated him. He brought the worst days to us. . . . *I have a rope for you and you will dance in the wind, with the branches*": Christianse, *Unconfessed*, 253.

65. Scott, *Extravagant Abjection*, 9.

66. Slavery is seen as a form of consumption. Sila tells a story about a "girl with a hole where her mouth had been. They said her white lover had eaten her mouth. And others said, no, it was her breast, he had eaten her breast. . . . That lover took the girl and he had a gold tooth and that tooth needed to be polished with blood and he sucked and sucked and sucked and sucked and her blood left her mouth and went into him and her blood left her breast and went into him": Christianse, *Unconfessed*, 201.

67. Judith Butler, *Precarious Life: The Powers of Mourning and Violence* (Verso: New York, 2004): 46–7.

68. Judith Halberstam, *The Queer Art of Failure* (Durham, NC: Duke University Press, 2011), 23.

69. "You are my good, quiet day, Lys. You make a place for my back to rest and all aching stops, and when my face relaxes I know that it was pulled up, strained. You are my good day, and my quiet, Lys. You make a place for my stomach to relax, and when it does I know that it was twisted and turned like a dirty old sheet taken away by a stream before I could catch it and wash it and lay it out. And my heart is what I thank you for the most, Lys, even though it is like a sore where a stick has broken skin. There is no safe place for a heart, but my good days are in you": Christianse, *Unconfessed*, 198.

70. Victoria Carrol, "Zanele Muholi's Work Documenting African Lesbians Stolen: Community Raises $9000 to Replace Lost Equipment," QWOC Media: Diversity Speaks, http://www.qwoc.org/2012/05/zanele-muholis-work-on-black-lesbians-stolen.

71. Matt McCann, "Theft Stalls, but Does Not Stop, a Project." *New York Times*, May 23, 2012, http://lens.blogs.nytimes.com/2012/05/23/theft-stalls-but-does-not -stop-a-project.

72. Rosalind C. Morris, "In the Name of Trauma: Notes on Testimony, Truth Telling and the Secret of Literature in South Africa," *Comparative Literature Studies* 48, no. 3 (2011): 397.

73. The frequent use of rape as a violent tool of enforcing heterosexuality and "cor-recting" women who "act like men" has had few to no consequences for the rapists due to official apathy and the prevailing ethos of black lesbians as expendable citizens of the "Rainbow Nation." One of the rare cases in which the rapists were convicted in-volved Eudy Simelane, star player for Banyana Banyana, South Africa's national soccer team. Simelane was gang raped and murdered outside Gauteng in 2008.

74. Pumla Dineo Gqola, "Through Zanele Muholi's Eyes: Re/imagining Ways of Seeing Black Lesbians," in *African Sexualities: A Reader*, ed. Sylvia Tamale (London: Fahamu, 2011), 82–89, 87.

BIBLIOGRAPHY

Abdur-Rahman, Aliyyah I. *The Erotics of Race: Identity, Political Longing, and Black Figuration*. Durham, NC: Duke University Press, 2012.

Abrahams, Yvette. "Disempowered to Consent: Sara Bartman and Khoisan Slavery in the Nineteenth-Century Cape Colony and Britain." *South African Historical Journal* 35 (1996): 89–114.

Adams, John. *The Portable John Adams*, ed. John Patrick Diggins. New York: Penguin Books, 2004.

Adams, Rachel. *Sideshow U.S.A.: Freaks and the American Cultural Imagination*. Chicago: University of Chicago Press, 2001.

Ahmed, Sara. *Willful Subjects*. Durham, NC: Duke University Press, 2014.

Allen, Jafari S. *¡Venceremos? The Erotics of Black Self-Making in Cuba*. Durham, NC: Duke University Press, 2011.

Allen, Richard B. "The Mascarene Slave-Trade and Labour Migration in the Indian Ocean during the Eighteenth and Nineteenth Centuries." *Slavery and Abolition* 24, no. 2 (2003): 33–50.

Anderson, Clare. "Convicts and Coolies: Rethinking Indentured Labour in the Nineteenth Century." *Slavery and Abolition* 30, no. 1 (2009): 93–109.

Appadurai, Arjun. "Dead Certainty: Ethnic Violence in the Era of Globalization." *Public Culture* 10, no. 2 (Winter 1998): 225–47.

Arondekar, Anjali. *For the Record: On Sexuality and the Colonial Archive in India*. Durham, NC: Duke University Press, 2009.

Ashforth, Adam. *Witchcraft, Violence, and Democracy in South Africa*. Chicago: University of Chicago Press, 2005.

Baak, Paul E. "Enslaved Ex-Slaves, Uncaptured Contract Coolie and Unfreed Freedman: Some Notes about 'Free' and 'Unfree' Labour in the Context of Plantation Development in Southwest India." In *Free and Unfree Labour: The Debate Continues*, eds. Tom Brass and Marcel van der Linden, 427–55. New York: Peter Lang, 1997.

Baderoon, Gabeba. "The African Oceans—Tracing the Sea as the Memory of Slavery in South African Literature and Culture." *Research in African Literatures* 40, no. 4 (Winter 2009): 89–107.

Bailey, Candice. "Muti Killing Is a Way of Life in Rural Areas." *IOL News*, January 16, 2010.

Ball, Terence. "Two Concepts of Coercion." *Theory and Society* 5, no. 1 (1978): 97–112.

Ballantyne, Tony, and Antoinette Burton, eds. "Introduction: Bodies, Empires, and World Histories." In *Bodies in Contact: Rethinking Colonial Encounters in World History*, eds. Tony Ballantyne and Antoinette Burton, 1–15. Durham, NC: Duke University Press, 2005.

Banet-Weiser, Sarah. *The Most Beautiful Girl in the World: Beauty Pageants and National Identity*. Berkeley: University of California Press, 1999.

Bank, Andrew, Hans Heese, and Chris Loff, eds. *The Proceedings of the Khoisan Identities and Cultural Heritage Conference*. Cape Town, South Africa: Institute for Historical Research Infosource, 1997.

Barnard, Lady Ann. *South Africa a Century Ago: Letters Written from the Cape of Good Hope (1797–1801)*, ed. W. H. Wilkins. London: Smith, Elder, & CO., 1910. http://digital.library.upenn.edu/women/barnard/letters/letters.html.

Barthes, Roland. *The Responsibility of Forms: Critical Essays on Music, Art, and Representation*. New York: Hill and Wang, 1985.

Berlant, Lauren. "Slow Death (Sovereignty, Obesity, Lateral Agency)." *Critical Inquiry* 33, no. 4 (Summer 2010): 754–80.

Bernstein, Robin. *Performing American Childhood from Slavery to Civil Rights*. New York: New York University Press, 2011.

Best, Stephen, and Saidiya Hartman. "Fugitive Justice." *Representations* 92, no. 1 (Fall 2005): 1–15.

Bhana, Surendra, and Arvinkumar Bhana. "An Exploration of the Psycho-Historical Circumstances Surrounding Suicide among Indentured Indians, 1875–1911." In *Essays on Indentured Indians in Natal*, ed. Surendra Bhana, 137–88. Leeds: Peepal Tree, 1991.

Bhana, Surendra, and Bridglal Pachai, eds. *A Documentary History of Indian South Africans*. Cape Town, South Africa: David Phillip, 1984.

Block, Sharon. "Lines of Color, Sex, and Service: Comparative Sexual Coercion in Early America." In *Sex, Love, Race: Crossing Boundaries in North American History*, ed. Martha Hodes, 141–63. New York: New York University Press, 1999.

———. *Rape and Sexual Power in Early America*. Chapel Hill: University of North Carolina Press, 2006.

Bogdan, Robert. *Pornography or Entertainment? The Rise and Fall of the Freak Show*. Chicago: University of Chicago Press, 1988.

Bradley, James. "The Colonel and the Slave Girls: Life Writing and the Logic of History in 1830s Sydney." *Journal of Social History* 45, no. 2 (Winter 2011): 416–35.

Braid, Mary. "Witchcraft Returns to Haunt New South Africa: Children Murdered and Their Bodies Used in Rituals." *The Independent*, January 21, 1998.

Bragard, Véronique. *Transoceanic Dialogues: Coolitude in Caribbean and Indian Ocean Literatures*. Berlin: Peter Lang, 2008.

Brantlinger, Patrick. *Rule of Darkness: British Literature and Imperialism, 1830–1914*. Ithaca, NY: Cornell University Press, 1990.

Brink, Andre. "Interrogating Silence: New Possibilities faced by South African Literature." In *Writing South Africa: Literature, Apartheid, and Democracy, 1970–1995*, eds. Derek Attridge and Rosemary Jolly, 14–28. Cambridge: Cambridge University Press, 1998.

———. *The Rights of Desire*. New York: Harcourt, 2000.

Brown, Wendy. *States of Injury: Power and Freedom in Late Modernity*. Princeton, NJ: Princeton University Press, 1995.

Burke, Timothy. "'Sunlight Soap Has Changed My Life': Hygiene, Commodification, and the Body in Colonial Zimbabwe." In *Clothing and Difference: Embodied Identities in Colonial and Post-Colonial Africa*, ed. Hildi Hendrickson, 189–212. Durham, NC: Duke University Press, 1996.

Burton, Antoinette. "'Every Secret Thing?' Racial Politics in Ansuyah R. Singh's *Behold the Earth Mourns*." *Journal of Commonwealth Literature* 46, no. 1 (2011): 63–81.

Butler, Judith. *Precarious Life: The Powers of Mourning and Violence*. New York: Verso, 2004.

Carpio, Glenda R. *Laughing Fit to Kill: Black Humor in the Fictions of Slavery*. New York: Oxford University Press, 2008.

Carsel, Wilfred. "The Slaveholders' Indictment of Northern Wage Slavery." *Journal of Southern History* 6, no. 4 (1940): 504–20.

Carter, Marina, and Khal Torabully. *Coolitude: An Anthology of the Indian Labour Diaspora*. London: Anthem, 2002.

Cazdyn, Eric. "Disaster, Crisis, Revolution." *South Atlantic Quarterly* 106, no. 4 (Fall 2007): 647–62.

Cervenak, Sarah Jane. *Wandering: Philosophical Performances of Racial and Sexual Freedom*. Durham, NC: Duke University Press, 2014.

Chasar, Mike. "The Sounds of Black Laughter and the Harlem Renaissance: Claude McKay, Sterling Brown, Langston Hughes." *American Literature* 80, no. 1 (2008): 57–81.

Chase-Riboud, Barbara. *Hottentot Venus*. New York: Doubleday, 2003.

Christianse, Yvette. "'Heartsore': The Melancholy Archive of Cape Colony Slavery." *Scholar and Feminist Online* 7, no. 2 (Spring 2009) http://www.barnard.edu/sfonline.

———. *Unconfessed: A Novel*. New York: Other Press, 2007.

Clark, Elizabeth B. "'The Sacred Rights of the Weak': Pain, Sympathy, and the Culture of Individual Rights in Antebellum America." *Journal of American History* 82, no. 2 (1995): 463–93.

Coetzee, J. M. *Disgrace*. New York: Penguin Books, 2008.

Cohen, Colleen Ballerino, Richard Wilk, and Beverly Stoeltje, eds. *Beauty Queens on the Global Stage: Gender, Contests, and Power*. New York: Routledge, 1996.

Comaroff, Jean, and John Comaroff. *Ethnography and the Historical Imagination*. Boulder, CO: Westview, 1992.

Conquergood, Dwight. "Performance Studies: Interventions and Radical Research." *TDR* 46, no. 2 (Summer 2002): 145–56.

Cook Jr., James W. "From the Age of Reason to the Age of Barnum: The Great Automaton Chess-Player and the Emergence of Victorian Cultural Illusionism." *Winterthur Portfolio* 30, no. 4 (Winter 1995): 231–57.

Coplan, David B. *In the Time of Cannibals: The World Music of South Africa's Basotho Migrants*. Chicago: University of Chicago Press, 1994.

Crais, Clifton. *The Politics of Evil: Magic, State Power and the Political Imagination in South Africa*. Cambridge: Cambridge University Press, 2009.

Crais, Clifton, and Pamela Scully. *Sara Baartman and the Hottentot Venus: A Ghost Story and a Biography*. Princeton, NJ: Princeton University Press, 2009.

Crush, Jonathan, and Clarence Tshitereke. "Contesting Migrancy: The Foreign Labor Debate in Post-1994 South Africa." *Africa Today* 48, no. 3 (Fall 2001): 49–70.

Davidson, Michael. "Universal Design: The Work of Disability in an Age of Globalization." In *The Disability Studies Reader*, ed. Lennard J. Davis, 117–28. New York: Routledge, 2006.

DeFrantz, Thomas. "The Black Beat Made Visible: Hip Hop Dance and Body Power." In *Of the Presence of the Body: Essays on Dance and Performance Theory*, ed. Andre Lepecki, 64–81. Middletown, CT: Wesleyan University Press, 2004.

Desai, Ashwin, and Goolam Vahed. *Inside Indenture: A South African Story, 1860–1914*. Durban, South Africa: Madiba, 2007.

Donham, Donald. *Violence in a Time of Liberation: Murder and Ethnicity at a South African Gold Mine*. Durham, NC: Duke University Press, 1994.

Douglass, Frederick. "The Heroic Slave" (1853). In *Frederick Douglass: Selected Speeches and Writings*, ed. Philip S. Foner, 219–46. Chicago: Lawrence Hill, 1999.

Enwezor, Okwui. "Reframing the Black Subject: Ideology and Fantasy in Contemporary South African Representation." In *Race-ing Art History: Critical Readings in Race and Art History*, ed. Kymberly N. Pinder, 371–89. New York: Routledge University Press, 2002.

Erlmann, Veit. " 'Spectatorial Lust': The African Choir in England, 1891–1893." In *Africans on Stage: Studies in Ethnological Show Business*, ed. Bernth Lindfors, 107–34. Bloomington: Indiana University Press, 1999.

Fausto-Sterling, Anne. "Gender, Race, and Nation: The Comparative Anatomy of 'Hottentot' Women in Europe, 1815–1817." In *Deviant Bodies: Critical Perspectives on Difference in Science and Popular Culture*, eds. Jacqueline Urla and Jennifer Terry, 19–48. Bloomington: Indiana University Press, 1995.

Ferguson, Roderick. "Race-ing Homonormativity: Citizenship, Sociology and Gay Identity." In *Black Queer Studies: A Critical Anthology*, eds. E. Patrick Johnson and Mae G. Henderson, 52–67. Durham, NC: Duke University Press, 2005.

Fitzhugh, George. *Cannibals All! Or, Slaves without Masters*. Cambridge, MA: Belknap Press of Harvard University Press, 1857.

———. *Sociology for the South; Or, the Failure of Free Society*. Richmond, VA: A. Morris, 1854.

Foucault, Michel. *Discipline and Punish: The Birth of the Prison*. Trans. Alan Sheridan. New York: Vintage Books, 1995.

———. "Nietzsche, Genealogy, History." In *The Foucault Reader*, ed. Paul Rabinow, 76–99. New York: Random House, 1984.

Frederickson, George M. *White Supremacy: A Comparative Study of American and South African History*. New York: Oxford University Press, 1982.

Frenkel, Ronit. *Reconsiderations: South African Indian Fiction and the Making of Race in Postcolonial Culture*. Pretoria: Unisa Press, 2010.

Fusco, Coco. *English Is Broken Here: Notes on Cultural Fusion in the Americas*. New York: New Press, 1995.

Gaines, Kevin. *Uplifting the Race: Black Leadership, Politics, and Culture in the Twentieth Century*. Chapel Hill: University of North Carolina Press, 1996.

Garland-Thomson, Rosemarie. *Extraordinary Bodies: Figuring Physical Disability in American Culture and Literature*. New York: Columbia University Press, 1997.

———, ed. *Freakery: Cultural Spectacles of the Extraordinary Body*. New York: New York University Press, 1996.

———. "Integrating Disability, Transforming Feminist Theory." *NWSA Journal* 14, no. 3 (Autumn 2002): 1–32.

Genovese, Eugene. *Roll, Jordan, Roll: The World the Slaves Made*. New York: Vintage Books, 2011.

Gilman, Sander L. *Difference and Pathology: Stereotypes of Sexuality, Race and Madness*. Ithaca, NY: Cornell University Press, 1985.

Gilroy, Paul. *The Black Atlantic: Modernity and Double Consciousness*. Cambridge, MA: Harvard University Press, 1993.

Govinden, D. *"Sister Outsiders": The Representation of Identity and Difference in Selected Writings by South African Indian Women*. Pretoria, South Africa: Unisa Press, 2008.

Gqola, Pumla Dineo. "Through Zanele Muholi's Eyes: Re/imagining Ways of Seeing Black Lesbians." In *African Sexualities: A Reader*, ed. Sylvia Tamale, 82–89. London: Fahamu, 2011.

———. *What Is Slavery to Me? Post-Colonial Memory and the Post-Apartheid Imagination*. Witwatersrand, South Africa: University of Witwatersrand Press, 2010.

Grossman, Jonathan. "The Right to Strike and Worker Freedom in and beyond Apartheid." In *Free and Unfree Labour: The Debate Continues*, eds. Tom Brass and Marcel van der Linden, 145–70. New York: Peter Lang, 1997.

Halberstam, Judith. *The Queer Art of Failure*. Durham, NC: Duke University Press, 2011.

Hansen, Thomas Blom. "The Unwieldy Fetish: Desire and Disavowal of Indianness in South Africa." In *Eyes across the Water: Navigating the Indian Ocean*, eds. Pamela Gupta, Isabel Hofmeyr, and Michael Pearson, 109–21. Pretoria, South Africa: Unisa Press, 2010.

Harris, Cheryl I. "Whiteness as Property," *Harvard Law Review* 106, no. 8 (June 1993): 1707–91.

Harris, Sharon M. *Executing Race: Early American Women's Narratives of Race, Society, and the Law.* Columbus: Ohio State University Press, 2005.

———. "Feminist Theories and Early American Studies." *Early American Literature* 34, no. 1 (1999): 86–93.

Harris, Theodore D. "Review of *Cannibals All! Or, Slaves without Masters.*" *Journal of Negro History* 48, no. 1 (1963): 57–58.

Hartman, Saidiya. *Lose Your Mother: A Journey along the Atlantic Slave Route.* New York: Farrar, Straus and Giroux, 2007.

———. "Review of Seymour Drescher, *Abolition: A History of Slavery and Antislavery.*" *American Historical Review* 115, no. 4 (October 2010): 1103–6.

———. *Scenes of Subjection: Terror, Slavery and Self-Making in Nineteenth-Century America.* New York: Oxford University Press, 1997.

———. "Venus in Two Acts." *Small Axe* 12, no. 2 (June 2008): 1–14.

Hassim, Aziz. *Revenge of Kali.* Johannesburg: STE, 2009.

Heese, Hans F. *Reg en Onreg: Kaapse Regspraak in die Agtiende Eeu.* Belville: Institute for Historical Research, University of the Western Cape, 1994.

Hoad, Neville. "Miss HIV and Us: Beauty Queens against the HIV/AIDS Pandemic," *CR: The New Centennial Review* 10, no. 1 (2010): 9–28.

Hofmeyr, Isabel. "Africa as a Fault Line in the Indian Ocean." In *Eyes across the Water: Navigating the Indian Ocean*, eds. Pamela Gupta, Isabel Hofmeyr, and Michael Pearson, 99–108. Pretoria, South Africa: Unisa Press, 2010.

Holland, Sharon. *The Erotic Life of Racism.* Durham, NC: Duke University Press, 2012.

Hyde, Alan. *Bodies of Law.* Princeton NJ: Princeton University Press, 1997.

Iton, Richard. *In Search of the Black Fantastic: Politics and Popular Culture in the Post–Civil Rights Era.* New York: Oxford University Press, 2010.

Johnson, Walter. "On Agency." *Journal of Social History* 37, no. 1 (Autumn 2003): 113–24.

———. *Soul by Soul: Life inside the Antebellum Slave Market.* Cambridge, MA: Harvard University Press, 1999.

Kakaliouras, Ann M. "An Anthropology of Repatriation: Contemporary Physical Anthropological and Native American Ontologies of Practice." *Current Anthropology* 53.S5 (2012): S210–21.

Kale, Madhavi. *Fragments of Empire: Capital, Slavery, and Indian Indentured Labor Migration in the British Caribbean.* Philadelphia: University of Pennsylvania Press, 1998.

Kant, Immanuel. *The Metaphysical Elements of Justice.* Trans. John Ladd. Indianapolis: Bobbs-Merrill, 1965.

Kapsalis, Terri. *Public Privates: Performing Gynecology from Both Ends of the Spectrum.* Durham, NC: Duke University Press, 1997.

Kessler, Charles, ed. *Berlin in Lights: The Diaries of Count Harry Kessler, 1918–1937.* New York: Grove, 2002.

Kolb, Peter. *The Present State of the Cape of Good Hope.* Trans. G. Medley. London: W. Innys, 1731.

Kooiman, Dick. "Conversion from Slavery to Plantation Labour; Christian Mission in South India, 19th Century." *Social Scientist* 19, no. 8 & 9 (August/September 1991): 57–71.

Kruger, Loren. "Black Atlantics, White Indians, and Jews: Locations, Locutions, and Syncretic Identities in the Fiction of Achmat Dangor and Others." *South Atlantic Quarterly* 100, no. 1 (2001): 111–43.

Kuppers, Petra. "Bodies, Hysteria, Pain: Staging the Invisible." In *Bodies in Commotion: Disability and Performance*, eds. Carrie Sandahl and Philip Auslander, 147–62. Ann Arbor: University of Michigan Press, 2005.

———. *Disability and Contemporary Performance: Bodies on the Edge*. New York: Routledge Press, 2013.

———. "Towards a Rhizomatic Model of Disability: Poetry, Performance, and Touch." *Journal of Literary and Cultural Disability Studies* 3, no. 3 (2009): 221–40.

Larson, Pier M. *History and Memory in the Age of Enslavement: Becoming Merina in Highland Madagscar, 1770–1822*. Portsmouth, NH: Heinemann, 2000.

Lavenda, Robert. "Minnesota Queen Pageants: Play, Fun, and Dead Seriousness in a Festive Mode." *Journal of American Folklore* 101, no. 400 (April–June 1988): 168–75.

Lee, Jin-Kyung. *Service Economies: Militarism, Sex Work, and Migrant Labor in South Africa*. Minneapolis: University of Minnesota Press, 2010.

Lee, Rebekah. "Death 'On the Move': Funerals, Entrepreneurs and the Rural-Urban Nexus in South Africa." *Africa: The Journal of the International African Institute* 81, no. 2 (May 2011): 226–47.

Legassick, Martin, and Ciraj Rassool. *Skeletons in the Cupboard: South African Museums and the Trade in Human Remains, 1907–1917*. Cape Town: Iziko Museum, 2015.

Levy, Andrea. *Small Island*. New York: Picador Press, 2004.

Li, Stephanie. *Something akin to Freedom: The Choice of Bondage in Narratives by African American Women*. New York: State University of New York, 2010.

Lindfors, Bernth. "Charles Dickens and the Zulus." In *Africans on Stage: Studies in Ethnological Show Business*, ed. Bernth Lindfors, 62–80. Bloomington: Indiana University Press, 1999.

Livingston, Julie. *Debility and the Moral Imagination in Botswana*. Bloomington: Indiana University Press, 2005.

Machado, Pedro. "A Forgotten Corner of the Indian Ocean: Gujarati Merchants, Portuguese India and the Mozambique Slave-Trade, c. 1730–1830." *Slavery and Abolition* 24, no. 2 (2003): 17–32.

Magubane, Zine. *Bringing the Empire Home: Race, Class, and Gender in Britain and Colonial South Africa*. Chicago: University of Chicago Press, 2004.

———. "Which Bodies Matter? Feminism, Poststructuralism, Race, and the Curious Theoretical Odyssey of the 'Hottentot Venus.'" *Gender and Society* 15, no. 6 (2001): 816–34.

Malchow, H. L. *Gothic Images of Race in Nineteenth-Century Britain*. Stanford, CA: Stanford University Press, 1996.

Malherbe, V. C. "In *Onegt Verwekt*: Law, Custom and Illegitimacy in Cape Town, 1800–1840." *Journal of Southern African Studies* 31, no. 1 (March 2005): 163–85.

Maloka, Eddy Tshidiso. "Basotho and the Experience of Death, Dying, and Mourning in the South African Mine Compounds, 1890–1940." *Cahiers d'Études Africaines* 38, no. 149 (1998): 17–40.

———. *Basotho and the Mines: A Social History of Labour Migrancy in Lesotho and South Africa, c. 1890–1940*. Dakar, Senegal: Codesria, 2004.

Markovits, Daniel. "Contract and Collaboration." *Yale Law Journal* 113, no. 7 (May 2004): 1417–518.

Mason, John Edwin. *Social Death and Resurrection: Slavery and Emancipation in South Africa*. Charlottesville: University of Virginia Press, 2003.

Mbembe, Achille. "Necropolitics." Trans. Libby Meintjes. *Public Culture* 15, no. 1 (Winter 2003): 11–40.

———. "On Politics as a Form of Expenditure." In *Law and Disorder in the Postcolony*, eds. Jean Comaroff and John Comaroff, 299–335. Chicago: University of Chicago Press, 2006.

———. *On the Postcolony: Studies on the History of Society and Culture*. Berkeley: University of California Press, 2001.

McClintock, Ann. *Imperial Leather: Race, Gender and Sexuality in the Colonial Contest*. New York: Routledge Press, 1995.

McKittrick, Katherine. *Demonic Grounds: Black Women and the Cartographies of Struggle*. Minneapolis: University of Minnesota Press, 2006.

McLagan, Meg. "Principles, Publicity, and Politics: Notes on Human Rights Media." *American Anthropologist* 105, no. 3 (September 2003): 605–12.

McMillan, Uri. *Embodied Avatars: Genealogies of Black Feminist Art and Performance*. New York: NYU Press, 2015.

McRuer, Robert. *Crip Theory: Cultural Signs of Queerness and Disability*. New York: New York University Press, 2006.

Mentzel, O. F. *A Description of the African Cape of Good Hope, 1787*. (Cape Town: The van Riebeeck Society, 1944), vol. 11.

Merians, Linda E. *Envisioning the Worst: Representations of "Hottentots" in Early-Modern England*. Newark: University of Delaware Press, 2001.

Miers, Suzanne. "Slavery: A Question of Definition." *Slavery and Abolition* 24, no. 2 (2003): 1–16.

Mohanty, Chandra. *Feminism without Borders: Decolonizing Theory, Practicing Solidarity*. Durham, NC: Duke University Press, 2003.

Moran, Mary H. "Carrying the Queen: Identity and Nationalism in a Liberian Queen Rally." In *Beauty Queens on the Global Stage: Gender, Contests, and Power*, eds. Colleen Ballerino Cohen, Richard Wilk, and Beverly Stoeltje, 147–60. New York: Routledge, 1996.

Morris, Rosalind C. "In the Name of Trauma: Notes on Testimony, Truth Telling and the Secret of Literature in South Africa." *Comparative Literature Studies* 48, no. 3 (2011): 388–416.

Morrison, Toni. *Beloved*. New York: Plume, 1988.

Moudileno, Lydie. "Returning Remains: Saartjie Baartman, or the 'Hottentot Venus' as Transnational Postcolonial Icon." *Forum for Modern Language Studies* 45, no. 2 (2009): 200–12.

Mpe, Phaswane. *Welcome to Our Hillbrow: A Novel of Postapartheid South Africa*. Athens: Ohio University Press, 2001.

Muñoz, José Esteban. *Disidentifications: Queers of Color and the Performance of Politics*. Minneapolis: University of Minnesota Press, 1999.

Munro, Brenna M. *South Africa and the Dream of Love to Come: Queer Sexuality and the Struggle for Freedom*. Minneapolis: University of Minnesota Press, 2010.

Naidoo, G. R. "Why Do Indians Kill Themselves?" *Drum* (August 1956): 27–31.

Noble, Marianne. "Sympathetic Listening in Frederick Douglass's 'The Heroic Slave' and *My Bondage and My Freedom*." *Studies in American Fiction* 34, no. 1 (Spring 2006): 53–68.

Noland, Carrie. "Introduction." In *Migrations of Gesture*, eds. Carrie Noland and Sally Ann Ness, ix–xxviii. Minneapolis: University of Minnesota, 2008.

Nymann, Ann E. "Sally's Rape: Robbie Mccauley's Survival Art." *African American Review* 33, no. 4 (1999): 577–87.

Oyewumi, Oyeronke. *The Invention of Women: Making an African Sense of Western Gender Discourses*. Minneapolis: University of Minnesota Press, 1997.

Painter, Nell Irvin. "Representing Truth: Sojourner Truth's Knowing and Becoming Known." *Journal of American History* 8, no. 2 (1994): 461–92.

Parle, Julie. "Death in Black and White: Suicide, Statistics, and Race in Natal, 1880–1916: 'Lies, Damned Lies, and Statistics.'" Paper presented at the WISER History Workshop, University of Witwatersrand, Johannesburg, July 5–8, 2001.

———. *States of Mind: Searching for Mental Health in Natal and Zululand, 1868–1918*. Pietermaritzburg: University of KwaZulu-Natal Press, 2007.

Pateman, Carole. *The Disorder of Women: Democracy, Feminism, and Political Theory*. Stanford, CA: Stanford University Press, 1989.

Patterson, Orlando. *Slavery and Social Death: A Comparative Study*. Cambridge, MA: Harvard University Press, 1982.

Peacock, Mabel. "Executed Criminals and Folk-Medicine." *Folklore* 7, no. 3 (September 1896): 268–83.

———. *Rogues, Rebels and Runaways: Eighteenth-Century Cape Characters*. Cape Town, South Africa: David Philip, 1999.

Peterson, Christopher. *Kindred Specters: Death, Mourning, and American Affinity*. Minnesota: University of Minnesota Press, 2007.

Phillips, Susan E. "Physical Graffitti West: African American Gang Walks and Semiotic Practice." In *Migration of Gestures*, eds. Carrie Noland and Sally A. Ness, 31–68. Minneapolis: University of Minnesota Press, 2008.

Povinelli, Elizabeth A. *The Empire of Love: Toward a Theory of Intimacy, Genealogy, and Carnality*. Durham, NC: Duke University Press, 2006.

Povinelli, Elizabeth A., and Kim Turcot DiFruscia. "A Conversation with Elizabeth A. Povinelli." *Trans-Scripts* 2 (2012): 76–90.

Pratt, Mary Louise. *Imperial Eyes: Travel Writing and Transculturation*. London: Routledge, 1992.

Qureshi, Sadiah. "Displaying Sara Baartman, the 'Hottentot Venus.'" *History of Science* 42, no. 2 (2004): 233–57.

Rabin, Dana. "Bodies of Evidence, States of Mind: Infanticide, Emotion and Sensibility in Eighteenth-Century England." In *Infanticide: Historical Perspectives on Child Murder and Concealment, 1550–2000*, ed. Mark Jackson, 73–92. Hants, UK: Ashgate, 2002.

Rama, Parbavati. *A Forgotten Diaspora: Forced Indian Migration to the Cape Colony, 1658 to 1834*. PhD diss, University of the Western Cape, May 2015.

Rapoo, Connie. "Just Give us the Bones! Theatres of African Diasporic Returns." *Critical Arts* 25, no. 2 (June 2011): 132–49.

Rassool, Ciraj. "Human Remains, the Disciplines of the Dead, & the South African Memorial Complex." In *The Politics of Heritage in Africa: Economies, Histories, and Infrastructures*, eds, Derek Peterson, Kodzo Gavua, and Ciraj Rassool, 133–56. Cambridge: Cambridge University Press, 2015.

Rassool, Ciraj, Leslie Witz, and Gary Minkley. "Burying and Memorialising the Body of Truth: The TRC and National Heritage." In *After the TRC: Reflections on Truth and Reconciliation in South Africa*, eds. Wilmot James and Linda van de Vijver, 115–27. Cape Town: David Philip, 2000.

Rastogi, Pallavi. "From South Asia to South Africa: Locating Other Post-Colonial Diasporas." *Modern Fiction Studies* 51, no. 3 (2005): 536–60.

Reiss, Benjamin. *The Showman and the Slave: Race, Death, and Memory in Barnum's America*. Cambridge, MA: Harvard University Press, 2001.

Richardson, Matt. "'My Father Didn't Have a Dick': Social Death and Jackie Kay's *Trumpet*." *GLQ* 18, nos. 2–3 (2012): 361–79.

Roach, Joseph. *Cities of the Dead: Circum-Atlantic Performance*. New York: Columbia University Press, 1996.

Robinson, John Robert. *"Old Q"; a Memoir of William Douglas, Fourth Duke of Queensberry, K.T., One of "the Fathers of the Turf," with a Full Account of His Celebrated Matches and Wagers, Etc*. London: Sampson Low, Marston, 1895.

Rodriguez, Juana Maria. *Sexual Futures, Queer Gestures and Other Latina Longings*. New York: New York University Press, 2014.

Ross, Marlon B. "Beyond the Closet as Raceless Paradigm." In *Black Queer Studies: A Critical Anthology*, eds. E. Patrick Johnson and Mae Henderson, 161–89. Durham, NC: Duke University Press, 2005.

Rushdy, Ashraf. *Remembering Generations: Race and Family in Contemporary African American Fiction*. Chapel Hill, NC: University of North Carolina Press, 2001.

Sam, Agnes. *Jesus and Other Short Stories*. Portsmouth, NH: Heinemann, 1994.

Samuelson, Meg. "'Lose Your Mother, Kill Your Child': The Passage of Slavery and Its Afterlife in Narratives by Yvette Christianse and Saidiya Hartman." *English Studies in Africa* 51, no. 2 (2008): 38–48.

———. *Remembering the Nation, Dismembering Women? Stories of the South African Transition*. Durban, South Africa: University of KwaZulu-Natal Press, 2007.

———. "(Un)settled States: Indian Ocean Passages, Performative Belonging and Restless Mobility in Post-apartheid South African Fiction." *Social Dynamics* 36, no. 2 (2010): 272–87.

Schneider, Rebecca. *The Explicit Body in Performance*. New York: Routledge Press, 1997.

Scott, Darieck. *Extravagant Abjection: Blackness, Power, and Sexuality in the African American Literary Imagination*. New York: New York University Press, 2010.

Scully, Pamela. "Narratives of Infanticide in the Aftermath of Slave Emancipation in the Nineteenth-Century Cape Colony, South Africa." *Canadian Journal of African Studies* 30, no. 1 (1996): 88–105.

———. "Rape, Race and Colonial Culture: The Sexual Politics of Identity in the Nineteenth-Century Cape Colony, South Africa." *American Historical Review* 100, no. 2 (April 1995): 335–59.

Scutt, Jocelynne A. "The Standard of Consent in Rape." *New Zealand Law Journal* 52 (January 1976): 462–67.

Sedgwick, Eve Kosofsky. *The Epistemology of the Closet*. Berkeley: University of California Press, 1990.

Semple, Robert. *Walks and Sketches at the Cape of Good Hope*. Facsimile ed. Charleston, SC: Bibliolife, 2009.

Serlin, David. "The Other Arms Race." In *The Disability Studies Reader*, ed. Lennard J. Davis, 49–65. New York: Routledge, 2006.

Sharpe, Christina. *Monstrous Intimacies: Making Post-Slavery Subjects*. Durham NC: Duke University Press, 2010.

Sharpe, Jenny. *Ghosts of Slavery: A Literary Archeology of Black Women's Lives*. Minneapolis: University of Minnesota Press, 2003.

Sharpley-Whiting, T. Denean. *Black Venus: Sexualized Savages, Primal Fears, and Primitive Narratives in French*. Durham, NC: Duke University Press, 1999.

Shell, Robert C. H. *Children of Bondage: A Social History of the Slave Society at the Cape of Good Hope, 1652–1838*. Hanover, NH: Wesleyan University Press, 1994.

———. "A Family Matter: The Sale and Transfer of Human Beings at the Cape, 1658 to 1830." *International Journal of African Historical Studies* 25, no. 2 (1992): 285–366.

Shukla, Sandhya. *India Abroad: Diasporic Cultures of Postwar America and England*. Princeton NJ: Princeton University Press, 2003.

Siebers, Tobin. "Disability in Theory: From Social Constructivism to the New Realism of the Body." In *The Disability Studies Reader*, 2nd ed., ed. Lennard J. Davis, 173–83. New York: Routledge, 2006.

Silvio, Teri. "Animation: The New Performance." *Journal of Linguistic Anthropology* 20, no. 2 (December 2010): 422–38.

Smith, Mark. *How Race is Made: Slavery, Segregation, and the Senses*. Chapel Hill: University of North Carolina Press, 2008.

Smith, Marquard. "The Vulnerable Articulate: James Gillingham, Aimee Mullins, and Matthew Barney." In *The Disability Studies Reader*, ed. Lennard J. Davis, 309–19. New York: Routledge, 2006.

Snorton, C. Riley. *Nobody Is Supposed to Know: Black Sexuality on the Down Low*. Minneapolis: University of Minnesota Press, 2014.

Soske, Jon. "Navigating Difference: Gender, Miscegenation and Indian Domestic Space in Twentieth-Century Durban." In *Eyes across the Water: Navigating the Indian Ocean*, eds. Pamela Gupta, Isabel Hofmeyr, and Michael Pearson, 197–219. Pretoria, South Africa: Unisa Press, 2010.

———. " 'Wash Me Black Again': African Nationalism, the Indian Diaspora, and Kwa-Zulu Natal, 1944–1960." PhD diss., University of Toronto, 2009.

Sparrman, Anders. *A Voyage to the Cape of Good Hope: Towards the Antarctic Polar Circle, and Round the World: but Chiefly into the Country of the Hottentots and Caffres, from the Year 1772–1776*. Trans. Georg Forster. London: G. G. J. and J. Robinson, 1785.

Spencer, Suzette. "Historical Memory, Romantic Narrative, and Sally Hemings." *African American Review* 40, no. 3 (Fall 2006): 507–31.

Spieker, Sven. *The Big Archive: Art from Bureaucracy*. Cambridge, MA: MIT Press, 2008.

Spillers, Hortense. "Mama's Baby, Papa's Maybe: An American Grammar Book." *Diacritics* 17, no. 2 (Summer 1987): 64–81.

Stoler, Ann Laura. *Race and the Education of Desire: Foucault's History of Sexuality and the Colonial Order of Things*. Durham, NC: Duke University Press, 1995.

Strother, Z. S. "Display of the Body Hottentot." In *Africans on Stage: Studies in Ethnological Show Business*, ed. Bernth Lindfors, 1–61. Bloomington: Indiana University Press, 1999.

Stychin, Carl F. "De-Meaning of Contract." In *Sexuality and the Law: Feminist Engagements*, eds. Vanessa E. Munro and Carl F. Stychin, 73–89. London: Routledge Cavendish, 2007.

Taylor, Diana. *The Archive and the Repertoire: Performing Cultural Memory in the Americas*. Durham, NC: Duke University Press, 2003.

———. "Performance and/as History." *TDR* 50, no. 1 (Spring 2006): 67–86.

Thompson, Krista. *Shine: The Visual Economy of Light in African Diasporic Aesthetic Practice*. Durham, NC: Duke University Press, 2015.

Tinker, Hugh. *A New System of Slavery: The Export of Indian Labour Overseas, 1830–1920*. Oxford: Oxford University Press, 1974.

Tinsley, Omise'eke Natasha. "Black Atlantic, Queer Atlantic: Imagining the Middle Passage as Queer Borderwaters." *GLQ* 14, nos. 2–3 (April 2008): 191–215.

Turner, Victor. *Dramas, Fields, and Metaphors: Symbolic Action in Human Society*. Ithaca, NY: Cornell University Press, 1974.

Underberg, Natalie. "Virtual and Reciprocal Ethnography on the Internet: The East Mims Oral History Project Website." *Journal of American Folklore* 119, no. 473 (Summer 2006): 301–11.

Urla, Jacqueline, and Jennifer Terry. "Introduction: Mapping Embodied Deviance." In *Deviant Bodies: Critical Perspectives on Difference in Science and Popular Culture*, eds. Jacqueline Urla and Jennifer Terry, 1–18. Bloomington: Indiana University Press, 1995.

Van Onselen, Gareth. "Pervasive Problem of Witchcraft Needs a More Urgent Response." *Business Day Live*, July 2, 2013.

Varma, Nitin. "Coolie Acts and the Acting Coolies: Coolie, Planter and State in the Late Nineteenth and Early Twentieth Century Colonial Tea Plantations of Assam." *Social Scientist* 33, nos. 5–6 (May–June 2005): 49–72.

Wåstberg, Per, *The Journey of Anders Sparrman*. London: Granta, 2010.

Weaver, Karol K. " 'She Crushed the Child's Fragile Skull': Disease, Infanticide, and Enslaved Women in Eighteenth-Century Saint-Domingue." In *Killing Infants: Studies in the Worldwide Practice of Infanticide*, eds. Brigitte H. Bechtold and Donna Cooper Graves, 25–44. New York: Edwin Mellen, 2006.

Weheliye, Alexander G. *Habeas Viscus: Racializing Assemblages, Biopolitics, and Black Feminist theories of the Human*. Durham, NC: Duke University Press, 2014.

Weiner, Marli F. *Mistresses and Slaves: Plantation Women in South Carolina, 1830–80*. Urbana: University of Illinois Press, 1998.

Wekker, Gloria. *Politics of Passion: Women's Sexual Culture in the Afro-Surinamese Diaspora*. New York: Columbia University Press, 2006.

Wenzel, Jennifer. *Bulletproof: Afterlives of Anticolonial Prophecy in South Africa and Beyond*. Chicago: University of Chicago Press, 2009.

Williams, Patricia. *The Rooster's Egg: On the Persistence of Prejudice*. Cambridge, MA: Harvard University Press, 1997.

Wiss, Rosemary. "Lipreading: Remembering Saartjie Baartman." *Australian Journal of Anthropology* 5, nos. 1–2 (1994): 11–40.

Wong, Edlie. *Neither Fugitive nor Free: Atlantic Slavery, Freedom Suits, and the Legal Culture of Travel (America and the Long Nineteenth Century)*. New York: New York University Press, 2009.

Worden, Nigel. "Coercion and Freedom in the Cape Colony, 1652–1836." In *The Face of Freedom: The Manumission and Emancipation of Slaves in Old World and New World Slavery*, ed. Marc Kleijwegt, 185–214. Leiden: E. J. Brill, 2006.

———. *Slavery in Dutch South Africa*. Cambridge: Cambridge University Press, 1985.

Worden, Nigel, and Clifton Crais. *Slavery and Its Legacy in the Nineteenth-Century Cape Colony*. Johannesburg: Witwatersrand University Press, 1994.

Worden, Nigel, and Gerald Groenewald, eds. *Trials of Slavery: Selected Documents Concerning Slaves from the Criminal Records of the Council of Justice at the Cape of Good Hope, 1705–1794*. Cape Town, South Africa: Van Riebeeck Society for the Publication of South African Historical Documents, 2005.

Wright, William. *Slavery at the Cape of Good Hope* (1831). New York: Negro Universities Press, 1969.

INDEX

Note: Page numbers followed by *f* indicate a figure.

performance studies, 2, 4–5, 7, 26

plakkaat, 17

poolsche bok, 15, 220n58

Popular Movement for the Liberation of Angola (MPLA), 126–27

Povinelli, Elizabeth, 8–10, 38, 40

property, 22, 70, 79, 116, 173, 183, 186–88, 201, 210, 244n15; bodily, 104–6; language of, 104; person and, 19–20, 25, 87–88, 91, 190, 195; relations, 18, 186–87; rights, 184, 195; use of, 93–95

prosthesis, 143–44, 165, 236n54, 238n78

prosthetics, 25, 109–11, 113*f,* 133, 136, 141–44, 236n54

prostitution, 56, 62

queering, 2–4, 26–27, 177–78

queer, 177; agency, 175; allegiances, 26; characters, 208; communities, 180; desire, 178, 180; ethics, 222n91; families, 208, 210; feminist theory, 78; intimacy, 211; kinlessness, 190; as performance, 177; relationality, 26–27, 209, 211, 213; rights, 213; sexual relations, 191; theory, 178; women, 213–14

queers: African, 27; of color, 212

Qureshi, Sadiah, 47, 61, 227n86

Rabin, Dana, 193

race, 4–7, 18, 39, 63, 86, 100, 111, 123, 156, 158, 164; denaturalization of, 177; discourses of, 5; ideology of, 150, 171; passing and, 237n75

racialization, 6, 9, 60, 79, 147, 156, 170

racism, 17, 22, 29–30, 32, 34–40, 54, 57–59, 61–62, 118–19, 160, 168, 172, 200, 224n27; culture and, 78; institutionalized, 239n17; olfactory, 118; scientific, 36; well-meaning, 127

rape, 25, 80, 87, 91, 102, 105, 187, 194, 201–2, 204–5, 209–10, 213, 221n79, 232n39, 247n64; enforcement of heterosexuality and, 247n73; of indentured women, 165; physical injury and, 93; as seduction, 91

Rastogi, Pallavi, 176–77

relational contracting, 22, 106–7

relationality, 11, 106–7, 197, 211; queer, 209, 213

relational ontology, 221–22, 26–27, 195, 212

resistance, 70; poisoning as slave, 8

Revenge of Kali (Hassim), 149–51

Rights of Desire, The (Brink), 25, 97–103

Roach, Joseph, 2, 29

Robben Island prison, 26, 73, 84, 182, 190, 202, 205, 209, 231n33

Rodriguez, Juana, 11–12

Rogers, David L., 113, 142

Rogues, Rebels, and Runaways (Penn), 2, 25, 79, 99

Ross, Marlon, 178, 243n79

Sam, Agnes, 26; *Jesus is Indian and Other Stories,* 26

Samuelson, Meg, 150, 199

science, 9, 38–40, 224n27; visual, 6

Scott, Darieck, 185, 190–91, 210

Scully, Pamela, 4, 30, 36–37, 41, 44–46, 48–50, 53, 55–56, 61, 63, 96, 191–93, 225n49, 228n103, 244n26

Scutt, J.A., 93

seduction, 25, 82, 87, 90–92; black women and, 77; narratives of, 79–80, 87–89

self-determination, 36, 80, 119, 145

self-harm, 153; as form of freedom, 195

sexuality, 80, 102, 104, 121, 123, 125, 127, 177–78, 190–91, 193, 244n27; black women's, 66, 186; deviant, 55; discourses of, 5; slave, 96; slave master, 187; violence and, 88

Sharpe, Christina, 79, 80, 91, 98, 186, 189

Sharpe, Jenny, 87, 231n39

Sharpley-Whiting, T. Denean, 57

Shell, Robert, 24, 79, 156, 230n2

Sims, J. Marion, 141–42

slave auctions, 57, 132; Baartman's performances and, 25, 44, 66; performances of slaves at, 25, 67, 69, 111, 113

slave trade, 6, 14, 47, 160, 172; abolition of, 45, 63, 160; in Africa, 13; India and, 152; Indian Ocean, 13; Red Sea, 13; transatlantic, 13; trans-Saharan, 13

Small Island (Levy), 53–54, 58, 226n71